Welcome to
the One Great Story!

For Corey and Eliece)
One of my bigger
efforts, both in time
and length, I hope
that you find it interesting
and perhaps illuminating!
Blessings,
George March 2022

Welcome to
the One Great Story!

Tracing the Biblical Narrative
from Genesis to Revelation

GEORGE B. THOMPSON JR.

foreword by
Mary Miller Brueggemann and Patrick D. Miller

WIPF & STOCK · Eugene, Oregon

WELCOME TO THE ONE GREAT STORY!
Tracing the Biblical Narrative from Genesis to Revelation

Scripture quotations, unless otherwise noted, are from the New Revised Standard Version of the Bible, © 1989, Division of Christian Education of the National Council of the Churches of Christ in the United States of America, and are used by permission.

Wipf & Stock
An Imprint of Wipf and Stock Publishers
199 W. 8th Ave., Suite 3
Eugene, OR 97401

www.wipfandstock.com

PAPERBACK ISBN: 978-1-7252-7731-1
HARDCOVER ISBN: 978-1-7252-7730-4
EBOOK ISBN: 978-1-7252-7732-8

Manufactured in the U.S.A.   08/26/20

In grateful memory of
THE REV. PATRICK D. MILLER JR., PHD
Charles T. Haley Professor Emeritus of Old Testament Theology
Princeton Theological Seminary
who died peacefully two nights after completing work on the
foreword for this book with his twin sister,
Mary Miller Brueggemann.

"Bless the Lord, O my soul, and all that is within me,
bless God's holy name."

—PSALM 103:1

Contents

Acknowledgments

Beverly and I had lived in Dahlonega, Georgia, for about a year when I was asked to lead the church's youth class for vacation Bible school. Having only several days with which to provide something from which I thought the teens would learn and still enjoy, I decided to try a biblical overview. We met in the sanctuary balcony, but I still managed to use a Post-It notepad easel for writing down key names and terms. Conversation seemed on topic most of the time, although I would not vouch for how much or how well they remembered any of our time together. Still, the germ of an idea for a book took hold with me. This idea grew in my mind for the next four or five years, as I led a weekly lectionary study at that church on Sunday mornings. Several faithful adult members explored texts with me and unknowingly helped me begin to formulate the thesis for this book.

Later, Beverly and I moved to Red Springs, North Carolina, as co-pastors of a congregation there, where the women of Circle 3 asked me if I would lead their monthly Bible study. It was all the excuse that I needed for organizing and expanding my notes, beginning with Genesis. Each month, I provided printed outlines to the Circle members and was gratified by the interest with which they listened, discussed, and asked questions. Surprisingly, they asked me back for a second year, so my file of notes grew in size and topics covered.

When Beverly and I moved to Whiteville, North Carolina, to be interim pastors there, I was invited once again to lead an adult class. This one had been meeting on Sunday mornings for thirty years or more and called itself the "Reformed Rebels," always willing to wrestle with theological issues that would give some church members pause. Then, over the summer, all the adult classes combined for one study, which I led from Walter

ix

Brueggemann's small but insightful volume, *The Bible Makes Sense*. By this time, I had an extensive set of notes and was anticipating time for getting this book started.

After the Whiteville experience, Beverly and I were participating in the life of Saint Andrews Covenant Presbyterian Church, Wilmington, North Carolina. There, I was asked to lead a winter study for the Wednesday night adult group who shared in a weekly intergenerational program, "Preparing Our People for Service (POPS)." By this time, most of the chapters of the book had been drafted.

Meanwhile, a friend of ours from the Dahlonega congregation, Dea Devereaux, agreed to read the entire manuscript—one chapter at a time—and give me feedback. Although an active church member, Dea never had joined a class or study group. After reading the first few chapters, Dea then asked if she could share them with another friend from church, Susan Reese, and I agreed. Their comments and observations on all the chapters strengthened my sense that this book could speak to folks inside, and along the periphery of, the church. Hence, the manuscript has been road-tested and, I believe, found sufficiently worthy.

Leisa McDonald tackled the formatting, copyediting, and sometimes tedious details and decisions involved in preparing the final manuscript for submission. I was glad to be able to work with her again.

As usual, I am grateful to Beverly for reading each chapter and commenting on each one—even though she knows that I don't necessarily heed her suggestions! To her, and to all of those who took part in the classes and presentations mentioned above, I extend heartfelt appreciation.

Finally, I am especially grateful to Mary Miller Brueggeman and her late twin brother, Patrick Miller, for the foreword. My respect for their biblical knowledge and experience makes their contribution a great honor.

Foreword

This book by George Thompson, *Welcome to The One Great Story!*, is offered to the whole church and especially to those who wish they understood the Bible better but feel or believe it is beyond them. It works for those who are joining the church or young people in confirmation. It works for the sometime church member who feels inadequate about the ways of God both near and far. It also works for the new Council or Session member who has been chosen to lead the church in the coming years. This book was made for study groups in the church as well. It is clear that Thompson draws on his extraordinary knowledge of biblical studies as well as an awareness of regular people who sit weekly in morning worship. That is the genius of his work. He understands where the church is in its educational task. You won't learn what each book of the Bible is about or be able to list the books of the Bible, however helpful that might be. What you will see and understand is the role of the faithful and reliable God among women and men, from creation until the "not-ending" of God's reign among us.

Thompson sees this story as a tapestry that is woven not only by the ancient near-Eastern world in which the story plays out. It is also part of the fabric of what is going on in our world today. No dust-covered Bible for him. Its worth is when the two worlds—the biblical world and our world of pandemics and war and love and family—meet. That is exhilarating and opens up for the reader a whole new future. Along the way are wonderful sidebars and excellent questions that will certainly help those who teach. Moreover, Thompson's "tapestry" urges the reader to move deeper into her or his life for new understandings and energy for the living of these days.

MARY MILLER BRUEGGEMANN and PATRICK D. MILLER
April 2020

Chapter 1

Once Upon a Time

A Sacred Story Line

What is the first Bible story that you remember hearing? Was it about the Israelites fleeing from Egypt? Samson pulling down the pillars to destroy a multitude of the Philistines? King Solomon deciding which of the two women would get the baby whom they both claimed was theirs? Elijah complaining to the LORD in the wilderness? The angel Gabriel visiting Mary? Jesus healing ten lepers and only one coming back to thank him? One of Jesus' followers using a sword to cut off the ear of the high priest's slave? Saul being struck blind on the road to Damascus? Peter being rescued from prison by an angel?

"YES, THAT'S THE BOOK FOR ME!"

Those of us who grew up in a church were very likely told Bible stories from an early age. If you were, and you were like me, you were not always sure what the story was supposed to be telling us. Part of that uncertainty would have been related to the story's setting—in a world so far removed in time, distance, and familiar customs from our own. I think the stories that I remembered the most were the hardest to understand—like a plague of locusts or Jesus making mud paste and healing a blind man with it.

What was it like for you to sit down and read something in the Bible on your own for the very first time? Where did you begin, and why? What do you remember about it? What questions did you have about what you read? What motivated you to keep reading—or did you give up out of frustration?

> *What was it like to sit down and read something*
> *from the Bible for the very first time?*

My home church had a practice of presenting Bibles to children when they entered the fourth grade. I remember the Sunday morning when I received mine, bound in black faux leather, with a presentation page in the front, a bunch of color maps in the back, and my name embossed in gold leaf on the front cover. It was my very own copy of the Bible, and I was excited! I received it with pride and carefully carried it home after worship. That night, I sat cross-legged in my pajamas on my bed, placing my Bible in front of me on the bedcovers. I was determined to read it—but where should I begin? It seemed to me like cheating to start anywhere other than at the beginning, so I turned to Genesis, chapter 1, and began to read.

Not many days later, I discontinued this nightly effort. I had made it to about chapter 17 or 18 of Genesis, but I could not understand what was going on. The translation was the Revised Standard Version, so it was not a matter of trying to make sense out of old-fashioned words and phrases. No one at church had suggested a place to start or a particular approach; no one oriented me on what I would be reading or how to find answers to my questions; no one checked in with me to see how it was going; and, for whatever reason, it never occurred to me to ask anyone for help. Granted, I was only nine years old at the time, so it was a challenge for a child to understand much about the characters and story lines. Even so, when I put that Bible aside, I quietly felt defeated and guilty.

Something similar happened to me at school in eighth grade. My literature teacher decided to challenge me so, one day in class, she handed me a copy of Tolstoy's *War and Peace* to read. I took the book home and plodded away at it for a couple of weeks, getting through about 200 pages of that 2,000-page novel—trying to keep track of characters, story line, events, and plot development. But I was lost, getting more and more frustrated and discouraged. Finally, I gave up and returned the book to her, apologetically—but that was that. I have never tried to read *War and Peace* again.

THE PARTS—AND THE WHOLE

My motivation to keep reading the Bible ebbed and flowed over the years, until my freshman year of college. There, I ran across a loosely knit fellowship of Christians, who didn't think much of organized church but were zealous in their faith. Perhaps not surprisingly, I read more of the Bible during college than in all the years before then. Introductory courses to the Old and New Testaments helped to broaden my perspective, but I was not able, at the time, to integrate that college-level learning into my devotional reading. Then I went to seminary, where (after testing out of the required Bible courses) I took classes in 1 and 2 Samuel, 2 Isaiah, John, and 1 Corinthians. By that time, I knew that I was preparing to become a pastor, so I was committed to using scholarly study tools in the service of preaching and Christian education.

You would think that, after all this formal and informal preparation, I would have had a clear and comfortable sense of the flow and overarching coherence of the Bible. At the time, I am not sure that I would have admitted anything to the contrary; however, it was not until some years of preaching were under my belt that it finally felt like I began to "get it." Perhaps there were professors and course readings along the way that had presented "it," but that comprehensive picture never, for me, had come into clear focus.

Reading the Bible—and feeling confident that you are following what is happening—can feel like dumping out the contents of a 1,000-piece puzzle and trying to figure out where to begin. But it doesn't have to be that way. Yes, the Bible is very long and consists of a dizzying number of distinct books and documents. And, yes, the Bible was composed, edited, and re-edited a long time ago, by many different people over hundreds of years, largely from oral traditions, in a geographical location that most people today see only on maps or electronic media. Yet, I am convinced that interested, devoted people can read the Bible and get a lot out of it, once they get oriented. You don't have to pursue a formal degree in order to understand and appreciate the Bible's rich, compelling message.

Reading the Bible can feel like dumping out the contents of a 1,000-piece puzzle and wondering where to begin.

My wife Beverly and I have been serving together as pastors for about a decade, during which time I have been regularly leading adult Bible studies. Over the years, I have preached about how Christians are called to find their story within the Bible's story. More recently, these Bible studies have allowed me to trace the story that holds the Bible together and to demonstrate how it echoes, time and again, from the Old Testament to the New, with fascinating consistency. I call this "The One Great Story," and it is the reason for this book. It is written for readers inside the church as well as those outside of it, for people of faith as well as people who might simply be curious—or even skeptical. For this reason, I have attempted to avoid "churchy" jargon—so that the story can speak vividly, both to church and non-church folks.

STARTING POINTS

Everyone who writes about the Bible does so guided by some set of assumptions, whether articulated or not. Here are the particular ideas that guide my understanding. The *first* one I already have begun to unpack: that what gives the Bible its basic integrity is a narrative—a story line. This narrative emerges in the first book, Genesis, and can be traced in its long development through most of the biblical books, all the way to Revelation.[1]

Second, although this story takes on more and more characters, places, events, and practices, its basic theme and goal do not waver. They concern God's call to establish a people who will bear witness to who God is and what God is doing in and for the world. The unavoidable flip side of this claim has to do with that selected people, what happened over many centuries as they sometimes trusted God in this call—but often did not. *Third*, this story, by definition, does not conclude with the last book of the Bible; it is our story too. Christians in all times and places are spiritual descendants of the people of God whom we discover, celebrate, cringe over, and certainly with whom we identify in the pages of the Scriptures.

Consequently, our *fourth* claim here is that the Bible retains a unique place in the life of believers in all times and places. It is intended to be our companion and our friend. Like any faithful and worthwhile companion, the Bible encourages us as it also sometimes tells us what we do not want to hear! This dual role is what makes the Bible so valuable and reliable.

Fifth and finally, I am aware that many adults in the church are embarrassed to admit that they don't know much of the Bible, or that they don't

---

1. More precisely, scholars would argue for the presence of more than one story line or tradition. Walter Brueggemann, for instance, distinguishes between the "primal narrative" that is revealed in Deuteronomy and Joshua, (and then is picked up in the New Testament Gospels), an "expanded narrative" revealed in Gen 12–50 (Abram/Sarai through the death of Joseph), and a "derivative narrative" that includes Judges through Nehemiah and the New Testament Acts of the Apostles. See Brueggemann, *The Bible Makes Sense*, chapter 3.

This book highlights elements that are common to these three narratives.

always understand what they read. Some even have concluded that it doesn't matter much to their faith anyway. This is a sad but all-too-common situation, and I think one of the main culprits is the church's failure to teach well. I remember once sitting in the board meeting of a large church and hearing one of the officers state quite firmly that he "did not need to go to Sunday school!" No one else in the room offered a response. When congregations get used to biblical ignorance, their life and witness are weakened and in danger of losing direction. The growing number of people in Western societies who show no interest in religion just might change their minds and hearts if they saw churches who engaged the Bible authentically, faithfully, and creatively.

THE NATURE OF THE BEAST

Approaching the Bible in terms of The One Great Story is a way to overcome our embarrassment of ignorance and confusion, and even our apathy. Before we enter this Story, though, let us make sure that we understand the basic nature of our subject matter. To do so, we want to be clear about some very well-established conclusions about the Bible itself:[2]

1. The Bible is *actually a library*. The version that mainline Protestant churches use includes sixty-six "books," which contain several kinds of literature—legal codes, short stories, songs, poetry, history, letters, oracles, and so forth. Genesis and Exodus, for instance, read quite differently than the Song of Songs or Paul's letter to the Galatians. Most of these writings also show evidence of having been handled by more than one storyteller, writer, or editor. In its great variety of detail, the Bible can appear daunting!

2. Even though we have inherited this library with its long, complex history, behind most of these texts and documents stands a spoken tradition that is much older and more dynamic. Writing is a fairly recent way for humans to transmit and preserve their community identity. Instead, what has dominated human history is the spoken word—storytelling through word of mouth, recitation, and response—passed on from one generation to the next. We are referring here to the universal phenomenon typically described as *"oral tradition."*

   Oral traditions still exist today, not only in non-Western or "less-developed" regions of the world but also in rural areas and

2. For a longer discussion of these conclusions, see McDonald, *Formation of the Bible*, 21–25.

working-class populations of Western countries.[3] Their continued re-silience and power can help us appreciate how our biblical ancestors would have preserved their stories, laws, and customs for many generations—initially and for a long time—only by oral practices.[4] What we read, therefore, in much of the Bible is derived from oral sources, which eventually were preserved by incorporating them into (and as) written documents. This is the case for both the Old Testament and the New Testament.

3. In spite of all of their diversity, the biblical books have a lot in common with each other in terms of themes and emphases. God is a major player virtually everywhere in the Bible. God's overall purposes come through consistently, as well as human responses to those purposes—whether faithful or otherwise. God's actions on behalf of a failed community appear from the very first book (Genesis) to the very last one (Revelation). These common themes will become quite clear throughout this book.

4. The Bible deals with circumstances and issues that were part of *life in ancient times*. The historically related events of the Bible cover a period of about two thousand years, ending in the late first century of the Common Era ("CE" or "AD"). The world was very different back then, compared to the twenty-first century with its satellites, democratic nations, mobile electronic devices, video conferencing, prevalence of the English language, etc. To read back into the Bible, an awareness—for instance—of specific historical or technological developments from our own time, is to insult the Bible's own integrity.

5. The *cultural world of the Bible* is specific to a time and place. It is often referred to, in scholarly studies, as "the Ancient Near East." This cultural world was affected by the conditions of male-dominated communities, as well as language, land, climate, assumptions about personal identity, and so forth. We do not readily understand, for instance, why blessings are so pivotal from father to son or what legal obligations a master had to his servants. Recognizing its own particular context, as puzzling as it often seems, is a necessary part of understanding the Bible.

6. Biblical writings serve very different purposes than those served by our typically modern assumptions about "objective and value-free"

---

3. For a brief, easy-to-read introduction to oral traditions in today's world, see Sample, *Ministry in an Oral Culture*, chapters 1 and 2.

4. See the summary of oral tradition in McKenzie, "The Hebrew Community and the Old Testament," 1073–74.

reporting and research. The Bible witnesses to a God who seeks to restore creation from the destructive rebellion of the very humans who were made to care for it. This goal of reclaiming, or "redeeming," humanity from its errant ways and their consequences becomes evident in The One Great Story at every turn. Details about characters, places, events, and practices are never included as ends in themselves or free of an interpretive framework or aim. Consequently, we today are challenged not to impose *our own assumptions about reality and truth* on how the Bible expresses itself.

Our typical, modern assumptions about "objective" study do not line up with ancient assumptions that frame biblical material.

7. In addition to all the other ways that the Bible is strange to our world, it was composed in languages that few of us can read. The oldest versions of biblical books were composed in ancient Hebrew or Aramaic (Old Testament) or Koiné—common Greek—(New Testament). Not only this, but it is likely that Jesus himself spoke Aramaic in daily conversation. This suggests that his sayings were translated from Aramaic into Greek by the time they appeared in the four Gospels. Most people on the planet cannot read, write, or speak any of those languages and thus rely on a translation in their own native tongues. Moreover, the process of translation itself still requires some interpretation, since word-for-word renderings sometimes do not convey the meaning of the original.

One example of the challenge inherent in language and understanding is Jesus' parable of the laborers in the vineyard (Matt 20:1–16). The landowner in the parable hires workers during different times of the day but pays them all the same wage at evening time. When those who worked longer complain, the landowner replies that he has done nothing wrong. His final comment to them comes in the form of a question: "Or are you envious because I am generous" (Matt 20:15b)? Actually, the Greek literally says, "Or is your eye evil because I am good?" At least five other English versions provide very similar translations to the one quoted here.[5] Instead of the literal Greek, each

---

5. These other translations include:
—*The Message*: "Are you going to get stingy because I am generous?"
—New American Bible: "Are you envious because I am generous?"
—New International Version: "Or are you envious because I am generous?"
—New Jerusalem Bible: "Why should you be envious because I am generous?"

translation team chose to provide an interpretation of those Greek words. Verses like this one remind us that there are places in a translation where we must make educated guesses about a text's meaning—whether the results fit into our preconceived notions or not!

8. Finally, the Bible that we know represents *a selection process*, or processes, that took place in the mists of history. The sixty-six books that are familiar to Protestants today were not the only ancient literature about the Israelites and Jews, as well as about Jesus and very early Christians. Evidence, from early history and from archeological discoveries, makes it clear that dozens of other documents about biblical characters and events were composed. Some of them survive today in a collection known as the Apocrypha (including such books as 1 and 2 Esdras and 1–4 Maccabees). Others are not extant, such as the Book of the Annals of the Kings of Judah (see, for instance, 2 Kgs 23:28). Some were known in the early Christian centuries, such as the Shepherd of Hermas and the Apocalypse of Peter, and others have been discovered much more recently, such as The Gospel of Thomas. The fact that an extensive list of these books exists suggests that, indeed, our Christian forebears made determinations along the way about the value of particular writings to the instruction and life of the church.

MEASURED DISCERNMENT

This last point, in other words, has to do with the question of *"canon,"* or standards by which any particular book would have been deemed suitable for circulation in the church. Evidence from history and archaeology is overwhelming: the Bible did not drop out of the sky, as though written by the finger of God, cut and dried, with no grey areas. Protestants, Catholics, and Orthodox Christian traditions still vary in their inclusion of what constitutes "the Scriptures." Not every ancient book written about Jesus "made it" into the Bible, for example, and neither did every letter attributed to the apostles Peter and Paul.[6]

Not only this, but our English translations are made from Hebrew and Greek collections that include variations, and sometimes even omissions, between ancient copies of the same texts. Some early Greek versions of the Gospel of Mark conclude with 16:8, while others include twelve more verses. Similarly, the oldest known documents of the Gospel of John do not

—Revised English Bible: "Why be jealous because I am generous?"

6. McDonald, *Formation of the Bible*, 21–25.

have the story of the woman caught in adultery (7:53—8:11). In the Old Testament, sometimes a Hebrew word or phrase is not clear, and translators have to rely upon early Greek or Latin translations to render an English reading (see, for example, Ps 16:2, Ps 18:43, Prov 24:21, and many others).

One of my Bible professors in seminary, James A. Sanders, told the story, in class one day, about a rare privilege that he was given. While a young scholar, Sanders became the first person allowed to view the Psalms scroll that was found among the famous collection known as the Dead Sea Scrolls. He had to travel to Israel to do so, and on the ship he memorized all the Psalms in Hebrew, since he would not be allowed to take any books or writing utensils into the room with him. During his examination of it, Sanders discovered that this scroll, dated from the first-century Common Era (that is, "AD"), included one extra Psalm—a total of 151, instead of 150!

Sanders's discovery is not the only one of its kind, and it reminds us that many decisions have been made across the centuries about what would be considered "in" and "out" of the canon. This matter of standards for what is acceptable as Holy Writ leads us also into the question of "interpretation," which we have mentioned a little already. In every era (even within the times of the Bible itself), people in the tradition of biblical faith have had to make sense out of what the Bible says. This kind of discernment is not as straightforward as we might wish—in part because every act of reading anything at all involves an attempt to see meaning in something. In our case here, scholarly study of the Bible has helped to open up a greater awareness of the way in which texts and passages were likely to have been understood by their earliest audiences.

Many decisions have been made across the centuries about what is considered "in" and "out" of the biblical canon.

GETTING FROM "THERE" TO "HERE"

These scholarly resources are invaluable but, by themselves, they are incomplete. We—and anyone who reads the Bible—interpret what we read out of our own context, too. It should not surprise us that our context (and any context, for that matter) lays a filter or two over the biblical text. What we see in the text through these filters might mislead us. Drastic differences between the ancient Mediterranean world and the modern, scientific world that affects us today illustrate the challenges of interpretation.

Still, one of the primary reasons that we have a Bible is because our spiritual ancestors assumed that the Bible's witness provides *meaning* that also is *significant* in every time and place.[7] In this book, we proceed with the conviction that evidence in the Bible itself witnesses to the dominating presence of The One Great Story that we will explore here. The meaning of that Story *then* offers us *here and now* a rich, challenging, and invigorating way to discover points of significance from it for our lives and for the life of this world that God still seeks to make whole. We can benefit from scholarship's capacity for *un*-covering those earliest meanings from a text, as we seek faithfully to *dis*-cover how that meaning might speak to our own situation and to the world today.

Thus, this book about the Bible is different from others. It aims to provide evidence for the claim that the Bible became what we know it to be because, across many generations and centuries, inheritors of a particular Story (The One Great Story) recognized its *meaning* as of major *significance* for themselves, in their changing circumstances. That recognition led, time and again, to explaining how that Story made sense out of their identity, purpose, and call. We are going to explore that Story here.

THE SECOND NAÏVETÉ

I write this book as a seminary-trained pastor and teacher, whose graduate work includes a degree in biblical interpretation. As a young adult, I struggled with matters of biblical inspiration and authority, and I have come out on the other side. My approach assumes that Christians take the Bible very seriously, even as those of us affected by modern, Western ways of viewing the world realize that the Bible speaks out of a quite different world and in a very different way. We impose assumptions on the Bible that did not exist in its time. Our opportunity now is to learn to discern how to throw out the bath water and keep the baby. For instance, Old Testament symbolic exaggeration, or its presentation of violence of many kinds, made sense in that biblical world. Today, these features often leave us scratching our heads or clucking our tongues. It is possible—perhaps necessary—for us to move from innocence through skepticism to what philosopher and

---

7. The distinction between a text's "meaning" (which does not change) and its "significance" (the relationship of that meaning to something else) is a critical distinction, one that I have found very helpful for preaching. A scholarly discussion of this argument is found in Hirsch, *Validity in Interpretation*, (see, for example 8–9, 62–63, and 140–43), which I adapted for my STD dissertation, "The Beckoning of Scripture: Meaning and Significance in Biblical Interpretation."

theologian Paul Ricoeur called "the second naïveté."[8] This kind of naïveté emerges when we move beyond a simple innocence, beyond even a scary or discouraging skepticism, to engage all the intricacies of biblical study with fresh enthusiasm. Once we get there, the Bible can become for us today an even deeper and more compelling witness to life and faith.

LAUNCHING OUT

This book does not provide an overview of every book in the Bible. Neither does it assume that every quotation of, or reference to, an earlier section of the Bible in a later section expresses the Story that I seek to illuminate here. Rather, here we favor those parts of any biblical book that reveal or allude to The One Great Story, that contribute to its trajectory throughout the Bible. We seek to discover how that Story itself influences and propels successive storytellers, scribes, and editors as they discuss later characters, places, events, and practices. In this way, The Story itself becomes expanded and developed, while maintaining its theme consistently. This theme, I believe, provides the heart and deepest energy driving the Bible as canon. It is within the energy of this Story that we, in our respective times and places, can discover how it still speaks.

It is within the energy of The One Great Story
that we can discover how it still speaks.

We are about to follow a Story that is long and involved! It includes many generations, many characters, a long list of locations, episodes, and developments—not to mention those storytellers and editors who preserved and interpreted various parts of it all along the way. What might not be apparent at first glance is that the most present and dependable of all the characters is not one of the many persons whom you might expect—not Abraham, Jacob, Moses, Ruth, David, Elijah, Isaiah, or Mary. Rather, it is God—a God who initiates things, who responds to what people are doing, who will shift action in order to maintain an overall purpose, and who never gives up.

Because of how The Story begins, *we could argue that its most central theme is whether the called, chosen ones will demonstrate their trust in the One who—because of the call given to them—promises, acts, expects, holds*

---

8. An academic summary of Paul Ricoeur's use of the term "second naïveté" is found in Mudge's essay, "Paul Ricoeur on Biblical Interpretation," esp. 6, 21–29.

accountable, and persists against the odds. Will they "do what is right in their own eyes," or will they follow the One who made them and keeps giving them one new chance after another? Will they live into the promise given to their ancestors, thus becoming a blessing for themselves and all peoples?

In the chapters that follow, we will see this Story begin, build, shift, peak, falter, start to echo, get revived, make a fresh appeal, and continue to speak. Along the way, we will reflect, now and again, on how the character of this Story is handled from one generation and set of circumstances to another, and how integrally rooted to the whole Story is the chapter that has to do with Jesus as Messiah. Finally, we will identify some of the issues about this Story for its hearers today—issues about interpretation, about the nature of biblical faith, and of life as a community of believers. These issues have a timeless-type quality to them, a feature that will both challenge and encourage us. Hopefully, this journey will allow you to grasp what took that earnest fourth-grader so many years to understand—and then you, too, can find the Bible opening up in fresh and exciting ways.

I invite you now to join me on the journey of a lifetime, a journey of Most High intent and human response. Welcome to The One Great Story!

FOR THE READER

1. What do you remember about your earliest exposure to the Bible? Was it through children's songs, a Bible story, or hearing someone read from the Bible? What were your impressions at the time?

2. With what parts of the Bible are you most comfortable—if any? Which parts bother you the most? Why?

3. Have you ever participated in an organized study of the Bible itself or of particular biblical books (as distinguished from devotional studies that draw from biblical stories and verses here and there)? What was that experience like? What did you get out of it? What wonderings did it bring up in your mind and heart?

4. What is easier for you to trust: a passage from the Bible or the evening news? Why?

SUGGESTED ACTIVITIES

- Without referring to a Bible, write down as many names of characters, events, locations, and customs or practices that you can recall. Allow yourself about 20 minutes to do this. When you finish, review your list and be aware of your thoughts and feelings. What interests you about the Bible? What turns you off? What might you like to understand better?

- Invite a friend to complete this exercise, too, and then share your results with each other. How does the conversation between the two of you help you think about the Bible?

Chapter 2

The Story Begins

Call, Creation, and Promise

" . . . and in you all the families of the earth shall be blessed."

—GEN 12:3C

Flames threw eerie shapes onto the blue-grey sky, as the women cleaned pots and utensils and the children gathered eagerly around the camp's main fire. Behind them, the men and older boys were securing the tents, flocks, and herds. Every night watch had been assigned, and each boy knew how vital it was to the voyaging clan that their animals be protected from wild predators. A few stars had begun to twinkle as the young ones settled in. Toddlers sat on laps of older siblings, and a few white-haired women quietly patrolled the circle. Muffled giggles, prankish glances, and wayward elbows quickly ceased, however, as the gathered audience sensed the approach of the one for whom they were waiting.

Roundish in appearance, bent over, with an untamed mane of receding hair matched only by a flowing beard stretching almost to an undefined waistline, one gnarled hand tightly grasping a slightly bowed but sturdy stick, it was as though a magnetic field followed the doddering figure into the center of the circle, not too close to the fire itself. Suddenly still and silent, the children were holding their breath. The figure by the fire now came alive, eyes wide open, head turning from one side of the gathered circle to another, growing in their mind's eyes to larger than life itself. Then, in a voice that sounded like heaven's, he spoke deliberately:

"A wandering Aramean was my ancestor; he went down into Egypt and lived there as an alien, . . . " (Deut 26:5).

By the time that the old man had finished speaking, the youngest ones were asleep in someone's arms, and discreet yawns could be detected around the circle. Women signaled to the children from their respective tents, and the spellbound assembly dispersed across the camp almost without a sound. If you had been there, you would have seen how their faces gave off a serene glow. Once again, they had heard from whence they came. Once again, they were reminded who they were—and whose.

"TELL US A STORY"

It is not difficult to imagine such a scene, is it? In days of old, long before social media or television, or radio, or telegrams, or newspapers, or pamphlets, or books, or even hand-printed scrolls—in those days, long ago, people learned many things through storytelling. As I have studied the Bible across many years, I have come to appreciate the power of story. I have realized that, even with all of the academic reading that I have done, what sticks with me most is a good story. Now, I understand more clearly how the medium of storytelling weaves the Bible together—how the strength of what we might sometimes think of as "the message" of the Bible depends on narrative. Now, I can imagine Hebrew nomads transmitting to their children a sense of their identity and purpose by telling a story, *their* Story—which eventually became The One Great Story.

The medium of storytelling weaves the Bible together.

In many respects, *this Story* begins not with accounts of the creation of the world, but with a childless couple who might have thought that when they had settled down in a place named Haran, their travels were over (Gen 11:30–32). The man's father, Terah, had taken the couple—Abram and Sarai—and a few other members of his family with him, from their hometown of Ur. Apparently the plan was to put down roots elsewhere but, instead, they stayed in Haran. Then Terah died.

Sometimes we want to ask the Bible questions that it simply does not answer—the way that a news reporter digs for more details about a breaking story. We are tempted to try to fill in what seem to us to be gaps in the story line, gaps that would help to satisfy our curiosity about what is going on. There are many places in the Bible where we could ask questions like these, and the transition from Terah's death to what happens next is one of those places. Did Abram and Sarai enjoy living in Haran? They seem to have prospered during the time there (Gen 12:5, 13:2). Did they feel welcome in a place that was not home? Were they bound by custom to remain with Terah as long as he was alive?

When we study biblical stories, it is important to be careful about "reading into" the text something that is not there. Much of the time, the Bible does not provide comment on the inner thoughts and feelings of characters as they decide and act. It was enough, to those responsible for the story as it appears in the text, merely to move to the next episode of Abram's and Sarai's life. Terah died in their adopted town of Haran, and—before you know it—God comes into the picture.

"Go," the LORD said to Abram and Sarai. And so, The One Great Story begins—with a call from God to a childless couple who still must have been grieving their patriarch's death. It was no small thing, this call from God. The two of them were to leave just about everything familiar and everyone they knew, to venture to a place as yet unknown. This call came with a big carrot dangling on a stick, too: the LORD said that the two of them would give birth to a people of distinguished repute. Not only this, but their pledged high regard would do something good for other peoples, too: " . . . and in you all the families of the earth shall be blessed" (Gen 12:3c).

God had high hopes for Abram and Sarai. And, again, without any fanfare or stream-of-consciousness commentary, the story continues. They go, Abram and Sarai, taking Lot, the nephew, their servants (slaves?), and "all the possessions that they had gathered" (Gen 12:5b). The entourage was on its way.

This divinely-selected couple encountered many adventures and moments of trial during the years of their journey. You might remember that the two of them never did make it to the land that God promised. That arrival comes many generations later in The Story. On their part of this long sojourn, Abram and Sarai covered a lot of territory. Based on archeological evidence, the move itself from Ur to Haran would have been no small trip. The latter was a few hundred miles north, up the Euphrates River from Ur. Leaving Haran for Canaan (Gen 12:5de) meant another long trip, this time in a southwesterly direction. Once they arrived, Abram received a promise from the LORD that this land would be given to Abram's descendants (Gen 12:7; compare Gen 13:14–18). Abram then marked the spot with "an altar." This act indicates that Abram was trusting the LORD and expressing his devotion to this one god, and not to other deities. As we will see many times throughout This Story, Abram and Sarai's descendants often waffled over their own ultimate trust and devotion.

> *Abram and Sarai's descendants often waffled over*
> *their own ultimate trust and devotion.*

Many locations appear as stopping points for this entourage, both regions and cities: Canaan, Bethel, Egypt, the Negeb, Mamre, Hebron, Sodom, Gomorrah, Kadesh, Gerar, the cave of Machpelah (where both Abram and Sarai would be buried), and others. These locations often figure later, in subsequent episodes with the couple's descendants. In our own understandable ignorance of their geography and history, today we probably find it easier just to follow the human interactions themselves, between Abram, Sarai, and others who came into this picture. At the heart of these interactions rested the question of succession and inheritance: who would carry this divine promise once the old couple died? They had no children.

Part of what makes the Abraham/Sarah (God later changed their names) episodes of The One Great Story so intriguing is the couple's way of handling their barren condition. Sarai was worried that she would not have a child, so she offered Abram her young slave, Hagar, as a second wife. Hagar indeed bore Abraham a son, who was named Ishmael. Yet it becomes clear that Ishmael would not be heir to the divine promise, although Hagar received assurance through a divine messenger that her son would be blessed anyway (Gen 16).

In the meantime, God came to Abram and reinforced the original promise, by making a covenant with him (Gen 15 and 17). This covenant assured the couple a very large number of descendants and their own land, Canaan, where they had been living, but as foreigners. For Abraham's part, he was to circumcise all males as "a sign of the covenant between me and you" (Gen 17:11b). In one version of this covenant episode, the story comments that Abram trusted in the LORD and the LORD's promise, which God then took "as righteousness" (Gen 15:6) for Abraham. In later chapters, we will see how this one sentence—like a comment that an early storyteller would have interjected into the account—became a key element of The Story's theological interpretation.

> **Pause to Reflect**
>
> When the LORD made a covenant with Abram, the text says that he "believed the LORD" (Gen 15:6). Three other English versions translate the verb in this clause as "put his faith in" (Revised English Bible; New American Bible; New Jerusalem Bible). In your mind, what are the distinctions between the concepts of "believing in," "trusting in," and "putting faith in?"

Still, how could this covenant be fulfilled without a male heir? One hot day, the couple was visited by three guests, for whom Abraham displayed gracious hospitality by providing them rest and a meal. The visitors then delivered a promise that Sarah would bear a son in the following year. Sarah laughed as she heard the promise, listening as she was, outside of the tent flap. The subsequent interchanges between God and Abraham—and then God with Sarah—reveal a very human response to an unlikely prediction. Sarah denied laughing, but God didn't let her off the hook! Yet it was God's remarks to Abraham that adds to the central theme of The One Great Story: "Is anything too wonderful for the LORD?" (Gen 18:14a). As with the comment just noted above, about Abram's trust of God for the covenant, this rhetorical question in the episode of Sarah's laughter becomes a theological linchpin for later episodes of The Story. It will echo often.

As the LORD promised, Sarah bore a son in due season (Gen 21:1–7), and Sarah marked the occasion with a statement about laughter—her own and that of "everyone who hears" (Gen 21:6b). Now Abraham's other son, Ishmael, and his mother, the Egyptian slave Hagar, were sent out of the camp; but God promised to Abraham that they would be okay and that the boy would establish a people as well, "because he is your offspring" (Gen 21:13c).

A strange twist comes into The Story at this point: God's command that Abraham sacrifice his only son, Isaac (Gen 22:1–19). Modern sensibilities leave many readers today wondering about the kind of God being represented in this episode, but the incident emphasizes something else instead. As Abraham was moments away from slaughtering Isaac, God stopped him and provided a ram for sacrifice instead. The death of Isaac would have eliminated Abraham's and Sarah's successor to the promise, the offspring who already had been promised for that purpose. Abraham's actions demonstrated complete trust in the LORD, despite the shocking nature of the divine request. His trust, flying in the face of a perplexing and even cruel command, led to a strengthened commitment by God to the promise. Isaac lived, and that promise still stood a chance.

Years of travel, temporary residence, international interactions, origins of new peoples, and divine punishment fill the story of Abraham and Sarah. When Sarah died, Abraham negotiated with the Hittites of Canaan for a burial site (Gen 23). Concern for an appropriate line of succession through Isaac led Abraham to arrange, through one of his servants, a marriage for Isaac with one of his own clan. The episode that tells of finding Rebekah carrying a water jar at a well is full of what must be ancient near Eastern customs and good old-fashioned charm (Gen 24). Not only does Isaac marry Rebekah but "he loved her" (Gen 24:67c). Even though Abraham himself married again and fathered several more children, his lineage, his property, and the divine promise, went with Isaac (Gen 25:5). Then Abraham died, "in a good old age, an old man and full of years" (Gen 25:8), and both Isaac and Ishmael oversaw his burial with Sarah. The first major chapter of The One Great Story comes to a close.

Abraham's lineage, his property, and the divine vow, did not go to his firstborn—Ishmael—but to the son of promise, Isaac.

THE BACKSTORY: CREATION, FALL, AND ALL THAT STUFF

You probably noticed that the telling of Abraham and Sarah's chapter in The Story is not where the Bible actually begins. Most of us have heard something about the creation accounts at the very beginning of the Book of Genesis. In the first chapter, God creates—in six days from "a formless void" (Gen 1:2a)—first light, then separation of waters, then dry land with vegetation, then lights separating day from night, then creatures in water and birds, then creatures on land, then humans. Chapter 2 provides some variation to the account: God makes a man (*adam* or "earthy"), situating him in the garden to cultivate it; then God makes birds and land creatures, to which the "adam" gave names; then God realized none of these animals would make a fitting companion for the "adam," so one of his ribs was fashioned into a woman. Everything now was as it should be.

In one of the earliest biblical episodes, both divine judgment and divine mercy appear together. This happens over and over again in the Bible.

Except that something went wrong—very wrong. Surely one of the most well-known of biblical stories—even if it is often misunderstood—is the one that happens next, the one often referred to as "the temptation." A wily creature is introduced, the serpent, who talked the woman into believing that it was okay to eat fruit from trees in the garden—even though God had said not to do so, or they would suffer terminal consequences (Gen 2:17). This lapse of judgment by the woman and the man led to severe changes in the terms of their circumstances in the world. Everyone would have a hard life from now on—man, woman, and especially the serpent, who received a curse from God (Gen 3:13–19). For centuries, Christian theology has called this change of circumstances "the Fall," since it represents how the divine purpose had been thwarted by human disobedience. Things never would be the same again.

> **Pause to Reflect**
> An old joke about the episode of "the Fall" (Gen 3)
> says that Adam blamed Eve, Eve blamed the serpent,
> and the serpent didn't have a leg to stand on! Based
> on your experience and observations about life,
> what do you think this episode was intended to say
> about human responsibility and accountability?

But life would go on anyway, although it was plagued soon enough by strife and murder. We also remember hearing something about Cain and Abel, Eve and Adam's sons. Cain killed Abel because Abel's offering to God was accepted, but his was not (Gen 4:2–8). The famous question, "Am I my brother's keeper?" comes from this episode. Yet, even though Cain was driven away, God promised to protect him (Gen 4:15). Thus, judgment and mercy appear together, more than once, in the earliest of biblical episodes. The Bible also demonstrates, early in its first book, an interest in connecting dots between persons and generations. A genealogy in chapter 5 leads from Adam to a character who then dominates the following five chapters, Noah.

Again, we are dealing with an episode from The Story that is fairly well-known, at least in some of its main elements. Things on earth were not going as the LORD had intended. The story says that "the wickedness of humankind was great" and that humans cared only about evil things (Gen 6:5). (This won't be the last time we hear about this issue before The Story is over!) So God decided that it was time to end the whole business, by eliminating all people, all animals, and all birds. There was only one glimmer of hope in the whole situation, which was this fellow Noah. Noah was "a righteous man, blameless in his generation; Noah walked with God" (Gen 6:9). He must have stood out like a sore thumb! So, as many of us remember, God called on Noah to prepare for a devastating flood by constructing a water-worthy vessel that would carry Noah's family and pairs of all creatures safely.

We also remember something about rain falling in torrents, the ark floating as the waters rose to cover even mountaintops, the report of complete destruction, and months of subsiding waters (Gen 7:6–24). Once Noah and his family were able to disembark, God commanded them to unload the ark so that the creatures could repopulate the earth (Gen 8:13–19). Noah then constructed an altar and worshipped the LORD, who decided never to do that again. God blessed Noah's family, as when the first humans were created (Gen 9:1; compare 1:22, 28). God set up a covenant with Noah and his family, using the rainbow as a sign of protection for all creatures on earth (Gen 9:8–17). This covenant brought an upbeat conclusion to an otherwise harsh episode: the Creator has not given up on the human enterprise.

> *The rainbow is a sign that the Creator has not given up on the human enterprise.*

Life started over again. Genesis lists Noah's three sons—Shem, Ham, and Japheth—and their progeny for a couple of generations each. This list also shows interest in details such as who ended up where and how certain peoples and places became settled—"in their lands, with their own languages, by their family, in their nations (Gen 10:5c; compare 10:20, 31–32)." Chapter 10 seems, in part, to set up the circumstances for the next episode, about the tower of Babel (Gen 11:1–9). Like the other episodes that precede it, the Babel incident appears designed to explain something significant and universal about the general human condition, framed in the setting of the prehistoric Near East. Such is the function and resounding power of the literary form known as "myth," once we understand it in this way.

In this legendary episode within The One Great Story, all people spoke one language (but compare the verses noted above in Gen 10) and had traveled to a location that looked good to them. They decided to build a city there, including a tower that would go far up into the sky—actually, "the heavens," where ancient cultures often imagined the gods to dwell. God, the LORD, did not like that idea, commenting (perhaps to the heavenly council) "this is only the beginning of what they will do; nothing . . . will now be impossible for them (Gen 11:6cd)." So God intervened, by "going down" and strewing the people every which way ("over the face of all the earth" [Gen 11:8]), which meant the end to their construction project. Hence, the people's effort to go *up* to heaven ("Come, let us build ourselves . . . a tower with its top in the heavens" [Gen 11:4]) becomes set in contrast with God's action in response ("Come, let us go *down*, . . . " [Gen 11:7]).

The name "Babel"—"Gate of God"—is used here as a play on the Hebrew verb *balal*, which means "to confuse." This episode, coming as it does following the great flood and repopulation of the earth, explains in an epic way how human beings kept trying things that went beyond God's intentions for them. Peoples and nations are flung across the world, far from each other, unable to communicate or understand each other. The divine purpose and hope waits again to be realized.

> *The Babel story explains in an epic way how human beings*
> *pursue things that are beyond God's intentions for them.*

The Story continues: yet another genealogy completes the chapter, filling in the names of several of Shem's descendants, all the way to a fellow named Terah, who lived in a Mesopotamian city called Ur. Terah had three sons, one of whom died young. Terah then moved from Ur with one of his surviving sons to another city, known as Haran. Then Terah died there in Haran, and Genesis says nothing else about it. What happened to his family? Ahh! We have heard their story already—that of Abram/Abraham and Sarai/Sarah.

Looking at the sequence of these mythical episodes early in Genesis, we can see how they are linked within this composite narrative. God, Creator of all that exists, had something wonderful in mind for Creation, but the humans went astray early on and brought pain and hardship on themselves. It got to a point at which God decided to get rid of the whole mess. And yet, God didn't want to give up on one character who still was devoted, so God spared that character, Noah, and his family, so that the Great Idea for Creation could stand another chance of working. After the Flood, God made a covenant with Noah and marked it with the rainbow in the sky. Sadly, though, things started getting out of hand again, many generations later. The humans again sought to become more than they were meant to be, by building a tower that would reach to the entrance of divine abode. God was not pleased with their intent and therefore dispersed them hither and yon. As the human generations continued, one line produced a man in whom God apparently had high hopes. His name was Abram, and his wife was Sarai.

TWINS! OY, WHAT TROUBLE!

The second major chapter of The One Great Story continues through Abraham and Sarah's "only son," Isaac. He married Rebekah after Sarah's death, and Rebekah became pregnant after Isaac prayed about her being "barren" (Gen 25:21). Rebekah hardly could have imagined what would transpire! She gave birth to twin boys, the second one with his hand on the first one's heel as they were born (Gen 25:25–26). What a great metaphor for the brothers' lives! They contended with each other for years, while their parents played favorites between them. Esau, the eldest, was a hunter and his father's favorite. Jacob, the one who "takes by the heel," was more of his momma's boy.

Because, in those days, inheritance went from the father to the eldest son, the first twin born received the favored birthright. In the case of Jacob and Esau, however, the younger twin outwitted his outdoorsy brother, tricking him out of that birthright (Gen 25:29–34). In the meantime, Isaac became wealthy through agricultural pursuits, although he moved around to some extent. He expressed his devotion to the LORD, whose favor for Isaac was acknowledged even by the king of the Philistines (Gen 26, esp. vss. 23–31). We will hear more about rivalry with the Philistines in later chapters of The Story.

> **Pause to Reflect**
> As some of the episodes in Genesis suggest, marriages in
> that time and place often were arranged for the benefit
> of the families involved. Given this context, what do
> you think is the significance to The Story that Isaac is
> reported to have "loved" Rebekah (Gen 24:67c)?

Speaking of rivalry, things got worse between Isaac's twin sons. Their father had become old and could not see well anymore. He asked Esau to make him a tasty meal from game that he would kill, after which Esau would receive Isaac's blessing. That blessing would overturn Jacob's tricking Esau out of his birthright. Rebekah overheard Isaac and quickly arranged with Jacob to prepare his own meal for him, one that he could take into his father by pretending to be Esau. She rigged up a "costume" of Esau's clothing and lambskin and dressed Jacob in them. When Jacob went into his father with the meal and the costume, he fooled his father into granting him the blessing. Esau returned with his meal just moments after Jacob left their father's tent. Isaac and Esau both were very upset when they figured out the deception; however, in those days, a blessing granted could not be revoked. Isaac could not take back his blessing. Esau wept and vowed to kill his brother after their father had died (Gen 27:1–41).

Jacob tricked their father Isaac and received the
blessing meant for his brother Esau.

This episode is told in quite dramatic detail and captures well the cunning and emotion among its four main characters. As a result, Jacob left their home—at his mother's urging—to live for a time with her brother (Gen 27:42–45). Jacob then dominates the story line for several chapters. He lived for a time as a vagabond, receiving assurance from the LORD that the promise given to Abraham surely would be his (Gen 28:10–22). Deceit followed Jacob, however; his uncle tricked him into marrying the older daughter (Leah) before being able to marry the one whom Jacob wanted, Rachel (Gen 29). Uncle Laban also cheated Jacob on wages for taking care of flocks of sheep (Gen 31:7). In spite of these circumstances, Jacob managed to trick Laban back in the matter of breeding sheep (Gen 30:25–43) and, as a result, became quite wealthy himself.

An angel of the LORD told Jacob in a dream to return to his homeland, so Jacob gathered up his family and all his property and left Laban, without telling him. When Laban finally heard of their departure, he took off after Jacob. Catching up to him, Laban chastised his son-in-law for leaving secretly without a proper farewell. He also asked for the return of the figurines of his gods ("the household gods" [31:35c]). Rachel was sitting on a camel's saddle, hiding them, so they were not discovered. After Jacob replied, by dumping his years of frustration about Laban in the father-in-law's lap, the two tricksters agreed to a deal. "The LORD watch between you and me, when we are absent one from the other (Gen 31:49)," known in many circles as the "Mizpah benediction," actually feels more like a mutual threat: neither man can depend on the other one, so God is invoked to make sure they both toe the line!

> **Pause to Reflect**
> Have you ever recited the "Mizpah benediction" or heard it used? How does its place in the episode between Jacob and his father-in-law, Laban, (Gen 31:43–50) change your understanding of the saying's original purpose?

Laban returned home, but Jacob's challenges were not over yet. He arranged to meet his estranged brother, Esau, and another dramatic episode develops. After praying to the LORD for deliverance, Jacob made careful plans, sending a huge gift of animals ahead of him to Esau (Gen 32:9–21). Now traveling alone (he sent his wives and children out of harm's way), Jacob spent the night in a wrestling match with a figure who is identified as "a man" but who seems at the end of the exchange to be something quite different. Some of what happens here is hard to interpret: the match appeared to be a stalemate, so the man injured Jacob's hip; Jacob wouldn't let go of the man without a blessing, which he received in the form of a new name—Israel ("the one who strives with God"); and the "man" would not tell Jacob his name. As often occurs in Old Testament stories, the main character—here, Jacob—names a location on the basis of a significant, often religious, event that took place there (Gen 32:30). The name *Peniel* means "face of God," so now the audience realizes that the "man" was a divine figure from the LORD.

It was morning, and Esau was on his way. Reunited with his family, Jacob approached his brother, bowing several times. Esau ran up to his brother, hugged and kissed him, and they wept together. The rest of their meeting was quite conciliatory, and they parted that day on good terms (Gen 33). With God's bidding, Jacob traveled back to Bethel, where the LORD had met him in a dream before his marriages and affirmed the promise with him (Gen 28:10-22). He traveled again, and Rachel died en route, giving birth to Jacob's twelfth and final son, Benjamin (Gen 35:16-20). Jacob finally made it back to Isaac, before the patriarch died. Once he had passed on, the twin brothers gave Isaac a proper burial (Gen 35:27-29).

Another major chapter closes. Even though Esau and his descendants and clans are listed (Gen 36), the attention shifts back again to Jacob's family. In spite of all the years of trickery within this extended family—all the calculating and questionable behavior that we would not want our children to emulate!—The Story maintains its underlying movement. God, the Creator of all, continues to hold a claim on the life and fortunes of this particular lineage. God—who is called "the LORD" in perhaps the oldest tradition that constitutes the Book of Genesis—continues to initiate contact with, and provide assurance and guidance to, a key figure in every generation of this clan. They are not ideal role models, but they are chosen.

After Isaac's death, the central character in the upcoming chapter of The Story is not so much Jacob, but his son Joseph. The fellow first appears as an indulged younger child who gets on his older brother's nerves. Yet, it is Joseph's faith and wit that help him to survive and, in the long run, to save his clan. Hence, the grand promise made to Abraham and Sarah will be rescued, once more.

Joseph's faith and wit help him survive and then save his family.

THE MAN WHO WOULD BE PHARAOH

He seems to have been a dreamer, this Joseph lad. All of Jacob's other sons were older, except for Benjamin, the only other son from Jacob's favorite wife, Rachel. The old man seemed to play favorites with her boys, especially with Joseph, who received a lavish gift from their father. It was a special garment of some kind, one that none of the other brothers possessed. This was not, however, the only reason that Joseph was not popular with them. He also told his brothers about two dreams of his—dreams suggesting that he, Joseph, would rise in authority and stature above them. Even Jacob was a bit perturbed in hearing about the second of the two dreams (Gen 37:3–11).

Joseph's brothers had had enough. They found a way to get rid of him, first by throwing him into a deep pit out in the hinterlands, then by selling him to some traders, who carried him with them to Egypt. Taking the fancy robe, the brothers covered it with goat's blood and took it to their father, saying that Joseph was killed by a wild animal. Jacob sorely grieved the news, but Joseph actually was very much alive, having been sold to none other than the captain of the Egyptian Pharaoh's guard (Gen 37:12–36).

Joseph's situation improved greatly—at least, for a time. Rather than ending up outside in a barn or field, Joseph must have impressed captain Potiphar with his skills. More to the point, the storyteller in Genesis emphasizes that "His master saw that the LORD was with him, and that the LORD caused all that he did to prosper in his hands" (Gen 39:3). Joseph thus was put in charge of the captain's house, which benefited greatly from the young man's acumen. Again, the storyteller is eager for the audience to see what is taking place from a particular vantage point: Potiphar's profit by Joseph's hand was "for Joseph's sake," not the captain's (Gen 39:5bc).

Trouble came calling, however. Potiphar's wife took a shining to the handsome young overseer and invited him to her bed. Joseph refused, out of his faith in God and loyalty to his boss, her husband. After days of tempting him, Potiphar's wife grabbed his shirt one day when they were alone and implored him to go to bed with her. Joseph ran out of the house, but the shirt stayed in her hand. She kept the shirt, fabricating a story that set up Joseph as the offending party. When she told her husband, Potiphar was enraged and threw Joseph in prison (Gen 39:7–20).

> **Pause to Reflect**
> In your own experience, what do you know of deep ill will and deception? Who was involved, and what took place? How did it affect you? What has it been like for you to come to terms with that experience?

This drastic turn of events could have been the end of the line for Joseph; he could have starved to death or contracted a deadly disease. But the storyteller continues to emphasize the LORD's favor with Joseph—so that he impressed the head jailer, who put Joseph in charge of all the other prisoners (Gen 39:21–23). As time went by, two of Pharaoh's top employees got on the king's bad side and ended up in prison with Joseph. Both of these men—the chief cupbearer and the chief baker—had dreams that they wanted to understand: in antiquity, dreams were thought to carry messages of a person's fate or destiny. Joseph interpreted their dreams, attributing the understanding to God. The cupbearer's dream was favorable, the baker's dream unfavorable. Soon, both interpretations came to pass, but the cupbearer forgot to credit Joseph before the Pharaoh (Gen 40).

The storyteller continues to emphasize Joseph's favor with the LORD.

Two years later, Joseph still in prison, Pharaoh himself had a couple of troubling dreams one night. His usual entourage of wizards and wise ones were at a loss to explain them. Then the cupbearer remembered Joseph, so the Pharaoh brought him from the dungeon, and he was allowed to clean up and dress. When Joseph heard Pharaoh recount the two dreams, the young Hebrew explained that Egypt had seven years to prepare for a major famine, itself to last seven years. Joseph gave credit where it was properly due: "God has shown to Pharaoh what [God] is about to do" (Gen 41:28b). Joseph urged the Pharaoh to appoint competent people to make proper arrangements, so Pharaoh looked at his servants and appointed Joseph! The monarch said to them, "Can we find anyone else like this—one in whom is the spirit of God?" (Gen 41:38).

This appointment was no minor decision or position. Pharaoh took off his own signet ring and placed it on Joseph's hand; he dressed him up in fancy clothing and gave him a gold necklace; Joseph rode in a big chariot, and the people shouted accolades (Gen 41:41–45). Now, the man who had been his father's pet child, who was sold away by his brothers, who managed a military officer's household, and survived in a dungeon caring for other prisoners, ascends to the second-highest rank of authority in the most powerful nation of the time. It is clear in the story that the listener is to see, not only the hand of God at work, but also Joseph's trust in God—and even the mighty Pharaoh's acknowledgement: "Since God has shown you all this, there is no one so discerning and wise as you" (Gen 41:39).

A BLAST FROM HIS PAST

Joseph proceeded with the plan of storing food all across Egypt. As he fore-
saw, the seven years of plenty ended, and a famine gripped the land, not only
in Egypt, but it "became severe throughout the world" (Gen 41:57b). Word
got out that Egypt had grain to sell, so "all the world" traveled to Egypt to
buy some from Joseph. Even Joseph's father, Jacob, heard the word and sent
his ten oldest sons to Egypt to buy grain (Gen 42:1–5). Once more, The
Story becomes filled with intrigue and deception.

> *Once more, The Story becomes filled with intrigue and deception.*

When the brothers arrived, they had to meet with Joseph in order to
make the transaction. Recognizing them (although they did not recognize
him), Joseph acted as though they were strangers. He accused them of spy-
ing on Egypt and threw them in prison. Then he made a deal with them:
leave one brother in Egypt, take your purchased grain home, and bring back
your youngest brother (Benjamin). The brothers consented, and then began
fussing with each other about this turn of events being retribution for what
they did to Joseph—although they had no idea that it was with Joseph with
whom they had just made this deal, and that he could understand everything they were saying (Gen 42:6–23)!

This segment of The Story—about Joseph, Egypt, and the eventual rescue of Jacob's clan—is the longest section in the Book of Genesis, comprising eleven or so chapters in a fifty-chapter book. It is filled with elaborate
details, an intricate story line, dramatic dialogue, emotional outbursts, and
surprising turns of events. On their return to drop off the grain and re-
trieve Benjamin, the brothers discovered that their money was back in their
sacks and became terrified. Once home, they told their father all that had
transpired in Egypt and the request by "the lord of the land"; but Jacob still
grieved for Joseph and would not let Benjamin go, even though Simeon was
imprisoned in Egypt (Gen 42:24–38).

> *The Joseph episode is filled with elaborate details, an intricate story line,*
> *dramatic dialogue, emotional outbursts, and surprising turns of events.*

Yet the famine worsened, and Jacob told the brothers to return for
more food. After a long conversation with them, Jacob agreed that Benjamin would accompany his brothers, along with extra money and gifts. All of
the remaining brothers traveled again to Egypt, and this time Joseph—still

incognito—arranged a small banquet with them. He released Simeon, asked about the family, and met Benjamin; the sight of his only younger brother moved Joseph so deeply that he left the room for a time and wept in private. During the meal, the brothers were stunned to see food from Joseph's table brought to theirs (Gen 43).

At this point, it looks like this episode with Joseph and his brothers would be drawing to a warm outcome. Not so! Joseph sent the brothers back on their way but secretly planted an expensive religious object in Benjamin's bag. Then Joseph sent his steward after the brothers, accusing them of theft. They denied the act, but the object—a silver cup—turned up in Benjamin's sack, for sure. On returning to Joseph's house, Judah pleaded their case, offering to become Joseph's slave if Benjamin were allowed to return home to Jacob (Gen 44).

Finally, the pressure overcame Joseph. He sent all of his Egyptian assistants out of the room and then began weeping, "so loudly that . . . the household of Pharaoh heard it" (Gen 45:2). He told his brothers who he actually was and asked about their father. Incredulous, the brothers stood dumb, so Joseph repeated himself and assured them that their action against him so many years earlier was used by God: "for God sent me before you to preserve life" (Gen 45:5c). Joseph urged them to return for the rest of the family, whom he would settle in Goshen, since the famine would last for five more years. Once the explanations were over, the brothers hugged Joseph, wept heartily, and talked together (Gen 45:1–15).

Pharaoh heard of this revelation and gave Joseph's brothers a royal escort for their return. Of course, Jacob was astounded when he heard the story that his sons recounted about Joseph, the "ruler over all the land of Egypt" (Gen 45:26b). So the old man and all of his family journeyed to Egypt to live. At night, Jacob had visions of reassurance from God that the trip to Egypt would turn out for good (Gen 46:2–4). Father and son wept together freely when they met in Goshen. Jacob's family settled with their flocks and herds, and Joseph supported them with food. As time went by, the clan grew in number and thrived there (Gen 46:5—47:12).

> *Jacob had visions of reassurance from God that*
> *the trip to Egypt would turn out for good.*

Joseph had wanted to see his father Jacob before the old man died, and his wish had come to pass. As Jacob's death drew near, the patriarch granted many blessings—first, to Joseph, through his sons Manasseh and Ephraim (Gen 48:8–22) and then to all his sons (Gen 49:1–28). His final request was to be buried in the cave near Mamre with Abraham and Sarah, Isaac and Rebekah, and Leah. Then Jacob died (Gen 49:29–33). Joseph wept over Jacob and then instructed the Egyptian doctors to embalm Jacob according to Egyptian custom. Pharaoh honored Joseph's request to take Jacob's body back to Canaan, to Mamre, for the burial that he requested. A grand procession with chariots and a large party accompanied Joseph. They all returned to Egypt following the burial (Gen 50:1–14).

For the last time in this segment of The Story, we encounter fear and deceit, but they are trumped by words that reinforce a key theological message throughout it. Joseph's brothers worried that he would seek revenge against them, now that their father was gone. So they made up a story that Jacob had asked them to ask Joseph to forgive them for harming him. Once again, Joseph expressed deep emotion—and honorable faith—as he responded to their effort to save themselves through their father's name. Once again, Joseph wept freely and assured them of his continued care for them and their families. He insisted that he could not act for God and that God had turned their harmful intentions into good: the clan was preserved (Gen 50:15–21).

> ### Pause to Reflect
> What is the most dramatic moment of forgiveness about which you have knowledge? What were the circumstances, and who was involved? Do you know what motivated the person to forgive? How did it change the situation, if at all? In what ways did blessing result?

This clan, as Joseph remembered and reaffirmed here, carried a promise from God, a promise that it would receive a land of its own. Before Joseph died, his kinfolk agreed to carry his bones with them, once God "comes to you" to take them to that land. And so Joseph died in Egypt and was buried there—for the time being (Gen 50:22–26).

This clan carried a promise from God, that
it would receive a land of its own.

CLOSING THIS CHAPTER

Creation, Fall, Flood, Rainbow, Babel, Abraham and Sarah, Isaac and Rebekah, Jacob, Rachel and Leah, Joseph and his brothers—The One Great

Story starts out in a cosmic-style setting and introduces one colorful set of individuals after another. Over their generations, these people visit, mark, and live in a number of locations, regions, and place names that will become central "players" in the journey to a fulfilled promise—and beyond. Not only the people, but *place* holds striking theological significance along the way. Every episode in the Genesis narrative leads to a moment or two that leaves the listener hanging. Characters display lapses of judgment, wily calculations, and sometimes ill intentions; even the righteous Noah got drunk and passed out (Gen 9:20–21)! As more chapters are added to The Story, however, many of these characters dominate. They will become part of The Story's appeal to later generations, in their own particular chapters.

In spite of all the questionable behavior from less-than-perfect men and women, The Story presses ahead. How? Through the unremitting persistence of the one character whose presence and purpose shadows every scene. The One Great Story contains a dizzying host of actors, but none is as central or as significant as God. That for which the Creator unceasingly hopes and adjusts impels The Story all along the way. We leave the Book of Genesis with a clan of folks whose tales of danger and exploitation remind us of a cat always landing on its feet. God has not given up on them.

The One Great Story contains a dizzying host of characters,
but none is as central or as significant as God.

FOR THE READER

1. Have you ever sat around a campfire at night and listened to someone tell stories? What was it like? How does that experience help you imagine the effect of these episodes of The One Great Story in Genesis on its early audiences?

2. What is a question or two that you wish you could ask the final editor of Genesis concerning details in one of its episodes? Why do you think your questions are not addressed there?

3. The chapters in Genesis about Joseph do not show him performing any religious acts or even praying. Yet at key points in several episodes, Joseph refers to God and God's purposes. What might this absorbing account be suggesting about how Joseph's faith developed?

SUGGESTED ACTIVITIES

• Select one of the characters from Genesis who is mentioned in this chapter and read all the sections in which he or she plays a part. In what ways is his or her trust in God (or apparent lack thereof) portrayed?

• Find a map displaying locations mentioned in Genesis; these would include areas around the Tigris and Euphrates Rivers, northwest to Haran, then roughly south, parallel to the eastern shore of the Mediterranean Sea, down to the Nile River in Egypt. What do you know about this region of the world? What questions come to mind as you look at the map? How do the places where you have lived and traveled affect who you are and what is important to you?

Chapter 3

The Story Builds

Toward a Land and a Renewal

"... go and take possession of the land that I swore to your ancestors, ..."

—Deut 1:8b

Good storytellers know how to keep an audience on the edge of its seat. As the Book of Genesis illustrates so clearly, The One Great Story begins like a roller coaster ride, with ups and downs, twists and turns that can leave riders breathless—and perhaps even screaming now and then, with surprise and anxiety. Just when we think that things actually might settle down, something else happens—someone new appears on the scene, or someone important to the story line dies, or circumstances change. At any given point in This Story, things can look great. More often, however, they are dire and heading toward seemingly hopeless.

The One Great Story begins like a roller-coaster ride.

YO-YO GOES UP—AND THEN DOWN!

Joseph's achievement in bringing his family to the security of Egypt is presented in grand terms: the most powerful empire of the day made room for a tiny band of wandering animal herders. The picture of patriarch Jacob being returned for burial near his grandfather Abraham's burial site—with a Pharaoh's escort, no less (Gen 50:7–14)—must have been, for Jacob's descendants, a tremendously dramatic symbol of divine irony. Their God, the One who called *them*, turned the world's political and economic powerhouse on its head! I can imagine that many descendants of Jacob might have wished that those circumstances would have stayed in place for a long, long time.

Well, as The Story goes, the good life in Egypt did last for a time. The Hebrews—descendants of Jacob—grew in number and strength in those years (Exod 1:7), but an era eventually passed, too. A new administration took over the empire: a new monarch ascended, one who did not know the story of Joseph's life-saving service to Egypt. This pharaoh was afraid that the Israelites would turn against Egypt under pressure, so he did what many imperial rulers have done over the centuries: he made the Hebrews' lives miserable. First, he made them construct cities and buildings for him and work on his crops; they were now his slaves. Then he told midwives to kill all boys born to Hebrew women. Although not all midwives obeyed this command, still the threat of male genocide hung over the now-enslaved community (Exod 1:8–22).

Within these ominous circumstances, a new episode is introduced—one that leads to another remarkable series of events, that becomes among The Story's most vivid and memorable. Like so many of the episodes that will follow it, this one consists of unlikely interplay between people of low regard and those of high estate. Even more, the wildly vacillating fortunes of its main character display classic literary power. Some of you already remember bits and pieces of this part of The Story, and certainly its central figure is no stranger. Enter Moses.

UNLIKELY

If you are like me, you can recall something of Moses' birth and early life from stories that you heard in Sunday school. When we were young, these accounts might have seemed cute, perhaps a little like a Shirley Temple movie. Make no mistake, however: the political ramifications of this baby's eventual status would not have been lost on the episode's early audiences.

How preposterous and delightful to hear that one of the Hebrew baby boys is saved from slaughter by a wily mother, who floated him down "the river" in a papyrus basket and sent his older sister to provide a report of his fate! How brave and clever of his sister to stay close enough to speak to the Pharaoh's daughter who saw the floating basket while bathing there! How so like an absorbing story that the baby boy returns to his own mother, to be nursed and raised—and paid by Pharaoh's daughter for the duty! How typical of an ancient story that the child becomes named because of the circumstances that led him to live in Pharaoh's court ("Mosheh"—Moses; *mashah*—draw out [of the water]) (Exod 2:1–10).

The adopted heir to the great empire now lived as a fugitive.

The early years of Moses' life are treated quickly and concisely; once again, his status changed radically. At this point, The Story leaves listeners a little unclear. By the time he was a young man, did Moses know that he was born a Hebrew? Details in The Story at this point suggest so but do not come right out and say it. When he saw the Egyptian man walloping one of the Hebrew workers, was Moses' response driven by ethnic loyalty? Murder is a serious offense, and Moses' attempt to hide his crime against the Egyptian guard did not succeed. He got scared the next day when another Hebrew worker mentioned the killing to his face, so Moses took off—and none too soon, for now Pharaoh knew of his crime and wanted his adopted son dead (Exod 2:11–15).

The adopted heir to the great empire now lived as a fugitive. After many days of travel, he ended up in a region known as Midian, southeast of Egypt, far away from Pharaoh's grip. Moses still looked like an Egyptian when he helped some sisters get water for their father's flock, after they had been harassed by some shepherds. This act of kindness led to Moses' marriage to one of the man's daughters, Zipporah. The man's name was Jethro, and he was known as a priest (Exod 2:16–22). Moses then named his first child, a son, "Gershom," a play on the Hebrew word *ger*, or "alien"—as though he still identified with his previous life in Egypt (Exod 2:22).

It looked like Moses could have settled into the nomadic, herding life, a safe distance from Egypt, raising a family, but The Story rarely allows its characters to sit still. Years went by, and the pharaoh—Moses' adopted grandfather—eventually died. Yet Moses' true people, the Hebrews/Israelites, continued to be enslaved. The storyteller, at this point, crisply notes that they sought God's help and that God observed their condition. More specifically, the story says that God's memory was jogged, that God recalled something from an earlier generation. What was it? Well, it was that promise, that pledge, that pact with those characters with whom The Story began—Abraham, Isaac, and Jacob (Exod 2:23–25). This reference to these three figures will occur again and again throughout The Story. Here, it signals to the listener that something significant is about to take place. God is going to act.

Moses named his first child "Gershom," or "alien."

RELUCTANT

I can imagine—can't you?—that the last thing on a fugitive's mind is to return to the place where he is wanted. Moses now was a family man, working for his father-in-law, sheltered by the breadth of a forbidding desert from any consequences for his youthful aggression (Exod 3:1). And then one day, . . .

> **Pause to Reflect**
> Whom do you know (or about whom have you heard) who at some time in their life escaped truly harrowing circumstances? What is their story? How do they talk about it—if at all? How does their story affect you?

A number of the Bible's most well-known scenes occur early in the Old Testament, and "the burning bush" surely is one of them. Moses was out in the boonies, far from any signs of civilization, minding his flock and his own business, when something happened that would change his life and that of his people forever. The story suggests that it took Moses completely by surprise. After all, encounters with the divine are not an everyday occurrence! When God saw that the bush (which "was burning, yet it was not consumed" [Exod 3:2c]) got Moses' attention, God called out his name. Without hesitation, Moses answered, and the words that he used—*"Here I am"*—also will appear a number of times on the lips of characters in later episodes (Exod 3:2–4).

God then kicked into high gear, calling the place "holy," ordering Moses to take off his footwear, and identifying the divine voice as that of the God of Moses' ancestors. Next, God issued a call to Moses, expressing concern for the enslaved Israelites, announcing the divine intention of freeing them and getting them "to a good and broad land." Oh, and by the way, God told Moses that he was to go to Pharaoh and secure their release (Exod 3:7–10).

Now the stalling began. Moses came up with one excuse after another: "Who am I that I should go. . .?" (Exod 3:11b); "What shall I say to them (about your name)?" (Exod 3:13cd); "But suppose they do not believe me or listen to me. . ." (Exod 4:1); "O my lord, I have never been eloquent," (Exod 4:10b); and the clincher, "O my Lord, please send someone else" (Exod 4:13). How ironic and fascinating, that a character who comes to play such a central role in The One Great Story is shown to hesitate at the call! I find some comfort in that—don't you? God did not accept any of Moses' excuses, instead telling him to get his brother Aaron to speak on Moses' behalf. In the final part of this scene, God gave Moses a staff which he will use to demonstrate the power of Israel's God (Exod 4:17).

How ironic that a character so central to The Story actually hesitated at the call!

CONFRONTATIONS—AND ESCAPE!

Before Moses and Aaron visited the (new) Pharaoh, they gathered all the Israelite elders and told them of God's intentions. The people must have been impressed with the "signs" that the staff from God made possible: they showed their trust in the men's story by worshipping the LORD (Exod 5:29–31). Then it was time to face Pharaoh.

The specific story line leading up to the eventual release of the Israelite slaves is long, sometimes complicated, and often ghastly by today's Western standards. As with all of the first five books of the Bible, this sequence can seem a little confusing, with evidence of two or three versions woven together in providing accounts of the tradition. From Sunday school days, some of us remember strange images referring to one or more of the "plagues" sent upon Egypt. Before these appear, however, Moses and Aaron fumbled ineffectively through their first clash with Pharaoh. The latter refused to allow the Israelites to leave for a religious observance, instead taking away one of the key ingredients that the slaves needed for making bricks (Exod 5). Moses complained to God about it, and God ("the LORD") reassured him again that, as the God who appeared to the ancestors Abraham, Isaac, and Jacob, God will rescue them and take them to the land of promise (Exod 6:1–8).

Not long afterward, the plagues began. In order, they were:

- the Nile River turned to blood (Exod 7:14–25);

- frogs throughout the land (Exod 8:1–15);

- gnats flying on people and animals (Exod 8:16–19);

- swarms of flies (Exod 8:20–31);

- deadly pestilence on Egyptian (only) livestock (Exod 9:1–7);

- boils on humans and animals (Exod 9:8–12);

- damaging thunder and hail (Exod 9:13–35);

- swarms of locusts eating all plants and fruits (Exod 10:1–20);

- three days of total darkness (Exod 10:21–29);

- and the final plague, death of all firstborn humans and animals (Exod 11:1–10, 12:29–32)

Each time the next plague arrived, Pharaoh would not let the people go, even though sometimes he said that he would do so—and then go back on his word. Plague number ten, death itself, indeed struck all the Egyptian households, but since the Israelites were instructed ahead of time to mark their doorposts with lamb's blood, the plague of death would not enter their homes (Exod 12:3–13, 21–23). Instead, the Israelites had prepared to leave quickly, and—once Pharaoh said the word—they did so. At last, they were free!

> **Pause to Reflect**
> What is the longest journey that you ever took?
> What were its high moments and low times? When
> it was over, how did you think and feel about it?

Escape from oppression. The Story says that the Israelites left Egypt with their possessions, including their animals, and unleavened dough for bread in slings on their backs. Not only that, but the Egyptians were so glad to get the Israelites out of their land, they gave them jewelry made of silver and gold (Exod 12:30–36)! As Pharaoh gave Moses and Aaron his sudden permission for the people to leave, he referred to their earlier request for a religious celebration. Now, perhaps with storytelling irony, Pharaoh urged them to worship—not Egyptian gods, but the LORD God (the one who is rescuing them). Even more ironic is Pharaoh's parting request—perhaps beseeching them—to seek favor from Israel's God for Pharaoh himself (Exod 12:32)! Thus, as will be the case many times throughout it, The Story reveals characters from a different, often oppressive, society almost begrudgingly acknowledging the God of the chosen people.

*The Story includes characters outside of the
Promise who acknowledge the LORD.*

IT'S NOT OVER

Tradition named this central part of The Story "the Exodus," from the Greek words that mean "a way out." The second book of the Hebrew Bible gets its name from this episode, and the Passover traditions in Judaism originate here (instructions for these traditions appear in the text, interrupting the flow of one dramatic escape episode to another). Yet we have not finished following the Israelites out of immediate danger. God's presence led the people as they began their journey away from Egypt: it was known as a pillar of cloud during the daytime and a pillar of fire in the darkness of night (Exod 13:21–22).

Meanwhile, Pharaoh and his court had a change of heart. They decided that they did not like the fact that their slaves had left, lock, stock, and barrel, so they went after the Israelites with everything they had. When the Israelites saw the chariots and army approaching, they panicked and complained mightily to Moses about their impending fate. Moses told the people not to be afraid, that the LORD, their god, would deliver them. First, the pillar of cloud protected them from Egypt's army. Then, after the Israelites passed through the sea that God divided with a strong wind, the Egyptian army got stuck in the mud as they pursued Israel. Finally, at the LORD's command, Moses once again stretched out his hand over the sea, and the sea went back as it was, sweeping up all the chariots and soldiers of Pharaoh's army. They all perished, but Israel survived on dry ground (Exod 14).

*Moses told the people not to be afraid, that their
god, the LORD, would deliver them.*

This episode concludes with the storyteller noting that the people recognized the LORD's action on their behalf—saving them from annihilation—and that they therefore put their trust in this God (and Moses) (Exod 14:31). As we heard earlier, this is the God of their ancestors Abraham, Isaac, and Jacob, the One who issued a call and a promise for blessing through a band of unlikely folks. Not even the grandiose and tyrannical intentions of the ruler of the world's strongest empire would thwart the purposes of God.

FROM THE FRYING PAN . . . ?

After such a spectacular rescue, Israel simply had to celebrate! The Story preserves some poetic verse that remembers the event with vivid imagery and gives all the credit to the LORD. Both Moses and his sister, Miriam, led the singing (Exod 15:1–21). But the celebration could not last forever: the people had a calling to fulfill, and The Story keeps making it clear that the LORD will guide and protect them.

If only the people could have trusted that promise! They did a lot of complaining as they traveled. First, it was about water that tasted bad—so Moses did what God showed him to do, and the water tasted better (Exod 15:22–25). Then they got hungry and were sure that life back in Egypt at least would have provided them food enough. So God gave Moses and Aaron a "heads up" about what would happen next, along with some instructions and restrictions. Each morning, "a fine flaky substance" appeared on the ground. This substance was edible and would sustain the Israelites on their journey. They were to collect only as much as they needed for the day; leftovers spoiled by morning. On the sixth day of the week, the people gathered twice as much, so that on the seventh day, Sabbath, they could rest and still have something to eat (Exod 16:1–30).

Those of us who went to Sunday school very likely remember that this substance was called "manna." The name appears to be a play on the Hebrew words, *man hu*, which in English is "What is it?" (Exod 16:15, 31). Don't think that God does not have a sense of humor—at least, the ancient storytellers did! God then told Moses to put some of this manna in a jar and keep it for posterity, to remind Israelite descendants of who sustained them on their journey out of Egypt (Exod 16:32–34).

> **Pause to Reflect**
> What do you complain about? What do the people
> whom you know best tend to complain about? What
> do these complaints reveal about you and them?

As The Story goes, the Israelites spent a lot of time in the wilderness, and much of the time, they did not display appreciation for the One who had rescued them. They complained—a lot! For instance, in the story about receiving the manna every morning, forms of the word "complain" appear seven times in just eleven verses (Exod 16:1–11). They complained, and fussed at Moses, when a new campsite had no water (Exod 17:1–7). (There are plenty more examples, but I don't want to get ahead of where we are in The Story.) As we will see soon, the Israelites also would stray from following the LORD. The Story makes it clear—sometimes in unadorned terms—that God expected their loyalty and trust.

The Israelites often did not appreciate the One who had rescued them.

"HERE'S THE DEAL"

On the move in a dangerous land, the Israelites traveled for several weeks before arriving at a place known as "Sinai." It was at this location that another series of significant events took place. Sinai also is part of the wilderness in that region, and the people set up camp there. God called Moses up to a mountain and reminded him of their rescue and of God's intention that they "be for me a priestly kingdom and a holy nation" (Exod 19:6). When they heard back from Moses, the people agreed to follow the LORD (Exod 19:8). So the people, by God's instruction, prepared for a divine encounter, with smoke, fire, the mountain shaking, and a trumpet blasting. The people did not get to "see" God, but they knew that Moses was going up and down the mountain. Now the stage was set for probably the most far-reaching part of their deal with God (Exod 19:9b–25).

Moses received from God ten "words," or laws, during this dramatic moment on the mountain. We know them today most commonly as "the Ten Commandments." These ten have to do with loyalty to the LORD and with relationships to other persons (Exod 20:1–17). Some of us remember trying to memorize these ten when we were in Sunday school. By this point in The Story, the people seemed suitably impressed by the natural display of power to ask Moses for protection (Exod 20:18–21). The moment is presented here and elsewhere as a very solemn episode in the life of the Israelites. Following the pronouncement of the ten words come long sections in the text that explain related laws, such as those about slaves (Exod 21:1–11), about different categories of persons physically hurting each other (Exod 21:12–27), about property (Exod 21:28–36), about making property amends (Exod 22:1–15), and some other social and religious practices (Exod 22:16–31).

Within the first books of the Bible, there are a number of other long sections that spell out regulations that the Israelites are expected to follow. The flow of The Story sometimes is "interrupted" by these sections. In general, they appear where they are in part to remind listeners that these divine expectations are not arbitrary: rather, following such "rules" expressed one's loyalty to the One who brought them out of the land of Egypt, the One who called Abraham, Isaac, and Jacob. Who is that One? It is none other than the God of the burning bush, the LORD, *YHWH* in Hebrew, a name that plays on the verb "to be" (see Exod 3:13–15). Israel's God is "I AM WHO I AM"—a god who cannot be manipulated by humans who try to use a divine name for leverage and advantage. The storytellers seek to keep this God and this narrative paramount; the codes, regulations, and law serve a bigger purpose. "We live a certain way, because we belong to this God."

> *Israel's God is "I AM WHO I AM"—*
> *a god who cannot be manipulated.*

It might seem difficult to keep religious rules in perspective when Exodus, Leviticus, Numbers, and Deuteronomy contain so many of them! Besides statutes about behaviors and consequences, the episode of Moses on the mountain with God also looks distracted by details of religious observances, objects, offices, and structures (see Exod 24–31). Yet, in the midst of these long sidebars, one short section stands out. It speaks of using the legal system for the purpose of justice, rather than one's own gain. Persons with whom one does not get along; those who are poor; non-Israelites who live among Israelites—these are people who are to be protected. In particular, the storyteller connects fair treatment of "strangers" with Israel's own Story: "you know the heart of an alien, for you were aliens in the land of Egypt" (Exod 23:9).

Thus, in the text as we have inherited it, the foundations of life as God's called community have been woven into the dramatic Story of oppression, rescue, wandering, and covenant. Eventually, Moses came down the mountain, carrying two stone tablets bearing those decisive ten words (Exod 31:18), the central symbol of what the LORD wanted from—and for—The People. In spite of all this, however, what Moses found when he returned led quickly to a crisis of immense magnitude.

WHEN THE CAT'S AWAY, . . .

Pause to Reflect
Try to recall your earliest memory of rules and laws.
What were they? How did you deal with them?
How have your attitudes toward rules and laws
changed as you have gotten older? What makes "the
ten words" different from other kinds of law?

As we continue to see over and over again, the People called by God to bless all the nations of the earth were not selected because of their superior faith and behavior. While Moses was away, This People seem to have forgotten their Story; they got impatient when he had not returned yet. In their minds, it was time to find someone else to get them out of the boondocks. So, they collected their gold jewelry and melted it down, to craft a statue of a calf. This imposing figure of strength was supposed to represent the god who had rescued them (Exod 32:4b). A big celebration kicked off, with lots of singing and dancing. You can guess, though, that God was ticked off—and so was Moses. This "golden calf" worship veered the people away from trust in the LORD. The people subsequently were punished, and yet—and yet—still God told Moses to keep leading them toward the land of Promise (Exod 32).

That Promise was made by the LORD to Israel's ancestors, to Abraham, Isaac, and Jacob (Exod 33:1). Through Moses, God gave them the ten words as a covenant, an agreement, a two-way deal. God will bring This People to a land, and they will be a blessing to all nations; This People will live with complete loyalty to God (*YHWH*, the LORD), expressing that loyalty in the ways that they worship God and treat others. Faith resulting in ethical behavior was intended to create and sustain God's purposes for the world, through The People called to this task.

God's purposes were to be sustained by faith and ethical behavior.

At this part of The Story, then, the LORD renewed the covenant. Moses prepared two stone tablets again, and God wrote the ten words on them again (Exod 34). Then The People received directions on constructing and fashioning a number of objects that they would use in their worship—an ark, utensils, lamps, altars, pillars and screens, garments for the priests, and so on (Exod 35–40). Such descriptions and directives are elaborated in more than one place: for instance, the Book of Leviticus contains twenty-seven chapters about sacrifices, offerings, dietary rules, ritual purification, and so on. To many Western readers today, these descriptions are impressive in detail but not necessarily instructive or appealing. The style of worship suggested by the many artifacts mentioned here speaks of a world remote and even vanished. Yet, in the text as we have inherited it, The Story includes these details. They do not advance The Story as such, but they do ground it in a specific time and place. The One Great Story rarely has the flavor of a generic brand: rather, its power draws from its distinctive particularity.

After receiving (again) the covenant with the ten words, Moses and the Israelites continued their journey, for they were still in the wilderness.

It turns out that, once again, their Story entailed a transition. In this case, it was something like a changing of the guard. The people who escaped oppression in Egypt traveled—or should we say, "wandered?"—through wilderness lands for a long, long time. Moses remained as the figure selected by God to lead them. In their many preparations for their next phase of travel (and adventure!), the Israelites seemed compliant overall with conditions of their covenant relationship (see Num 1–10). Their attitude suddenly changed, however, once they broke camp and were back on the road. In the first instance, "the rabble among them" (Num 11:4) stirred up discontent about the available diet (this theme sounds familiar). Eventually, so many years went by that everyone who had left Egypt died on the journey (Num 26:64–65).

God's people still were having a hard time trusting the One who had called them and saved them. They were heading toward Canaan, an area in the region that has figured in their Story from generations past. At the LORD's instruction, Moses sent out spies to bring back information about the land, the towns, and the people. The spies returned, saying good things about the land and its fruits but holding no hope that its occupants could be conquered (Num 13). The People panicked, wailing and complaining, even talking of a mutiny to return to Egypt! Even Joshua and Caleb, two of Moses' assistants, could not reassure them: the people ("the whole congregation") were ready to kill them (Num 14:1–10).

Moses prayed hard to the LORD on their behalf, and the journey continued—however, Moses now knew that it would be the next generation who would get there. All those complainers would not live long enough to enter the land of the Promise, only their children (Num 14:13–25). They did not trust in God to fulfill this promise.

> **Pause to Reflect**
> What does it take for you to continue working toward
> a goal once you discover that it is not as quick or
> easy to achieve as you might have thought?

This journey toward Promise faced many challenges. Sometimes the challenges were political (as with Edom, Num 20:14–21); sometimes they took on military aspects, as with the kings of the Amorites and Bashan (Num 21:21–35) and of Midian (Num 31). Other times, there were religious overtones to circumstances, as with the Moabites, Balak, and Balaam (Num 22–24) and with the gods worshipped by the residents of Shittim (Num 25). According to one summary of the journey, the Israelites pulled up stakes, traveled, and set up camp in thirty different places (Num 33:1–37)! Some of the accounts of battles and spoil strain our twenty-first-century sensitivities—even though many of today's television programs and movies are at least as violent. However, what remains consistent throughout this early phase of The Story, in our inherited configuration of it, is that the LORD God intended to fulfill a promise and a vision.

This journey toward Promise faced many challenges.

For Moses himself, some of this fulfillment would end up tasting bittersweet. The reluctant "leader" of this stiff-necked band of escaped slaves remains the central figure throughout many episodes of The Story. Death comes to us all, and it finally came also for Moses. There was a wrinkle to his death, though, as the Israelites prepared for what would be their final chapter of post-Egypt wanderings. Moses would not go with them, but another one would lead them. God authorized Joshua to take over from Moses, to head the people's final push (Deut 31:1–8). The reason? Lack of trust in God, sinful behavior—whether the particular storyteller was blaming Moses (Num 20:12–13), Moses and Aaron (Deut 32:50–51), or the people themselves (Deut 3:26). So God showed Moses all the land waiting for the Israelites, as he stood on Mt. Nebo; then he died in a place called "the plains of Moab" and was buried there. He was still a vigorous guy at his death, and the people mourned for him thirty days (Deut 34:1–8).

Now it was Joshua's turn. He was chosen by God to succeed Moses, and he also would have his hands full.

"JOSHUA FIT THE BATTLE . . . "

The most detailed versions of what often has been called "the conquest of the land" appear in the Book of Joshua (2–12). It contains dramatic speeches and predicaments, acts of valor, wondrous and unlikely military victories, disobedience, and regular reminders of Who ultimately is leading the Israelites and providing for them. This conquest includes strategic support from none other than a local prostitute, named Rahab (Josh 2)—and this will not be the last time that we hear of her! Perhaps the most well-known place name from this series of episodes is Jericho. Once the Israelites had the town surrounded (they characteristically were protected on all sides by strong, high walls), Joshua received an odd set of divine instructions. They followed those instructions to the letter.

For six days, early in the morning, the Israelite soldiers marched around the city walls, silently and just one time, followed by seven priests who blew trumpets made of rams' horns. On the seventh day, they marched around the city seven times and, at Joshua's command, all the Israelites shouted. When they did so, those walls hit the ground, and the city was defeated. The only residents who were spared were Rahab and her family, because she had helped Joshua's spies (Josh 6). Military success also took place at a city known as Ai (Josh 8) and against a number of "kings" in the region (Josh 10:16—11:21; 12:7–24). The locations of these conquests, and of the peoples who lived there, clearly held a high value within the storytelling traditions. Those places serve to spell out the geographical parameters of what descendants claimed as "the Promised Land" from God.

Once the land was secured, God made it clear that its settlement by the Israelites would be no free-for-all. Clans would receive apportionments as inheritances (Num 33:53–54); the boundaries were delineated (Num 34:1–15; see also Josh 13–19 for more detail); specific persons were selected to oversee the apportionment of the land (Num 34:16–29). The Promise was almost here! The descendants of Abraham, Isaac, and Jacob—all twelve tribes of them—were about to begin the life which the LORD had pledged a long, long time earlier. Their leader, Joshua, had taken over from Moses and led them to this place. For a time, they lived in peace (Josh 23:1).

The Promise was almost here!

Now Joshua himself was nearing the end. Like Moses before him (Deut 32, 33), and the patriarch Jacob before them (Gen 49), Joshua gathered all the people and their officials, to a place called Shechem, and delivered a final speech. It was not as long as the one that Moses is reported to have made, but its brevity perhaps makes it more compelling. Joshua began this address first by summarizing their Story: "Long ago your ancestors . . . lived beyond the Euphrates and served other gods" (Josh 24:2). The voice in this part of the speech, however, is not Joshua's, but God's—"The LORD, the God of Israel." Joshua here speaks God's word to the people, "Thus says the LORD, . . ." Surely the contrast between "other gods" and "the LORD, the God of Israel" would have been strikingly apparent to its listeners.

> **Pause to Reflect**
> What was the most important thing to you as a child? Do you remember why? Now finish this sentence: "At this point in my life, I have given my heart to _____." Why this?

This recital is tightly delivered, beginning with a mention of Abraham's father, Terah, and moves quickly to Abraham's own journey. Abraham's "legitimate" son Isaac is mentioned, along with Isaac's twins, Jacob and Esau. Jacob's eventual settling in Egypt is mentioned, as are Moses and Aaron. The escape from Egypt, the Red Sea rescue, the years of wilderness wanderings, successful battles—including Jericho—also are included. In this condensed version of The Story, in the English translation, the LORD speaks in first person about eighteen times in twelve verses (Josh 24:2-13). God's part of Joshua's speech ends with a reminder that the Israelites did not achieve victory or gain their land by their own power. They now had the land, its towns, and its bounteous harvests, simply and only because God had provided them (Josh 24:13).

Yet the speech did not end there: it immediately shifted, to a "therefore" clause in the line of thought. Joshua threw down a gauntlet before The People: follow the LORD only. Get rid of those other gods—whether the ones that came from Terah's homeland, or the ones that they found in Egypt, or the ones that already were in the Land before the people took it over (Josh 24:14-15). The point is clear: for Joshua, there was only one god whose actions on The People's behalf warranted their loyalty and complete commitment. He and his clan would throw in their lot with the LORD.

In response to Joshua's call for a decision, the people also said "yes" to the LORD. They acknowledged what this God had done for them, and they declared their loyalty as well (Josh 24:16-18). Two more times, Joshua pressed the people about this decision, and twice more they pledge their allegiance: "The LORD our God we will serve, and [this god] we will obey" (Josh 24:24). At that point, Joshua wrote it all down and moved a big stone to mark the location of their affirmation. The renewal ceremony was concluded, and all the people returned to their allotted lands (Josh 24:25-28). Then Joshua died and was buried; from there, the storyteller noted that the people remained loyal to the LORD throughout the lifetimes of those elders who had served with Joshua (Josh 24:31). Once more, a major chapter comes to a close.

Two more times, Joshua pressed the people, and
both times they pledged to serve the LORD.

WHEN "OVER" IS NOT OVER

Yet The Story does not end here, and it certainly does not contain the words "and they lived happily ever after." The Israelites were faced with developing many aspects of their community, as they began to live into their calling;

numerous passages in Leviticus, Numbers, and Deuteronomy signify the ways in which social, economic, judicial, and international dimensions were infused with the religious foundation of their existence. This people belonged to the LORD God—no other—and was expected to live that way. As with previous periods of their existence, the Israelites quickly discovered that life in the Promised Land also was a time of transition itself, another shift in their life and charge. One key element of that shift was the absence, shall we say, of a single human position of authority that was recognized by all the tribes. Once they all had settled in, there was no Jacob, or Joseph, or Moses, or Joshua to speak for God or lead the people through crisis.

What could provide the people of Promise with the confidence and security that they needed? How well would they remember The Story of how they became who they were, and of their purpose? What would happen to this People? Answers to these questions are not simple, and they lead us into the next part of the journey that comprises The Story.

FOR THE READER

1. Moses became a leader in great crisis for the Israelites. Why, then, might the early storytellers have included episodes that reveal a reluctant, and sometimes angry, Moses?

2. Read Exod 21:1–17, the "ten words" that God spoke to Moses on Mt. Sinai. Which one is the easiest for you to understand? The most difficult? How do you think those earliest Israelites thought about these "words" as a way of life?

3. Whom do you find it easiest to trust? Hardest? Why? Why do you suppose the Israelites during exodus, wilderness, and entrance into the land found it so hard to trust in the LORD?

4. Do you think that the presence of military activity in the Bible constitutes a blanket justification of war? How would you explain your answer?

SUGGESTED ACTIVITIES

- Jot down a list of groups of people you can name, from history or today's headlines, who were or are being used by others for their benefit. How might such peoples interpret Pharaoh's enslavement of the Hebrews?

- Find an edition of the Bible that includes a map showing the possible route of the Israelites through the desert and eventually into the land. There was a much shorter way to get there! What is there about this part of The Story that might explain why their route became so circuitous?

- Ask a friend what she or he knows about these stories with Moses, Pharaoh, the Exodus, wilderness, and entering the Promised Land. What impressions do they have about the value of these stories?

Chapter 4

The Story Shifts

Status and Security

" . . . for they have not rejected you, but they have rejected me
from being king over them."

—1 SAM 8:7B

Perhaps you have heard someone make this comment, with a certain degree
of exasperation: "It was like herding cats!" Those of us who have lived around
domesticated felines for a period of time know too well that they do not take
kindly to any request for cooperative behavior. Sheep can be herded—and
cattle, too—but cats will squirt off in any direction imaginable, thwarting all
ill-devised efforts to keep them under some form of control.

Hearing what life was like for the Israelites, after they had settled into
the land of Promise, can leave an impression that you are listening to a bunch
of scatterbrained cats. While the twelve tribes (or ten, if you follow Judg 5)
had solemnly pledged before their leader Joshua that they would follow the
LORD their God, things often went off the rails. The People of the Promise
seem to have put themselves into a distressing cycle: they would turn away
from God; one of their neighboring nations would threaten to undo them;
the people would "cry to the LORD" for help; God would "raise up" a judge

to save them from the mess—and then it would start all over again. This period of time after the covenant with Joshua was not stable! There were heroes along the way, but their heroism always was in response to what the storytellers remember as Israel's forsaking of their covenant with the LORD.

> *When Israel would forget its covenant with God, the*
> *People depended on heroes to rescue them.*

The period of the "judges" eventually faded out—or, perhaps it is more accurate to say that it was forced out. We also follow in this chapter the Israelites' move to a more centralized form of government, that of a monarchy. Life under the rule of kings seemed like a smart change to some: it promised an elevated position among Israel's neighbors and, hopefully, more political and military stability. As we will see, however, monarchy did not "solve" the ongoing, fundamental challenge to those people of the Promise. That challenge was to trust in the One who had called them into existence, for a purpose bigger than themselves.

Let's pick up the story line, now in Judges.

JUDGES FOR ISRAEL

Unlike The Story as we have heard it so far, life after settlement in Canaan produced no figures who led Israel as dramatically or as long as Moses, or even Joshua, did. Instead, we discover a collection of characters—including one very notable woman—who stand out at different times and places. Sometimes in the texts that we have inherited these people are called "judges." However, their function typically was not judicial, but military; furthermore, their rise to power was charismatic. That is, these "judges" were selected by God: the LORD would "raise up a deliverer" to deal with a particular threat. Their authority from God was recognized in acts that the people accepted as divinely inspired.

Here is a quick rundown of several of these characters and their accomplishments. Othniel from the tribe of Judah received "the spirit of the LORD" and led a successful campaign against the king of Aram, which brought peace for forty years (Judg 3:7–11). Ehud, a Benjaminite, used stealth and military skill to defeat Moab and bring peace for eighty years (Judg 3:12–30). Deborah was known as a prophetess and provided services in Ephraim that, if not judicial, were recognized as wise and prudent. At Barak's request, Deborah accompanied an army of Israelites that defeated a

Canaanite army, with help from the LORD (Judg 4:1–16). Their victory was remembered in a poetic, jubilant recounting of the incident (Judg 5).

In a much longer account, Gideon was visited by an angel and called to deliver Israel from the Midianites. Gideon displayed his loyalty in several ways—by building an altar to the LORD; by tearing down the altar to Baal, a Canaanite god; by reducing the size of the army; by using trumpets, jars, and torches as part of his military tactics; and by defeating the army of Midian (Judg 6:11–7:25). His achievements so impressed the Israelites that they asked him and his male descendants to rule over them. Gideon refused the offer, saying "the LORD will rule over you (Judg 8:23c)." Yet Gideon himself stumbled in his faith, even though the Israelites enjoyed another season of peace. According to the text as we have inherited it, Gideon fashioned a gold object out of donated gold earrings (does this sound familiar?), which became associated with worship of other gods (Judg 8:24–28). When he died, Gideon was remembered for his leadership—but, once again, the Israelites quickly abandoned the LORD and went back to the gods of Baal (Judg 8:27–35).

> *Gideon refused the request to become Israel's*
> *ruler: "The LORD will rule over you."*

At Gideon's death, one of his sons, Abimelech, aspired to gain the power that his father had turned down. He used his mother's side of the family to gain support, and then murdered all but one of his father's other sons (the one, Jotham, hid and survived) (Judg 9:1–5). Then Abimelech got certain men of standing to crown him their king (Judg 9:6). His reign lasted only three years, however. For one thing, Jotham was still alive and did not accept his half-brother's authority. More significantly, however, Abimelech died in battle, after being hit on the head with a millstone thrown over a tower by a woman and then begging his armor bearer to finish him off with a sword—rather than being remembered as having been killed by a woman (Judg 9:50–57)! Following Abimelech's death, two other men—Tola of Issachar and Jair from Gilead—judged in succession for more than forty years (Judg 10:1–5).

Pause to Reflect
How likely is it today that someone would be chosen by God for a special task? How would she or he know it? How might others be able to perceive it as genuine—or not?

One more time, the Israelites again forgot their pledge to the LORD. Their neighbors on all sides (Aram, Sidon, Moab, Ammon, Philistia, and others) worshipped their own gods (Judg 10:6), who apparently had some kind of strong appeal—perhaps akin to keeping up with the Joneses? This time, it was someone named Jephthah who led the People. He was an effective soldier who was asked by a group of elders to command an army against Ammon. Jephthah hesitated to do so, because his half-brothers had threatened him years earlier, and he consequently left home to live elsewhere. Yet he finally agreed, with commitments from the elders and the people (Judg 11:1–11). Jephthah was known to have had "the spirit of the LORD" (Judg 11:29) and led Israel to a decisive defeat of the Ammonites (Judg 11:29–33). However, he made a vow to God that unexpectedly led to the gruesome death of his own daughter (Judg 11:34–40).

After Jephthah died, Ibzan (seven years), Elon (ten years), and Abdon (eight years) served as judges (Judg 12:8–15). Little is known about them or their ministry, although the story line implies that the people remained faithful to the LORD during this time. When the story picks up after Abdon, we see the cycle beginning once again to repeat itself. To be clear, Israel's threatening consequences for abandoning the LORD are viewed in retrospect as not accidental: the storyteller speaks of "the LORD [giving] them into" one or another of their neighboring enemies. This time, it was the Philistines, who had kept the Israelite tribes under their thumb for a generation (Judg 13:1). This time, the one who was chosen to deliver them left behind episodes and escapades that have reverberated with awe and wonder throughout history.

SAMSON THE MIGHTY

Stories of Samson appear to focus on his physical strength, as he used it to defeat Israel's enemies. What sometimes gets lost in the hubbub is the divine action and human faith that led to Samson's achievements. He was born as the fulfillment of a divine visitation to a barren woman to parents who displayed humble trust in Israel's god, the LORD (Judg 13). The couple committed to raise the child so that he would be ready "to deliver Israel from the hand of the Philistines" (Judg 13:5b). Samson was prepared for his mission as he grew up: the storyteller mentions that "The spirit of the LORD began to stir him . . . " (Judg 12:25) before any of his exploits are told.

What makes Samson so memorable across the ages are the extraordinary feats that tradition preserved about him. His first one concerns a young lion that he killed by ripping it apart with his bare hands; later the lion's carcass housed a beehive with honey, which Samson scooped out, ate and shared with his parents (Judg 14:5–9). Later, he caught three hundred foxes and turned them into a huge running torch, to destroy the Philistines' grain, vineyards and olive trees (Judg 15:3–5). Some of his countrymen then found Samson and bound him with strong ropes, to offer him up as a payment to the Philistines. When the Philistines drew near, Samson broke out of the ropes, saw a donkey's jawbone laying on the ground, and used it to kill one thousand of the Philistines (Judg 15:9:17). After this wondrous conquest, he prayed to the LORD for something to drink, so that he might revive his strength (Judg 15:18–19). On another occasion, Samson pulled out the posts and doors of the city gates of Gaza and muscled them up a hill (Judg 16:1–3).

Almost as an afterthought, the storytelling tradition here mentions that Samson judged in Israel for two decades (Judg 15:20, 16:31c). His character and legacy, however, have been dominated by the stuff of popular legend, not the least of which is the episode that led to his death. One of the promises that Samson's mother made was never to cut his hair (Judg 13:5), as a sign of his consecration to God. Apparently only Samson and his parents knew this. In spite of this dedication, however, Samson had a weak spot for women. He was known for visiting prostitutes (see Judg 16:1–2) and eventually fell hook, line, and sinker for a woman in a Philistine-controlled location; her name was Delilah. We don't know her ethnic origin, but her actions reveal her character. High-ranking members of the Philistine community found out about this love affair between Delilah and their archenemy Samson. So they all agreed to pay her a huge—and I mean huge!—sum of money for her to find out how to overcome Samson's tremendous physical prowess (Judg 16:4–5).

Three times, Samson gave Delilah phony answers to her question about his strength, and three times he escaped subjugation by the Philistines (Judg 16:6–14). Each time, Delilah would plead with Samson to tell her the truth, and eventually he gave in: "she had nagged him with her words day after day, and pestered him, [and] he was tired to death" (Judg 16:16). This time, as he slept in her lap, someone came in and shaved Samson's head, and Samson could not escape. His eyes were gouged out, and they took him to a prison in shackles, where he turned the mill (Judg 16:17–22). Gradually, Samson's hair grew back. His Philistine captors decided to hold a great celebration to their god, ironically bringing in Samson from the prison mill to amuse the huge crowd of Philistine dignitaries. The house was packed as Samson felt for the two middle pillars of the building, praying to the LORD for the strength to avenge his blindness and die with his reveling captors. When he pushed as hard as he could, the entire structure fell down, killing everyone, about three thousand men and women (Judg 16:23–30). So ends the story of Samson, antiquity's superman.

During the time of judges, Israel would "cry out to the
LORD," as did their ancestors when in Egypt.

In the text as we have inherited it, we can detect a handful of particular phrases that sum up Israel's life during the judges. One of those phrases is the sentence, "The Israelites did what was evil in the sight of the LORD," which appears eight times in Judges (2:11, 3:7, 3:12 [twice], 4:1, 6:1, 10:6, 13:1). This sentence often is used to signal a shift by the Israelites, away from loyalty to their God and toward gods in surrounding nations. Often, this sentence is followed by a second phrase, "when the Israelites cried out to the LORD," which appears six times in Judges (3:9, 3:15, 4:3, 6:6, 6:7, 10:10). This phrase echoes an earlier episode in The One Great Story, in which the Israelites cried out because of their slavery in Egypt (see Exod 2:23). A third phrase then follows the second one in four of the cases: "the LORD raised up" (Judg 2:16, 2:18, 3:9, 3:15), twice called "judges" and twice called "deliverers." Finally, a fourth phrase in Judges emphasizes the source of power and authority given to those who were raised up—"the spirit of the LORD came upon . . ." (and slight variations). Four times this phrase is used about Samson (Judg 13:25, 14:6, 14:19, 15:14), and three other times for other judges who were raised up (Judg 3:10, 6:34, 11:29).

> **Pause to Reflect**
> What is the value of loyalty? To whom are
> you loyal? Why? Have you ever taken a risk
> to yourself as a result of staying loyal?

Whether these phrases appeared in the very earliest recitations of these old episodes, or whether they became included as the episodes took written form, the intent seems pretty clear. They serve to signify the theological framework out of which Israel's descendants were expected to understand their own history. It is a history about a God who required something from This People, who often were very fickle about their ultimate allegiances. When The People wised up and genuinely sought deliverance, the LORD their God selected someone in particular to lead them. That person was empowered by the very breath of the LORD, whose presence with him (and her) was confirmed by an outcome favorable to Israel.

RUTH, THE UNLIKELY LINK

The One Great Story tends to be dominated by men, but the women who receive attention play pivotal roles along the way. Even more significant are those women who technically would not be expected at all—women who were not born into the Promise given by the God of Abraham, Isaac, and Jacob. During this period of time in which "judges ruled" (Ruth 1:1), one such woman character was remembered by the storytelling tradition. She was from Moab, and her name was Ruth; yet her episode as part of The Story includes another key female character—Ruth's mother-in-law, Naomi.

On the surface, the two women's story seems quaint and, although at points a bit strange and questionable by Western moral standards, demonstrates how personal loyalty leads to happy endings. A closer reading, however, will uncover a more dramatic trajectory, as the tradition and theology of The One Great Story once again become evident.

In a quick look, we find that Naomi and both of her daughters-in-law have become widowed. Naomi's husband, Elimelech, had been from Judah, but her sons had married Moabites, because their family had moved to Moab to live there during a famine back home. Naomi encouraged the young widows to remain in Moab while she returned to Judah, but Ruth pledged to stay with Naomi:

> Where you go, I will go;
> Where you lodge, I will lodge;
> Your people shall be my people,
> and your God my God.
> Where you die, I will die—
> there I will be buried. (Ruth 1:16b–17a)

To any descendant of Abraham, Isaac, and Jacob, this pledge by a "foreigner" would have been considered not only decisive, but quite remarkable. So the two women returned together, to Bethlehem in Judah. The daughter-in-law asked Naomi for her help, presumably so that she could marry again. Ruth wanted to go gleaning in the field of a man who might "find favor" (Ruth 2:2c) with her. Naomi told her to go, and it so happened that the field where she began gleaning was owned by a respected and devout relative of her deceased husband; his name was Boaz. Ruth worked hard while gleaning, catching the attention of Boaz's field servants. Boaz inquired of her and then approached her, expressing his gratitude for Ruth's loyalty to Naomi. Boaz began showing favor toward Ruth, at mealtime and during the reaping of the fields (Ruth 2).

After a time, Naomi instructed Ruth to go to the threshing floor one night and wait for Boaz to fall asleep, before lying down at his feet. When he awoke, he was alarmed to find Ruth there but seemed to understand her purpose. Boaz blessed her and promised to help "redeem" her (and, indirectly, Naomi's) situation. Before daylight, Boaz gave Ruth a large amount of grain to take home to Naomi. Then he tried to negotiate with one of his male kinsman a deal to buy some land from Elimelech's estate; but, in order to get the land, the man also had to "take" Ruth—in order "to maintain the dead man's name on his inheritance" (Ruth 4:5c). However, because the man had an inheritance of his own, one that would be adversely affected by accepting Boaz's proposal, this male kinsman turned it down (Ruth 3:1—4:6).

Through a simple legal ceremony, Boaz then claimed right to Elimelech's property and to Ruth. He married her and, when she had a baby boy soon afterward, Naomi's friends rejoiced with her: "He shall be to you a restorer of life and a nourisher of your old age" (Ruth 4:15a). These women also named the baby, Obed. At this point, the storyteller leaves Ruth and Naomi, closing the narrative by mentioning—without any fanfare—that Obed's grandson was David.

Those of us who are following The One Great Story for the first time don't know who David is, or why the storyteller thought it important to mention him here. Yet I will claim, with the weight of scholarly support, that this narrative about Naomi and Ruth might not have made it into the Bible if it were not for its link with the person of David. In the life of the Israelite people, the period of the judges—roughly three centuries long[9]—would come to an end. It is time for us to find out why, and to see what, as a result, happened next in this Story about the People of the Promise.

THE LAST OF HIS KIND

Throughout the period of the judges, Israel seemed to accept the idea that the twelve tribes were subject to the LORD's authority as it appeared from time to time through charismatic leaders. At the same time, religious practices and offices also appear to have become quite well-established. Sometime after Samson and any subsequent judges, an Israelite priest named Eli served in a town called Shiloh, with his two sons. A man named Elkanah visited Shiloh every year with his two wives, to offer sacrifices to the LORD. Elkanah's wife Hannah had no children, but Elkanah loved her greatly and would provide her with special offerings for the sacrifices. Hannah would be taunted so greatly by Elkanah's other wife that, over the years, Hannah

9. See Olson, "The Book of Judges," 724.

became very unhappy. Elkanah tried to cheer her up by reminding her of his loyalty to her (1 Sam 1:1–8).

One year, when Hannah entered the designated room to make her sacrifices, she began to cry. Eli was sitting nearby as Hannah prayed earnestly; she promised that, if God gave her a son, she would dedicate him to God (the same dedication that was made for Samson—see Judg 13:3–5). The old priest was watching Hannah pray and concluded that she was drunk! When he began to chastise her, Hannah explained her situation and her prayer. Eli then blessed her, and she went on her way. The next year, Hannah gave birth to a boy and named him Samuel. When he was weaned, Hannah took him (with Elkanah's blessing) to Eli with a sacrifice and left him with the old priest (1 Sam 1:9–28).

Hannah would visit Samuel each year during the visit for sacrifices and bring him a new robe. Eli would bless her husband Elkanah and Hannah for Samuel (1 Sam 2:18–20). The boy was faithful to his service and well-regarded (1 Sam 2:11, 26). Yet all was not well. Eli's sons stole meat brought for the sacrifices, to eat it themselves; they showed no regard for the sacrificial practices (1 Sam 2:2–17). Eli received an ominous prophecy from a divine messenger, that both of his sons would die on the same day, and that God would establish another family to take over the priestly duties (1 Sam 2:27–36). This tragic warning sets up the next scene, in which Samuel is called by the LORD.

Hannah's dedication to the LORD made Samuel's birth possible.

It was nighttime, and the old priest and Samuel were in bed in their respective spaces at the temple. Suddenly, Samuel heard a voice calling his name. Thinking it to be Eli's, the boy got out of bed and went quickly to Eli's room, ready to be of service. Yet Eli told the boy to go back to bed, because he had not called for Samuel. Samuel returned to his bed, but a second time he heard a voice calling for him. A second time he went to Eli, and a second time Eli sent him back. When Samuel came into Eli's room a third time, the old man realized that the boy was hearing the voice of the LORD, so he told the boy what to say aloud if he heard the voice again (1 Sam 3:1–9).

Sure enough, the voice came again—only this time the storyteller mentions that "the LORD came and stood there . . . " Samuel repeated aloud what Eli told him to say: "Speak, for your servant is listening." Then God delivered that fateful message about Eli's house that Eli himself had heard earlier. In the morning, Eli told the boy to repeat everything that he had heard, and Samuel reluctantly did so. Then Eli knew that it surely was the LORD speaking to Samuel, and the old man accepted the message (1 Sam 3:10–18).

This nighttime vision of the LORD was the beginning of Samuel's long ministry to Israel. He seems to have functioned over the years in more than one recognized office—certainly as a prophet, but also as a judge and a priest. The nation needed someone to steer the ship! In spite of all the generations that had passed since settling the Promised Land, Israel still had trouble with its neighbors. The Philistines engaged them in war, and Israel's elders decided to take the Ark of the Covenant with them to the battle. (The ark was a specially constructed trunk-like container in which were kept the two tablets of stone with the ten words, brought down from Mt. Sinai by Moses.) By the end of the battle, many Israelite soldiers were killed, the ark ended up in the hands of the Philistines, and Eli's two sons—who had been there with the ark—also died (1 Sam 4:2–11). When a messenger ran back to Shiloh to tell Eli the bad news, the old man fell backward off his seat, broke his neck and died as well (1 Sam 4:12–18).

After transporting the ark to their own place of worship, the Philistines began to fear its power. Three times they moved it to different towns, but no Philistine community wanted the ark of the covenant in *their* backyard (1 Sam 5)! So they put together a "guilt offering" of appeasement and found a way to get the ark back over the border into Israel, by placing it on a cart pulled by a pair of milk cows and sending it down the road. Once the Philistine officials (who watched safely at a distance) were satisfied that the ark was back in grateful hands, they headed home (1 Sam 6:1–16).

TO BE "LIKE THE NATIONS"

Samuel was respected in Israel as a judge, for many years. He led them in a ceremony of repentance and recommitment when the ark was returned (1 Sam 7:1–6). He prayed for them when the Philistines threatened to attack them again, and they were spared defeat (1 Sam 7:7–14). Samuel judged Israel annually in three other locations besides his hometown (1 Sam 7:15–17). Despite all this, though, he ended up with the same problem that the old priest Eli had—rascals for sons! They became judges once Samuel got old, but they took advantage of the office and did not rule fairly. This seems to have been the last straw for Israel's local rulers.

Samuel was respected in Israel as a judge, for many years.

Perhaps it was because of the rotten apples who were Samuel's sons, or having endured two sets of rotten apples consecutively. Perhaps it was fear of losing the ark again, or weariness over having to defend their borders time and again against aggressive neighbors. Perhaps those elders of Israel felt like their nation was not getting the respect—and status—on the international scene that they thought they deserved. The Story does not provide explicit reasons for their action. Yet they chose to assemble and meet with Samuel to talk about the nation's governance. They told him that he was getting on in years—implying, of course, that Samuel would not be around much longer to function as judge. They also pointed out to Samuel—which must have been a painful reminder to a deeply disappointed father—that his sons clearly were not following in their father's footsteps. The elders were leading up to something, for sure.

> **Pause to Reflect**
> What kind of transitions have you experienced? Which ones did you choose? Which ones were out of your control? What did you fear? For what did you hope?

Our storyteller at this point does not beat around the bush: "appoint for us, then, a king to govern us, like the nations" (1 Sam 8:5), the elders said. We don't know if the elderly Samuel was surprised by the request, but we do know that he was unhappy about it. So he consulted the LORD, who gave Samuel an earful. God's reply almost sounds like something an attentive parent might be thinking when the child asks for something out of line—"I figured this was coming!" The LORD emphasized to Samuel that the elders were not rebuffing Samuel, but God as the One to rule over them. Samuel was told to go along with the elders but to enumerate for them what a monarchy would require. Besides manpower for an army, the king also would require personnel to take care of his fields and to make weapons. "He will take . . . he will take . . . he will take . . . he will take . . . he will take . . . he will take" (1 Sam 8:6–18). The result for The People: "and you shall be his slaves" (8:17b). (Sounds like an ironic reference to Egypt, doesn't it?)

God told Samuel to tell the people how much
a king would demand of them.

Undeterred, it was "the people" (not just their elders) who repeated the request—so that the allure of "be[ing] like other nations (1 Sam 8:19b)" appears more evidently to have been a driving motivation. Samuel reported the news to the LORD, who told Samuel to do what they asked. Now the old judge and prophet had the task of finding someone to anoint to this new position for Israel. Prepare to meet the unlikely choice—tall and handsome Saul.

THE MONARCHY ESTABLISHED

We should not be surprised to find that the selection of Israel's first true king was carried out through divine guidance. The LORD told Samuel that a man from the tribe of Benjamin would arrive in town and that he, Samuel, was to anoint that man to be Israel's king. This young man was named Saul, from a well-to-do family. Recently, he had traveled from home, trying to locate some of his father's donkeys that had gotten away. After their unsuccessful searches in several locations, Saul's young servant suggested finding the "man of God" (Samuel) in the next town, to ask for help. They eventually found him, and—upon seeing Saul approach—the LORD told Samuel who it was. Now, Samuel was preparing for a religious ceremony, and he invited Saul to share in the meal that followed the ceremony. The old man assured Saul that his donkeys had been located, and then strangely hinted at something very important to come for him. Saul brushed off the suggestion, since his tribe Benjamin was considered low on the Israelite totem pole. Still, he and his servant ate there and spent the night as Samuel's guest (1 Sam 9).

Early the next morning, Samuel started Saul and his companion on their way, but he stopped Saul when they were alone for a moment. That pause was a life-changing one: Samuel was ready to "make known to you the word of God" (1 Sam 9:27d). With a vial in his hand, Samuel poured oil on Saul's head, kissed him, and told him the big news—that he was chosen by the LORD to rule over Israel, and to deliver them from their feisty neighbors. Samuel went on to prepare Saul for some signs that would confirm his divine anointing—news that the donkeys were safe; two loaves of bread received from three travelers on the road; and an encounter with the LORD's spirit, in the company of prophets playing instruments. Saul would be overtaken in a burst of spiritual emotion with these prophets, which would change him forever. After these things will have taken place, Samuel then told Saul that he was to go to a town called Gilgal, where Samuel would meet him (1 Sam 10:1–8).

All of what Samuel prophesied came true, but Saul kept the matter to himself for the time. Soon Samuel called all the Israelites together to introduce Saul as their king. The crowd was enthusiastic. After going over with everyone what was expected, Samuel wrote it all down and sent everyone home. A few naysayers questioned Saul's selection, but soon he would prove himself (1 Sam 10:17–27). A threat from their old nemesis the Ammonites got Saul riled up, and he designed a battle that led to a great victory. Rather than punishing the naysayers, Saul and Samuel held a celebration to reaffirm the new king's status. The mood at that point was very upbeat (1 Sam 11).

Tragically, however, conditions for Saul would not stay positive for very long. Military activity continued to demand his attention and, with it, appropriate religious offerings. In preparing for yet another battle with the Philistines, Saul became impatient in waiting for Samuel to arrive, so he undertook the offering on his own. Upon his arrival, Samuel was upset, since Saul's action departed from the divine requirement. Thus, in the prophet's eyes, Saul had forfeited the opportunity to reign long and prosperously (1 Sam 13:2–15).

Saul's poor decisions led to his losing God's favor as the chosen king.

Saul made other decisions that showed poor judgment. One day, he told the soldiers not to eat anything until evening, as part of a tactical maneuver. His son Jonathan did not hear of this order and made a small snack out of a piece of honeycomb. When Saul finally found out what Jonathan had done, he was ready to kill him, but the people interceded for the young soldier (1 Sam 14:24–46). On a different occasion, he went to a medium to get advice (1 Sam 28:3–25). So, even though he was continuing to lead in battle and gain some victories (1 Sam 15:1–9), Saul lost favor with God. Samuel made it clear to Saul that he was not doing what the LORD expected of him; Saul confessed his wrongdoing, but it was too late (1 Sam 15:10–31). At the end of this conversation between Samuel and Saul, the storyteller mentions both Samuel's grief and God's regret: "And the LORD was sorry that he had made Saul king over Israel" (1 Sam 15:35c).

AN AWKWARD TRANSITION

Samuel did not get much time to lament Saul's loss of divine favor. The LORD sent him once more to anoint a king for Israel. Yet again, the process of selection—and the selection itself—took place quite improbably, from a human point of view. Samuel followed God's directions by traveling to see a certain man in Judah, who hailed from a town called Bethlehem. The pretense for his visit was a sacrificial ceremony, to which the man, Jesse, brought his several sons. As each son walked by Samuel, the LORD said "No" to Samuel. So the old prophet and judge asked the father if these seven sons were all that he had. Jesse replied no, that the youngest one was out tending sheep. Samuel asked for him and, when he arrived, the LORD told Samuel to anoint him. As he did with Saul, Samuel anointed Jesse's youngest son with oil, while all his brothers were watching. There was no fanfare, no parades, no speeches—just a simple anointing. Samuel then went home (1 Sam 16:1–13). But the story-teller wanted listeners to know that God would be present and active with this next unlikely, as-yet-unknown monarch: "the spirit of the LORD came mightily upon David from that day forward" (1 Sam 16:13b).

Yes, it was true: the next king chosen by God was a shepherd boy, named David, hailing from the least of the twelve tribes of Jacob. His grand-father was Obed, born to Ruth, the Moabite woman whose marriage to Boaz "redeemed" her widowed mother-in-law Naomi. No one could have seen this turn of events coming! Yet David's legacy will become very prominent within The One Great Story.

Those days, however, were in the future. At this point, immediately fol-lowing his anointing, David was in an awkward and dangerous situation. His predecessor was still in power; there had been no "dethroning" announce-ment or ceremony. Saul knew nothing of David, until he was recommended to play the lyre (a stringed instrument) for Saul when Saul was suffering from what was called "an evil spirit" (1 Sam 16:14–15). So well-received was David that he became Saul's armor-bearer, playing his lyre and calming Saul during his episodes of anguish (1 Sam 16:2–23). The storytelling traditions here do not indicate that anyone yet was speaking of David's own anoint-ing—for the position that Saul currently held.

What these traditions do indicate was an early recognition of David's skill and style. The popular story of "David and Goliath" demonstrates the way in which the young shepherd's reputation built up. In the ongoing struggle that Israel experienced with the Philistines, the two armies were getting ready to face off once again. One of the Philistines' soldiers walked out of their camp and issued a challenge to the Israelite army: "Send out one of your soldiers to fight me. If he wins, we will serve you; but if I win, you will serve us." Everyone in Israel, including King Saul, was petrified: this Philistine soldier, Goliath, was a huge and terrifying figure, reportedly standing ten feet tall. Even his armor and weapons were oversized; his spear head alone weighed nineteen pounds (1 Sam 17:1–11)!

Pause to Reflect
In what religious ceremonies have you witnessed or shared in your life? What were they intended to do or represent? What difference did they make to those who were involved?

Goliath issued his challenge to the Israelite army morning and evening for many days. Meanwhile, Jesse sent his youngest son, David, with some supplies for his brothers and their officer at the Israelite's army camp. When he arrived, David could hear his people still talking about Goliath, wringing their hands in fear. The shepherd started asking questions, and his eldest brother got annoyed, accusing the lad of abandoning his responsibilities with their father's sheep to watch the two armies fight. Saul heard that David was there and sent for him. The (anointed) shepherd persuaded Saul to let him face Goliath, appealing to his experience protecting the flocks from lions and bears. Saul suited up David in his own armor, but David did not want to wear any of it. Instead, he took his staff, his shepherd's sling, and five smooth stones (1 Sam 17:12–40).

Goliath clearly was not intimidated by the sight of David walking toward him. He cursed and taunted the young man, promising that his body would be consumed by birds and animals. But David countered with his own promise—not only of Goliath's impending death but also of the Philistine army's demise. Goliath was not deterred and walked closer to face David. In a matter of seconds, David ran to the battle line, put one of the stones in his sling, and launched it toward the huge, menacing enemy soldier. The stone smacked Goliath hard, almost boring right into his forehead, whereby he fell forward to the ground. With Goliath now helpless, David was able to run up to him, take the Philistine's own sword from its sheath, kill him, and behead the Philistine army's most-feared human weapon (1 Sam 17:41–51).

That was all the Philistines needed to see! Their army ran off and was chased and subdued by the Israelites. It was a decisive victory for Israel, with favorable consequences for David. For one thing, Saul made David commander of the army, since he continued to triumph in battle. Saul's son Jonathan became a special friend to David; he shared with the shepherd-warrior his own royal robe and military possessions, because "he loved him as his own soul" (1 Sam 18:1c). David became quite popular. After Goliath's defeat, Israelite women danced and sang a song that gave more credit to David for the army's success (1 Sam 17:52—18:8).

David served King Saul and, because of his military successes, became very popular with the people.

This news upset Saul, whose attitude toward David began to shift. The king became jealous and, during one of his fits of rage, tried to kill David in the house by throwing his spear. He also gave David his daughter Michal in marriage, thinking that it somehow would lead to a military misstep on David's part with the Philistines. But David's popularity grew even more as his military effectiveness continued; Saul was out to get this man whom he viewed as an upstart and a threat. Even two of Saul's children, his wife

Michal and his son Jonathan, sought to protect David from their father, by devising elaborate escapes. Saul even chased David when he visited Samuel to tell the old judge what Saul was doing to him (1 Sam 18:9—19:24).

ON THE RUN

The popular young military hero (and anointed king) now was on the run in earnest. Despite being in such danger, David met secretly with Jonathan to see what his dear friend (and the mad king's son) had to say about the situation. Jonathan was sure that Saul would not harm David, but David could not accept that assessment. The king's son seemed to begin to realize that the LORD would grant the kingdom to David, rather than to himself, as Saul's heir. They talked a lot about how to figure out if it were safe for David to return and how Jonathan would convey messages to David. Later, when David was not present for a festival, Jonathan made up a story to try to keep his father Saul from being suspicious. It didn't work: Saul became enraged toward Jonathan, who tried to defend David. Yet the king's son now clearly realized that David indeed was not safe from his father. So, when their plan for conveying this message was completed, the two friends met secretly once more. They wept and embraced each other, pledging God's presence between them and their descendants. It was a most sorrowful parting (1 Sam 20:1–42).

David's life as a vagabond took him to various places, running into certain people, trying to avoid others (1 Sam 21), hiding in a cave where other "discontents" gathered to join David's army (1 Sam 22:1-2). That army rescued a town first from the Philistines and then from Saul's threat (1 Sam 23:1-13) before heading out into the wild country. It was a cat-and-mouse game for a while out there. Three times, the storytelling traditions report that Saul and his troops came close to David and his band, and twice David was in a position to kill Saul. In both cases, what David did, instead, was steal something from Saul's personal effects—to prove that he had been that close to the king—leave the spot, and then display those personal effects to Saul and his entourage. David's words were not taunting, however, but expressed his loyalty in God's name to Saul as king. Both encounters ended with pledges of peace between the two (1 Sam 24, 26).

> *David's life as a vagabond took him to various places;*
> *he ran into certain people and avoided others.*

Yet David still was not convinced that he was safe. He and his volunteer army went to a Philistine city and stayed for more than a year. He gained the trust of the king of that city, Achish, who appointed David his bodyguard (1 Sam 27:1—28:2). When other Philistine lords met Achish to prepare for another assault on Israel, they did not want David with them; they had heard of his military reputation and did not trust him. So Achish, somewhat apologetically, asked David to leave peaceably, which he did (1 Sam 29). The vagabond army traveled south, only to discover that the Amalekites had retaliated for one of David's earlier victories against them, by burning the town of Ziklag to the ground and carrying off all of its inhabitants—including David's wives. His standing among the people hit a low point for the first time, since his army's family members were among those kidnapped (1 Sam 30:1–6).

With the local priest's help, David asked the LORD for guidance, and God assured him that he would achieve a successful rescue. On the way, some of his soldiers found an Egyptian man who had been abandoned by his Amalekite master due to the man's illness. After eating and drinking, the man was revived and confirmed what had happened at Ziklag. David promised to protect the man if he showed David where "this raiding party" had gone. He showed them where the Amalekites were camped, as they were reveling in the spoils of many raids. David's army overcame the Amalekites and recovered all the property and all the kidnapped people—including David's wives. He returned everything but was granted some of the herds as his spoil, which he shared with those who lived in every location where David's ragtag army had journeyed (1 Sam 30).

> **Pause to Reflect**
> Have you ever had a moment in your life when
> everything seemed to be going your way? What was
> it like? How long did it last? What changed?

Without his knowing so, David's time of wandering exile was drawing to a sudden, brutal end. Sometime around the Ziklag campaign, Saul also had been out in battle—not surprisingly, against the Philistines. Israel's longtime nemesis routed Saul's army this time; three of Saul's sons—including David's beloved Jonathan—were killed, and Saul was shot up with arrows. There was no way out. Saul asked his armor-bearer to kill him by sword, so that the Philistine soldiers would not have the pleasure of taunting and torturing him to death. The armor-bearer was shocked by the whole situation and would not carry out his king's order. So Saul got out his own sword, fell down on it, and died. His armor-bearer, seeing the king dead, did the same to himself. The Philistines took over the towns in the region, beheaded Saul, moved his armor into the temple of their god Astarte, and hung his body on a wall. Some "valiant men" of a nearby town journeyed at night to rescue the king's and his sons' bodies, which they burned and then moved the bones to a burial site (1 Sam 31).

AT LAST—DAVID'S REIGN

A tragic era at the beginning of the chosen People's new monarchy was drawing to a violent close. It took a few days for the news of the defeat of Saul's army and of Saul's and Jonathan's deaths to reach David back in Ziklag. When it did, David and his entourage mourned, wept, and fasted, and David composed a song of lamentation (2 Sam 1). When the mourning was over, the LORD sent David to Hebron with his men and his family, where they settled. Here, David was acknowledged king—specifically, to reign over Judah, the southernmost territory of the tribal allotments (2 Sam 2:1–4).

Yet peace and stability continued to evade the people of the Promise. One of Saul's sons, named Ishbaal, became the king of Israel, that is, the northern territories of the original tribal allotments. Fighting between the two factions began almost immediately, with casualties on both sides, escalating to full-fledged war (2 Sam 2:12—3:1). To speak of the intricacies of intrigue during this period would amount almost to understatement! Characters appear, take action, kill, or get killed. The chess game eventually moved to David's favor: Saul's army commander, Abner, was murdered in vengeance (2 Sam 3:20–34); and Ishbaal was assassinated in his bedroom while resting on his couch (2 Sam 4). In all these deadly schemes, the traditions that we have inherited are clear in protecting David's innocence and reputation (see 2 Sam 3:28 and 4:9–11). Finally, the people came together to acknowledge David as the LORD's anointed; the elders agreed to a covenant with him, and the political division was over—for the time being (2 Sam 5:1–4).

David mourned the death of Saul and Saul's
son Jonathan, David's dear friend.

Right away, David claimed Jerusalem to be the capital city (2 Sam 5:6–12) and then moved the Ark of the Covenant there, with great celebration (2 Sam 6:1–19). David had a house built in Jerusalem (2 Sam 5:11–12), and there were no battles to fight. Things were settling down, at last! At this point, the storytellers recount a holy moment of covenant between David and the LORD, as well as introducing Nathan, a prophet of God. With no introduction, Nathan appears at this point in the narrative as one who was trusted by the king to bring the LORD's messages. In a vision at night, Nathan heard from the LORD about David's promised place in The Story—that God will "make for you a great name" (2 Sam 7:9c) and that David's "throne shall be established forever" (2 Sam 7:16b). This vision, placed where it is the narrative, also anticipates David's successor and what he will do for the LORD: "He shall build a house for my name" (2 Sam 7:13a), that is, construct a temple (more on that soon enough). David's prayerful response to Nathan's reported vision displays humility, obedience, and praise before God. It expresses a key element of the complex character that not only dominates this part of the narrative, but also adds to the overall trajectory of The Story itself.

In the traditions as we have inherited them, David was remembered for bringing Israel peace and security. After a time, he initiated military actions against several of Israel's longstanding antagonists and was quite successful, receiving gifts and spoils of valuable metals (2 Sam 8:1–12; see also chapter 10). King David put in place military and religious officials (2 Sam 8:16–18) and was known as a fair king to all Israel (2 Sam 8:15). He tracked down the last few descendants of Saul ("for Jonathan's sake" [2 Sam 9:1b]) and took care of them for the rest of their lives (2 Sam 9). For a time, then, the People of the Promise seemed to live in a manner that fulfilled that Promise.

Yet peace and security would not last—and David himself contributed to the coming instability. First, David committed adultery and tried to cover it up. This episode is well known to students of the Bible; its consequences reverberated through the rest of David's own life, as well as fractured the well-being of the nation.

TRUTH AND CONSEQUENCES

We often refer to this episode as "David and Bathsheba," although other characters play key—and tragic—roles. David was strolling around on the roof of the royal residence one day, when he spotted a good-looking woman who was bathing, presumably at her house. Even though David found out that the woman was married, he sent for her and had sex with her. After some time, the woman—named Bathsheba—sent word to the king that she was pregnant (2 Sam 11:1–5).

This pregnancy would not necessarily have caused a stir—except that Bathsheba's husband, Uriah, served in the army and was away at a siege of a town called Rabbah. Under these circumstances, he could not have been the father of this baby. So David hatched a plan: he had Uriah called back from the front and tried to get him to go home to Bathsheba. Uriah, however, was loyal to the military code and would not do so, even when the next day

David hosted him at the royal residence and got him drunk. Instead, Uriah again slept outside with David's servants (2 Sam 11:6–13).

David then moved to another plan. He sent a letter to Joab, the army's commander (that very letter being carried there by Uriah himself), instructing Joab to put Uriah on the front line of the next battle. Then, when the fighting became fierce, Joab was to pull back other soldiers, so that Uriah would be vulnerable and more likely to be killed. Joab did what David instructed; indeed, Uriah was killed, along with some other soldiers. Upon hearing the news, David sent word back to Joab not to let the incident bother him but to continue the siege and take the city. Bathsheba mourned her husband's death for the required period; then David married her, and their baby was born, a boy (2 Sam 11:14–26).

If David had thought that his actions went unnoticed, he was wrong. Nathan, the LORD's prophet, approached David with a message, and he delivered it first by telling David a parable. It presented two men, one rich and another poor, one with many animals in his flocks, and the other with just one lamb that he treasured like a daughter. When the rich man received a guest, instead of using one of his many sheep for the guest's meal, he took the poor man's precious lamb and slaughtered her (2 Sam 12:1–4).

David took the bait: he renounced the rich man's actions vehemently, calling for his death and a fourfold restitution to the poor man, pointing out the rich man's lack of compassion. This was all that Nathan needed to hear. In a short, direct statement, Nathan began his divine message to his king: "You are the man!" (2 Sam 12:7b). The prophet immediately spelled out the LORD's selection of, rescue of, and material blessings to David. Nathan made it clear that David "despised the word of the LORD" by having Uriah killed—especially by an enemy—and marrying Bathsheba (2 Sam 12:9–10). There would be long-term consequences, Nathan declared, among David's family—and the baby would not survive (2 Sam 12:11–12).

In having Uriah killed, David violated his covenant
with the LORD, and consequences followed.

In the ancient world, rulers had a tendency to keep close at hand persons who supported their agenda and did not question the ruler's actions. David could have banished Nathan, or even have had him killed, for the prophet's forceful pronouncements: after all, David *was* the chosen king! Yet what adds to the fascinating complexity of this story—and of David as a biblical character—is his response to Nathan. David confessed his wrongdoing:

"I have sinned against the LORD" (12 Sam 2:13a). He did not hedge or qualify his confession; it was as straightforward as the accusation itself.

Now, the fate that David had declared deserving of the rich man in the parable did not come to David; he lived for many more years. However, the baby did die from an illness, in spite of David's prayer and fasting (2 Sam 12:15–19). After a time, Bathsheba bore another son, whom David named Solomon (2 Sam 12:24). Soon afterward, the siege of Rabbah was successful, and the rest of the Ammonite territory was subdued (2 Sam 12:26–31).

A CHALLENGED MONARCHY

As Nathan's prophecy declared, David's reign as king would be marked by internal strife that would sabotage his legacy. David's oldest son, Amnon, raped his half-sister Tamar and then abandoned her—thus assuring that she never would marry (2 Sam 13:1–19). Tamar's brother Absalom, finally impatient with his father's lack of response, lured Amnon into an apparently safe situation but then had him killed while he was tipsy (2 Sam 3:20–29). Then the retaliating son left the country and stayed away for three years, while David mourned for Amnon and missed Absalom (2 Sam 13:34–39). David's commander, Joab, sensed David's heart on the matter and devised a plan.

Joab found a woman from his hometown and prepared her to visit the king. She told David a story of Joab's concoction, one that would sound plausible, in which the woman would ask for help to preserve the life of her supposed, only remaining, son. As the two talked, David figured out that Joab had put the old woman up to this, so he instructed Joab to bring Absalom back to Jerusalem. Yet the father and son still did not meet, for two more years. Joab would not meet Absalom to arrange the visit, until Absalom had one of his servants set fire to one of Joab's fields. Once Joab finally spoke to David, the king called for his wayward son. Absalom bowed before David, who gave him a royal kiss (2 Sam 14).

Still, all was not well. Absalom was good-looking like his father and had a wily streak. He would ride in a chariot with fifty men running in front of it (2 Sam 15:1)—surely to make a public show of his importance. He spoke to people who came to the king for a legal decision and would say things to call into question the fairness of their pending treatment (2 Sam 15:2–5). Absalom became quite popular and eventually set in motion the plans for a royal coup, to begin during a visit to Hebron for sacrifices (2 Sam 15:7–12). David was tipped off by a messenger and left Jerusalem with his officials and household (2 Sam 15:13–18). The chosen king now was on the run once more!

Absalom betrayed his father, and yet David
mourned his son's ignominious death.

It now was clear, as David and his entourage were on the move, that the king did not have universal support of the people. Some were loyal and others were not (see 2 Sam 15:19–23; compare 16:5–14). Meanwhile, Absalom had sex with David's concubines who were left to take care of the royal house (2 Sam 16:20–23), to show that he, Absalom, had assumed the kingship. He sought advice from what the young upstart supposed were two of David's royal advisers, Ahitophel and Hushai, on how to complete the coup by removing his father as a threat. Although Ahitophel had an esteemed reputation, Absalom and his followers decided that Hushai's proposed plan would work better (2 Sam 17:1–14).

> **Pause to Reflect**
> What kind of "plotting for advantage" have you ever witnessed
> or taken part in? How did it work out? Who benefitted
> by the outcome? Who might have been hurt by it?

Once Hushai realized that his plan was Absalom's choice, he secretly sent word to David to have his entire entourage cross the Jordan River that very night (2 Sam 17:15–22). They did so and then received food and rest from some supporters there (2 Sam 17:27–29). Even as he prepared for battle with Absalom's troops, David was greatly concerned for his wayward, conniving son: he directed Joab to "deal gently for my sake" (2 Sam 18:5b) with the usurper. Alas, David's request would not be honored. The fighting went heavily against Absalom's troops, spreading from field to forest. Absalom ended up riding through the forest and saw some of David's servants coming. Before he could stop his mount, Absalom found himself suspended in midair, hanging by his long hair from the branches of a large tree. Once Joab heard this news, he ordered Absalom's death, promising a large reward. The man who reported the scene had heard David's plea for Absalom's well-being and would not comply with Joab's order. The commander then thrust three spears into the helpless rebel's chest, and Joab's armor-bearers finished off the deadly deed (2 Sam 18:6–15).

When David heard the news from a messenger, he wept and mourned for Absalom (2 Sam 18:19–33). Hearing of the king's response, Joab went to David and told him that he was shaming the very soldiers who had just saved his life. David would lose the loyalty of the people, Joab continued, if he did not go out to his public seat to be seen and greeted by the troops. David heeded

his commander's advice (2 Sam 19:1–8) and discovered that the people were
ready to have David back as their king. He did return, having replaced Joab as
commander—since Joab himself was responsible for the death of the grieving
king's son (2 Sam 19:11–18a). Along the way, David dealt with some of his
predecessor Saul's former supporters and made some mostly generous decisions about their status with the new monarch (2 Sam 19:16–40).

Seeds of rivalry were evident, however, even in this time of stabilizing
the kingdom again. Israel, the northern section, felt that Judah, the southern
section, was trying to squeeze Israel out of its rightful place in the celebration of return (2 Sam 19:41–43). Tragically, this rivalry was not to disappear.
A man named Sheba soon called for a rebellion against David's claim to be
king. He gained the support of the northern tribes of Israel, but Judah stayed
loyal to David (2 Sam 20:1–2). Amasa, David's new commander, was given
orders to gather the army before David, to prepare for battle. Joab, David's
former commander, tricked Amasa as he went to greet him and disembow-
eled him with a sword. Then Joab took over the army again (2 Sam 20:4–13).

Joab's victory over Sheba was aided by another "wise woman." Joab had
set up equipment to knock down the wall of the city of Abel, where Sheba
and his forces were holed up. The woman talked Joab into sparing the city,
by promising to have Sheba's head thrown over the wall. She went into the
city and talked to its residents, who complied with the plan. Once the rebel's
head was in Joab's possession, the siege was over, the rebellion was crushed,
and Joab returned to Jerusalem as commander, including of Israel's troops
(2 Sam 20:14–23).

A TUMULTUOUS ERA ENDS

David's reign as king of God's chosen People was a long one and marked
by both glory and tumult. He clearly was remembered as an effective soldier and military leader, one who displayed loyalty to Saul's name (2 Sam
21:1–14) and courage on the battlefield (2 Sam 21:15–22). Those who fought
most closely with David were remembered as almost larger than life (2 Sam
23:8–38). As their king, David conducted a census of the People and then
regretted the decision, praying earnestly for the People's well-being (2 Sam
24:1–25). David's trust in the LORD also was expressed through the inherited traditions by songs, or "psalms," that are attributed to him (see 2 Sam
22 and 23:1–7). A number of the psalms in the Old Testament book of that
name have David's name attached to them (see, for example, Pss 3–9, 10–17,
and 19–32). David's life would come to an end, by natural causes—perhaps
remarkably so. As he aged, it appears that he also was losing health and

physical strength (1 Kgs 1:1–4) and thus perhaps was considered not fit for the throne. Apparently, the choice of a successor was not a foregone conclusion: royal intrigue surged to the forefront again in The Story. Absalom's next-younger brother, Adonijah, figured that the throne was his—and, like his brother, he acted the part, riding in chariots and flanked by horsemen. Those of the royal court, however, were divided in their support of Adonijah (1 Kgs 1:5–10). Nathan, the prophet who once more appears in the narrative, met with Bathsheba, Solomon's mother, bringing advice. Nathan urged her to remind David of his vow that Solomon would succeed him as king (a vow, by the way, that does not appear in the narrative until now). Bathsheba went to David in his room. She asked David if he knew about the sacrificial ceremonies that Adonijah was holding and the threat that they posed to her and her son. Then Nathan showed up to add to this report, saying that those attending the ceremonies were calling Adonijah the king (1 Kgs 1:11–27).

Immediately, David had Bathsheba return to him, and he swore his vow that Solomon would succeed him. Then he gave three of his court members (including Nathan) orders to proceed forthwith to anoint Solomon as king. They did so, with great pomp and ceremony, with music and a large, enthusiastic crowd. When word of Solomon's anointing and celebration reached Adonijah and his guests, they dispersed with fear, and Adonijah ran to "grasp the horns of the altar." Solomon sent word that his half-brother's life would be spared, as long as he remained loyal and worthy. After Adonijah appeared before Solomon and properly expressed his loyalty, he was allowed to return home (1 Kgs 1:28–53). The crisis of succession was over: Bathsheba's son was now the king of Israel and of Judah, the land of the twelve tribes of the LORD, the God of Abraham, Isaac, and Jacob.

David's reign demonstrated the sometimes dangerous challenges involved in royal succession.

Before he died, David spoke words of encouragement and advice for the new king. He reminded him to continue being faithful to the LORD, by following the law of Moses; in this way, the promise that David's house would maintain the monarchy forever would remain. David also gave directions concerning three particular persons, two who were potential threats and one who had been hospitable to David and his troops. Then as ancient stories often do, after his final words were spoken, David breathed his last. A new king was in place, and a new era was beginning (1 Kgs 2:1–12).

ISRAEL AFTER DAVID

The People of God had changed. Beginning centuries earlier more like a band of nomads (although often wealthy ones), they had reached a point in historical development that put them on a par with surrounding nations. No longer did they live at the mercy of other peoples whose claim to property and power eclipsed their own. When it came to status and security, the monarchy gave them some skin in the international game. As we will see soon, Solomon's reign brought this people to the height of its position in the world. Yet, in all of that glory, where was The One Great Story?

In the next chapter, we first follow Solomon, as he builds an empire and a temple for the LORD. Solomon's achievements, actions, and ultimate loyalty offer a wondrous, yet perhaps contradictory and compromised, study of biblical faith. We then will watch his unified political achievement gradually fall apart and get swallowed up. Why did it happen like this? The traditions that we have inherited through these texts seem to have one fundamental answer—trust in the God of their ancestors was not sustained. In spite of a few brief, bright moments, what follows is marked by more strife, abandonment, intrigue, tragedy, and heartache—with an occasional flicker of hope.

FOR THE READER

1. Much of the Old Testament is dominated by male characters. What might our spiritual ancestors have thought of the story of Naomi and Ruth—which includes a woman not even of the twelve tribes? How does this story strike you?

2. The Israelites gave up their God-chosen judges, so that they could have a monarchy instead. What were they gaining? What were they losing? What were they afraid of?

3. Why was the "David and Goliath" episode so memorable for the people of Israel?

4. What do these episodes in this part of The One Great Story suggest about why David and his legacy were so important to the keepers of the traditions?

5. What do The Story's episodes in this chapter suggest about the effectiveness of Israel's new monarchy?

SUGGESTED ACTIVITIES

- Read Judg 6:11–27, about the LORD's call to Gideon to deliver Israel. What themes do you recognize in this call episode that we have seen in earlier accounts of other biblical characters? What do these themes contribute to your understanding of The One Great Story?

- Make a list of notes on the women who are prominently featured in the episodes covered by this chapter. Discuss their stories with a friend. Why were they remembered? What do their lives suggest about how trust in God makes a difference to a community?

- Read 1 Sam 8 (22 verses) and make a list of all the things that Samuel told the elders of Israel that the king would do. How do the items on this list compare with the activities of the judges, as seen for instance in Judg 2:11–3:30 and/or 4:1–23? In what ways are they similar? Different? What do the differences represent for the life of the chosen people?

Chapter 5

The Story Peaks and Falters

"Is it because there is no God in Israel that you are going
to inquire of Baal-zebub . . . ?"

—2 KGS 1:3C

It must be part of our general human nature to love grandeur, to savor conspicuous displays of command, and to bask in symbols of permanence. During Solomon's reign as king, we could imagine people—especially in the capital city, Jerusalem—saying to each other, "Now, this is more like it!" Perhaps they would have strut a little down the street, whistling battle tunes as they thought about their nation at peace. Perhaps the children would have taken turns playing Moses leading the Israelites in the wilderness, or Samson pulling down the pillars, or the young shepherd David against Goliath, or the warrior David defeating the Ammonites, or their king Solomon receiving heads of state. Even the scribes might have wondered if the divine promise, made so long ago to Abram and Sarai, had reached the apex of its fulfillment at last.

One could argue convincingly that this chosen People certainly had waited a long time! For readers like ourselves—who are so accustomed to seeking quick results for our aspirations and daily needs—a promise of blessing that seemed to hang in mid-air for centuries would be just about impossible to endure. This was about Israel's identity and purpose, for gosh sakes! Those who paid careful attention to their heritage and its story line now must have been breathing a collective sigh of relief. In many ways, Solomon's reign brought a degree and quality of well-being to the nation that it never had known previously. That well-being, however, would not last long.

In this chapter, we will summarize King Solomon's achievements and influence, and then watch as the Promise loses its way. Kings came and kings went. Their names for us often are hard to remember (and will not try here to recount them all), and their actions sometimes were startling, but the theme of their legacies follows a familiar tune. Eventually, tragedy greets the Called People again, this time on the other side of what they thought would have been fulfillment. Like flies on honey, the question of Israel's ultimate allegiance would continue to pester the people of Promise. It should come as no surprise to us, then, that the character who emerged to prominence amidst this distressing era hails back to "the good ol' days" before Israel asked for a king.

SOLOMON AND HIS EMPIRE

What we have inherited from the traditions that are represented in the biblical texts portray Solomon's overall achievements as the realization of promises made before his time. As we saw in the previous chapter, David would not be the one to see the worldly splendor and glory come to pass. His son with Bathsheba inherited these hopes—and he made the most of them. Solomon's legacy covers a wide range of enviable accomplishments— expansion of territory and cities, construction projects including an impressive temple for the LORD, international dealings, and a reputation as a wise, fair monarch.

Solomon's legacy covers a wide range of enviable accomplishments.

First, though, Solomon had to clear the deck of threats. In typical Old Testament fashion, he had two men put to death—one, Joab, for killing two of David's warriors without the king's approval (1 Kgs 2:28–35); and the other, Shimei, for breaking a "house arrest" order imposed by Solomon at the start of his reign (1 Kgs 2:36–46a). Our narrators emphasize that this action gave Solomon control of Israel's national interests and political power: "So the kingdom was established in the hand of Solomon" (1 Kgs 2:46b).

Our narrators also spare no details as they pass on descriptions of Solomon's authority and prosperity. The new king seemed to have had possessed a clear sense of order and structure, for he set up administrative positions to make the country run smoothly. Solomon appointed priests, secretaries, a recorder, a head of the army, a palace chief, a director of "forced labor," and twelve officers for the twelve tribal allotments, who oversaw distribution of food (1 Kgs 4:1–19). He made what appears to have been a diplomatic move in marrying the daughter of the current (unnamed) Pharaoh (1 Kgs 4:1)—a feat that must have given the priests and scribes, keepers of The Great Story, immense delight. The borders of his control extended north to the Euphrates River, south to the northeastern edge of Egypt, east to the deserts beyond Edom and Ammon, and west to most of the coastline of the eastern Mediterranean (see 1 Kgs 4:21). Lists itemizing the king's provisions for the royal dining table reflect an opulent lifestyle (1 Kgs 4:22–23); even the people enjoyed abundance and freedom from danger (1 Kgs 4:20, 25). The count of royal stables, chariots, and horsemen ran into the many thousands (1 Kgs 4:26).

Besides these grand-scale features of his daily life, Solomon built big things—a building for the palace's treasury and armory (1 Kgs 7:2–5; see also 10:16–17), a large columned porch (1 Kgs 7:6), a hall for dealing with legal matters (1 Kgs 7:7), a house for his Egyptian wife (1 Kgs 7:8), and his own palace, which took thirteen years to complete (1 Kgs 7:1, 8). None of these edifices was erected with cheap materials but rather of "costly stones, cut according to measure" (1 Kgs 7:9a), requiring extra skill and expense. All of this building was overseen by a man named Hiram, a skilled artisan of repute whose mother had been an Israelite (1 Kgs 7:13–14; see also 5:1–12).

> **Pause to Reflect**
> What is the most impressive, inspiring human-made structure
> that you ever have seen? What makes it so impressive?
> What thoughts and feelings does it prompt in you? If it is a
> religious structure, what does it suggest to you about divine
> things? If it is not religious, what does it seem to symbolize?

Probably Solomon's most important—and certainly most enduring—building achievement was constructing a temple for worshipping Israel's god, the LORD. The traditions that we have inherited went into great detail describing the materials used, the pillars constructed, as well as items such as a huge bronze basin, bronze carts with elaborate carvings, a golden altar, pots, bowls, latticeworks, lampstands, cups, dishes, firepans, and more (1 Kgs 7:15–50). Cypress was used for the floor; cedar lined the walls, carved with gourds and flowers; gold covered the inner sanctuary, the altar, and "the whole house" (1 Kgs 6:15–22). Two large cherubim (winged sentries of sacred spaces) were carved for the inner sanctuary and covered with gold (1 Kgs 6:23–28). The doors opening to the inner sanctuary were of olivewood and elaborately carved, then covered with gold (1 Kgs 6:31–32). The entire project took seven years (1 Kgs 6:38d).

Probably Solomon's most enduring building achievement
was constructing a temple for the LORD.

For overall effect and significance, I suppose that Americans could compare the construction of the Temple in Jerusalem to that of the Congressional complex on Capitol Hill in Washington, DC. Although no explicit or specific religious value or authority is assigned to Capitol Hill, the parallels between it and the temple in Jerusalem—in terms of political bearings, judicial process, national identity, and solemn pride—seem clear. When Solomon's temple built for the LORD was dedicated, the ark of the covenant was brought into the inner sanctuary and ceremoniously placed "underneath the wings of the cherubim" (1 Kgs 8:6c). Then, reminiscent of the cloud in the tabernacle in Moses' day (Exod 40:34–38), a cloud representing "the glory of the LORD" engulfed the temple. King Solomon rose, blessing the People, and affirmed for them that the temple fulfilled a promise made by his father, and that Solomon's place as king fulfilled a promise made by the LORD (1 Kgs 8:1–21).

After these words, Solomon dedicated the temple with a long, sincere prayer. In it, the narrators see Solomon linking the covenant with David's line to the much older covenant made at Sinai—the ark being the most cherished artifact of that earlier covenant. Solomon's prayer also asked for God's faithfulness, for righteous judgments, for forgiveness of the people's sins, for non-Israelites who pray to the LORD, to support the people when they defended the LORD, to bring the people back if they are ever exiled. After another blessing of the people, the king commanded the People to "devote yourselves completely to the LORD our God" (1 Kgs 8:61a), and then sacrificed thousands of oxen and sheep. The dedication having concluded, the entire nation celebrated for seven days and then returned home (1 Kgs 8:22–66).

In case you can't tell yet, this temple construction and dedication was a really big deal! It symbolized for Israel the completion of things for which the people had hoped, for a very long time. From the perspective of their One Great Story, it was almost too good to be true. So many generations of their ancestors had wandered and struggled and fought and sought solace in idols—could this promise from Abram's and Sarai's days be trustworthy? As the people gazed at their new, grand temple, and listened to their eloquent, faithful young king, on that dedication day, the whole experience must have had a surrealistic feel to it. A new day was dawning for the People of the Promise. They had arrived!

During the rest of his reign, Solomon maintained expansive fame and influence.

The traditions responsible for the biblical texts remember that the temple dedication was followed by a second "theophany" for Solomon—that is, another appearance to the king by the LORD. Not surprisingly for those who follow The Story, this appearance came with both good news and bad news. Its formula is familiar—"*if this, then that; but if not this, then not that.*" In this case, the LORD will keep the promise of maintaining David's royal line, as long as Solomon and his successors stay loyal to the LORD "with integrity of heart and uprightness" (1 Kgs 9:4c). However, if Solomon or his descendants go after other gods, the entire nation of Israel will fall; it will lose its land and its respect among other nations (1 Kgs 9:1–9). These are sober, cautious—and also familiar!—words from the God of Abraham, Isaac, and Jacob to the king who has promised to reign faithfully and with justice.

During the rest of his reign, Solomon maintained expansive fame and influence. He had an armada of ships built, which brought back a large amount of gold to the king (1 Kgs 9:26–28) that was fashioned for drinking vessels and other purposes (1 Kgs 10:21). His renown spread to such an extent that he even received a visit from another head of state, a queen from a place known in the text as Sheba. This queen was very impressed with Solomon's wisdom and with the entire presentation of Solomon's house, food, and staff. She gave credit to Israel's god for all of the greatness that she saw there. The wording of this episode also suggests that the two monarchs worked out a trade agreement. Once again, an episode from Solomon's reign emphasizes how striking, even imposing, his monarchy appeared to everyone (1 Kgs 10:1–13).

From a historical perspective, the territory that Solomon claimed was not the largest in the world, during his or any other era. Still, the biblical traditions pulled out all the stops when it came to other measures of his prominence and distinction. They summarized it simply: "Thus King Solomon excelled all the kings of the earth in riches and in wisdom (1 Kgs 10:23)." They might have been overstating their claim, but nonetheless, the point was well-taken: here was a monarch whose accomplishments on the world stage left his people feeling very proud.

All was not well, however, for the acclaimed king of Israel. He "acquired" many hundreds of women as wives, according to the biblical sources, many of whom came from nations with whom Israel had had military struggles, even in the recent past. These nations worshipped their own gods, not the God of Abraham, Isaac, and Jacob. As Solomon aged, he became more interested in some of these other gods that his wives worshipped. He even built places within Israelite territory for them to worship those gods. This shift of loyalty was to have serious consequences, as the traditions responsible for the biblical texts recall this part of Solomon's reign. They remember the LORD being angry with Solomon and telling him that his kingdom would be torn apart after he died (1 Kgs 11:1–13).

> *As Solomon aged, he became more interested in*
> *gods that his many wives worshipped.*

From that point on, the stability that Israel had so relished for many years began to unravel. Three different men, from various places and stations among the People, challenged Solomon's legitimacy in various ways. One of them, Jeroboam, worked for the king overseeing laborers. He was visited by a prophet named Ahijah, who told Jeroboam that he would become king of ten of the tribes, as a result of Solomon's apostasy. Word of this prophetic message got back to Solomon, who tried to have Jeroboam eliminated; the man who would be king—Jeroboam—however, escaped to Egypt and was protected by the Pharaoh. Not long afterward, Solomon died, and his son Rehoboam replaced his father as king in Jerusalem (1 Kgs 11:14–43).

THE KINGDOM DIVIDED

Seeds of national division had been sown in years past, and they were about to sprout quickly and dramatically. Those who had gathered for Rehoboam's selection as Solomon's successor immediately asked the new king to ease up on the heavy taxes and the required labor. Jeroboam had heard of Solomon's death and, having returned from Egypt, joined his countrymen in this request. Rehoboam first consulted the men who had served Solomon; they approved of the request, saying that it would foster the People's loyalty. But when Rehoboam posed the same question to his childhood friends now in his court, they gave him the opposite advice. Rehoboam followed his young, inexperienced peers' advice. He told the People that they would work even harder for him than for his father Solomon (1 Kgs 12:1–15).

Seeds of national division had been sown in years past, and they were about to sprout quickly and dramatically.

That royal response from Solomon's son was all that the people of Israel needed to hear! In no uncertain terms, they denounced their legacy with David's lineage and left the meeting place. King Rehoboam's effort to talk them out of their decision led to the death of Rehoboam's messenger, by stoning. Then Rehoboam quickly escaped the place, before anything could happen to him. Meanwhile, that same assembly crowned the recently returned Jeroboam as their king. Only the tribes of Judah and Benjamin acknowledged Rehoboam as the rightful king. A prophet brought word from the LORD to Rehoboam not to fight against Jeroboam for the kingdom. Thus, from then on, the hope for a single kingdom under David's name forever was lost: the nation-state that had achieved so much worldly success under Solomon was now two rival kingdoms (1 Kgs 12:16–24).

Pause to Reflect
What kind of divisions exist in your community?
What do you know about their history? Who benefits
from them? Who suffers because of them?

Jeroboam felt compelled to strengthen the loyalty of the northern tribes that followed him. First, he set up the new capital in Shechem, where Rehoboam himself had recently been crowned. Then he had two calves of gold made and housed in religious buildings in Dan and Bethel, so that his people would not travel to the temple in Jerusalem to worship. Jeroboam said, "Here are your gods, O Israel" (12:28d), as though the golden calf in the wilderness centuries earlier had been their ancestors' savior. Because he continued to set up religious sites and offices like these, Jeroboam received a harsh message from an old, faithful prophet, Ahijah. The king's aim to consolidate his supporters had led to actions that were evil in the LORD's sight—just as they had been named as evil centuries earlier. Ahijah made it clear that Jeroboam's line would not continue in the monarchy. Moreover, the blind prophet said, the nation of Israel itself (that is, the northern ten tribes) would be "scattered"; it would not survive, because of Jeroboam's sins (1 Kgs 14:1–16).

The two kingdoms would be served by a combined total of more than three dozen kings (and one queen!) in the next two and three centuries.

Although he was king over Israel for twenty-two years, Jeroboam died with this tragic prophecy hanging over him. Meanwhile, King Rehoboam of Judah apparently had died some years earlier (see 1 Kgs 14:21). Judah's loyalty to the LORD had been not much better than that of Israel's—high places for worship, pillars and wooden idols, even male prostitutes in the temple (1 Kgs 14:22–24). Five years into Rehoboam's reign, Egypt raided Jerusalem, carting away all the precious possessions and gold objects from the Temple and the royal palace (1 Kgs 14:25–26). Watching these symbols of grandeur and fortune leave their capital city and land must have delivered a searing blow to Judah's sense of identity.

Indeed, this loss of expensive religious and political artifacts stands in retrospect as a turning point in the life of the Chosen People. The two kingdoms would be served by more than three dozen kings (and one queen!) in the next two and three centuries. Judged by the traditions responsible for the literature that we have inherited, few of these monarchs sought to help their people honor their covenant with the LORD. None of the northern (Israel) kingdom's monarchs were remembered as faithful to the covenant, and only two of those received even mixed reviews. Jehu got rid of those who were worshipping Baal, but he left the golden calves that Jeroboam had made (2 Kgs 9 and 10). Jehoahaz seems to have had a temporary change of heart—resulting in a period of relative peace—but the ghost of Jeroboam's sinful ways cast a long shadow over his reign (2 Kgs 13:1–14). It comes as no surprise, then, that internal intrigue and violence marked many of the royal tenures: five of Israel's kings were murdered, as well as its one queen, Athaliah, (2 Kgs 11:1–16); two of Judah's kings suffered the same fate.

From the record, six of the southern (Judah) kingdom's kings remained faithful to the LORD—Asa, Jehoshaphat, Jehoash, Jotham, Hezekiah, and Josiah. Evidence of their covenant loyalty is reported often concerning objects of worship, whether the king got rid of idols to Baal and Asherah. The reigns of these faithful kings occurred here and there over three centuries and more, hardly consistent enough to establish strong momentum. Enticements to worship the gods of the surrounding nations—who were the Chosen People's perennial enemies—must have been tremendous.

Internal intrigue and violence marked many of the royal tenures.

Studying this part of the Old Testament can leave a reader wondering at times whether God had anything much to do with this period of The One Great Story! If most of the kings had more interest in other gods and political posturing, what happened to signs of the presence of the LORD? Where, and who, was tuned in, paying attention, and giving witness to the God of this People's ancestors and the covenant? The answer to these questions takes us away from the royal palace, and even the fabulous Temple, and into the world and lives of an unlikely cadre of folks. They were known as "prophets," and two of them retained a distinctive place among the middle generations of the monarchies. They are Elijah and Elisha, whose ministries were directed to the Northern Kingdom.

PROPHETS AMID KINGS

Prophets appear now and then in this broad stretch of The Story, and they played a particular role in the life of kings. For instance, we remember Nathan, a prophet who served during David's reign: he spoke sternly to young King David about the Bathsheba-Uriah situation; much later, near David's death, Nathan was instrumental in assuring that Solomon would succeed his father. The role of prophet clearly was recognized—not unlike the role of judges, in this regard—as a valid position within most of Israelite religious tradition. Indeed, the Hebrew word for "prophet" appears more than 300 times, in writings from Genesis to Malachi, and referring to individuals of various personalities and behaviors.[10]

> *The role of prophet clearly was recognized as a valid position in Israelite religious tradition.*

During the era of the kings, prophets show up often as incidental characters, except in the cases of Nathan, Elijah, and Elisha. We see evidence of them in two, sometimes overlapping, ways. One way is as a group of prophets who apparently lived and ministered together, known as a "company of the prophets" (see 1 Sam 10:11, 19:20; 1 Kgs 20:35). The other kind of evidence for prophets is of those who speak falsely, acting as though their words are divinely inspired and true (as in Jeremiah 14:13–14). Sometimes kings preferred to hear what these "false prophets" had to say, since their utterances typically reinforced what the king wanted to do. In other occasions—such

---

10. See the long, detailed article by Napier, "Prophet, Prophetism," 896.

as an upcoming, dramatic episode involving Elijah—prophets were false because they followed a god other than the LORD.

ELIJAH: "YOU TROUBLER OF ISRAEL"

Both Elijah and Elisha stand out within The One Great Story, in part because of the dramatic nature of their acts, and in part because they appear among the most faithful followers of the LORD in their day. Elijah came first, introduced abruptly into the narrative during the reign of Israel's seventh king, Ahab. Elijah was remembered for performing wondrous works that confirmed his divine vocation. He revived the son of a non-Israelite widow who was hospitable to him (1 Kgs 17:8–24). Even more consequential, Elijah went to King Ahab and told him that a drought was coming over the land (1 Kgs 17:1); much later, he would lead Ahab's chariot as the rains returned (1 Kgs 18:41–46).

Elijah was remembered for performing wondrous
works that confirmed his divine vocation.

It is the series of events that occurred before the drought ended for which Elijah perhaps has been most famously remembered. Ahab had married a princess of the Sidonian king. Her name was Jezebel, and her nation served Baal. Ahab built an altar for Baal in Samaria, which now was Israel's capital city. Jezebel was doing her best to rid Israel of the LORD's prophets (see 1 Kgs 18:4). These actions were considered by our inherited texts as the worst of any Israelite king to that time (1 Kgs 16:31–33).

The drought was getting worse, and Ahab tried to find springs of water and grass for the royal horses and mules. Elijah appeared during Ahab's hunt and challenged him to a showdown of sorts, at the holy place, Mt. Carmel. When everyone had gathered there, Elijah chastised the Israelites for giving their loyalty to both Baal and the LORD. So the prophet—who thought that he was the only one left—threw down the gauntlet. He told them to bring two bulls and let the prophets of Baal, all 450 of them, choose one and prepare it for sacrifice. Elijah urged them to call on their god, which they did, for several hours. During that time, Elijah poked fun at the prophets of Baal, who by then were gashing themselves with swords and wailing loudly. Yet, as the whole assembly watched, nothing at all happened to their prepared offering (1 Kgs 18:1–29).

*Elijah's defeat of the prophets of Baal led to a
death threat from the queen, Jezebel.*

Then it was Elijah's turn. First, he fixed up the LORD's altar, one that
had been erected there and used in earlier times. As part of this repair, Elijah used twelve stones, representing the twelve tribes of Jacob. After digging
a large trench around the renovated altar, he set up the wood for burning,
prepared the bull and set it on the wood, and—as a final act of readiness—
instructed that large jars of water be poured over the entire site, three times!
Elijah's preparation of the offering to the LORD hardly could have been
more astonishing. Standing next to it, the prophet then prayed. He identified
the LORD as "God of Abraham, Isaac, and Israel" (1 Kgs 18:36b), affirming before everyone gathered there the origins of the people's covenant and
his intentions in that moment: "so that this people may know that you, O
LORD, are God, and that you have turned their hearts back" (1 Kgs 18:37).
When Elijah's prayer was finished, his drenched offering became completely
and totally engulfed in flames, incinerating even the dust and the water. The
people's response to this act of their God was immediate: "they fell on their
faces and said, 'The LORD indeed is God; the LORD indeed is God'" (1 Kgs
18:39). At Elijah's command, all the prophets of Baal were taken down by
the river and executed (1 Kgs 18:30–40).

> **Pause to Reflect**
> In what ways do prophets exist today? What do
> they do? Where do they receive their authority?
> How do people respond to them?

You would have thought that this wonderful occasion of the LORD's
display of power would have put Elijah on top of the world. Ahab's wife Jezebel, however, was not one to concede defeat. She sent word to Elijah that she
intended to have him dead within twenty-four hours. Scared, the mighty
prophet ran, even leaving his servant and traveling alone for a day into the
wilderness. What happened next is an episode to which preachers over the
generations have returned again and again. Elijah requested of the LORD
to take his life. He sounded very discouraged: "for I am no better than my
ancestors" (1 Kgs 19:4d). He slept for a while and then was awakened by a
divine messenger, so that he could eat. After doing so (from where did the
food come?), Elijah slept again, and once again was awakened, eating in
preparation for a journey. Many days of traveling brought him to Horeb, a
mountain also known in other biblical traditions as "Sinai." Early listeners to

the Elijah cycle of wondrous works immediately would have thought about what an earlier episode of their Story says about Sinai—where Moses met God and received the Ten Words (see chapter 3 of this book and Exod 19). Once there, Elijah took shelter in a cave overnight (1 Kgs 19:1–9a).

The LORD spoke to Elijah in that cave, asking him why he was there. This fugitive from royal wrath unloaded, appealing to his earnest ministry on God's behalf, pointing out his people's apostasy, and reminding the LORD that he was a sought-out, lonely guy. God's response was to tell Elijah to stand up and observe. When he did so, displays of natural force appeared before him that would strike terror in anyone's heart. First came a powerful wind that shattered rocks apart; then an earthquake rattled the ground; then a fire appeared. Yet, unlike earlier, centuries-old stories of God's presence made known through spectacular signs from nature, our inherited text here says that God "was not in" any of these. Instead, Elijah next saw nothing— but he heard something. It was quiet, almost as no sound at all. English translators have rendered the Hebrew phrase with wording such as "a still, small voice," "a sound of sheer silence," "a gentle whisper," "a low murmuring sound," and the like.

In The Story, it didn't matter that Elijah's moment to meet the LORD has an almost anti-climactic feel to it. Up to this point, the Chosen People recognized the presence of God through wondrous signs appearing in the natural world: after all, Moses' story of being on Mt. Sinai was filled with smoke, clouds, thunder, and lightning (Exod 19:16–19). For Elijah, recognition of standing in the company of the Divine occurred on the weak end of the "wow!" spectrum. For reasons not readily apparent in the inherited text, the storytellers wanted their audience to see something distinctly significant going on here about God. This "sound of sheer silence" perhaps means that we don't need to depend on magnificent spectacles in earth or sky to discern the presence of God. Perhaps this tradition realized that God is always closer than our breath.

*God meets Elijah in the wilderness, not through
dramatic display, but as "a gentle whisper."*

What happened next, in the rest of this unexpected divine-human encounter, might seem to fly in the face of what Americans of the present generation seem to expect. Once Elijah heard the sound, he went out of the cave and stood there. He then heard a voice asking him the same question that Elijah had heard inside the cave: "What are you doing here, Elijah?" (1 Kgs 19:9c, 13d). Elijah repeated the same answer that he had given earlier, which—to a psychologically sensitive, caring, and supportive listener—most likely would call for a bit of hand-holding, a soothing voice, a word of comfort. How might we today imagine Elijah being able to move beyond his funk otherwise? However, the text here says nothing along these lines, nothing at all. Instead, the LORD immediately gave Elijah new orders, such as would befit the ministry of a prophet. He was instructed to get going, to anoint two new kings (one being a rival to the north) and to anoint someone to become prophet in Elijah's place. Finally, God reminded his downcast servant that there will be many more of the Chosen People who remain loyal to the LORD and not to Baal (1 Kgs 19:13–18).

Unlike the traditions in Exodus that show Moses constantly complaining to God, Elijah here complied readily with his new mission. He found the person whom the LORD said would continue his prophetic ministry, a man named Elisha, plowing in a field with a large team of oxen. The sequence of actions in this episode implies that Elisha realized who had approached him, once the prophet threw his own cloak over the farmer. His readiness to leave his family and way of life was evident in the feast that Elisha prepared and shared with his community. From that point, Elisha was one of Elijah's helpers—and would he have known, at that time, his eventual role (1 Kgs 19:19–21)?

As we have seen, prophets and kings did not always get along, because true prophets spoke "the word of the LORD," whether it was a word that the king liked or not. Ahab was still king in Israel, and his wife Jezebel devised a plan for him to get some neighboring property that he wanted badly. The owner of that property, Naboth, refused to sell, because the parcel was part of what his family had inherited in the tribal allotment and could not be sold on a long-term basis (see Lev 25:23–28). Jezebel found two "scoundrels" who publicly accused Naboth of cursing God and the king; even though the charges were false, Naboth was stoned to death. Then Ahab took over the land of Naboth's that he wanted. Elijah went to Ahab and told him that he had done evil and would be punished. Ahab put on sackcloth and fasted—as signs of repentance—so God told Elijah that the punishment would come to Ahab's house after his death (1 Kgs 21).

Prophets and kings did not always get along, because true prophets spoke "the word of the LORD," whether the king liked it or not.

Elijah's ministry continued after Ahab died from an arrow wound sustained during battle (1 Kgs 22:29–40). Ahab's son, Ahaziah, succeeded his father on the throne. He was injured in an accident at the palace and sent servants to seek a divine word about his prognosis—but from Baal, not the LORD. Elijah was directed by the LORD to intervene, and he told Ahaziah's envoys first—and then Ahaziah himself—that his lack of trust in the LORD would lead to his death from the injury. And so it happened (2 Kgs 1). The ministry of this itinerant prophet, whose wonder-working stories fueled his reputation and legacy, was drawing to a close. Its conclusion, however, was not to be what anyone could have anticipated!

ELISHA: "A DOUBLE SHARE OF YOUR SPIRIT"

For many of the major characters in The One Great Story, death is the final thread woven into the tapestry of their particular tale. People like Jacob, Moses, and David don't just fizzle out of the picture: sometimes they make final speeches, distribute blessings, or figure out who will succeed them. One way or another, though, they all go the way of all flesh; they all die. All of them, except for Elijah.

We know by now that Elijah was directed by the LORD to anoint Elisha to carry on the prophetic ministry and that Elisha had joined his master's company. The traditions passed on through our inherited texts also indicate that Elijah was aware of his impending departure. Hebrew storytelling in many texts like this one feels sparse and sometimes repetitive to our modern ears, but its dramatic buildup is impossible to miss. Everyone close to Elijah seemed to know what was coming—the band of prophets who followed him asked Elisha about it, and he told them to stay quiet. They all were traveling together on this particular day. As they would arrive in one location, the elder prophet would instruct his protégé to remain where they now were but, each time, Elisha swore that he would not leave Elijah. This exchange took place three times, in three different locations (2 Kgs 2:1–6).

Tradition remembers Elijah being "taken up" into the heavens and his protégé, Elisha, receiving "a double share" of God's power.

Finally, the two prophets were standing alongside the Jordan River, while the rest of their company stood back, as though waiting to see what would take place. Like Joshua before him (Josh 3:13–17) and Moses at the Red Sea (Exod 14:21–22), Elijah parted the water in front of them, and the two prophets navigated the river on dry ground. Then the elder prophet inquired whether his protégé had a favor to ask before the elder's departure. Elisha replied by requesting to "inherit a double share of your spirit" (2 Kgs 2:9c), that is, to receive the same prophetic power from the LORD that had animated Elijah's own life of ministry. Elijah made no promise about this request except to hope that Elisha would see him ascend (2 Kgs 2:7–10).

There was no warning. The text says that the two men were "walking and talking" when a fiery chariot with horses appeared between them, and Elijah was caught up by a twister-like wind. Elisha called out and watched as his mentor disappeared into the sky. When Elijah was out of sight, Elisha—as an expression of mourning—tore his clothes in two. The elder prophet's outer garment was lying on the ground, so Elisha picked it up and, as Elijah had done a little earlier, hit the water in the Jordan River with it. Just as before, the water opened up so that Elisha could return to the other side of the river. Now the prophets who had been watching from a distance knew that Elisha was to carry on the ministry, even though they sent out a contingent that searched three days for Elijah—to no avail (2 Kgs 2:1–18).

> *Even on his deathbed, Elisha was approached by the*
> *king of Israel for a word from the LORD.*

Elisha thus became known for wondrous deeds and for bringing the word of the LORD to the king of Israel. He made bad water clean (2 Kgs 2:19–22), helped a widow get out of debt and support her own children (2 Kgs 4:1–7), fed more people than the food would have fed otherwise (2 Kgs 4:42–44), raised a child from death (2 Kgs 4:8–37), healed the commander of a non-Israelite army (2 Kgs 5:1–19), helped a woman get her land back (2 Kgs 8:1–6), and the like. Even on his deathbed, Elisha was approached by the king of Israel for a word from the LORD (2 Kgs 13:14–19). At his death, his power from God still was seen as potent: the tradition remembered that a body got pushed into Elisha's grave, and immediately the man came back to life (2 Kgs 13:20–21).

> **Pause to Reflect**
> In what ways has war touched your life? How
> did the eventual "victory" affect you? What
> happened to those on the losing end?

AN END BEGINS

In spite of the long and dramatic witness of the prophets Elijah and Elisha, the northern kingdom of Israel did not return to the LORD and their covenant. This long and persistent pattern of neglect, as well as of varying degrees of interest in the gods of their old enemies, is viewed in retrospect by The Story as the reason for the conquest and eventual destruction of Israel as a nation-state. A king named Hoshea took over the throne of Israel. Already, for about twenty years, Israel had been under the thumb of an empire known as Assyria. It appears that many Israelite officials had been deported to Assyrian lands at the time of the initial invasion. Hoshea became king by killing his predecessor, Pekah (who himself killed his predecessor), in a conspiracy (2 Kgs 15:27–30). Even though Hoshea also was giving tribute to the Assyrian king, he was not trusted by the latter and so ended up jailed. Consequently, the Assyrian king laid siege to Samaria and, after three years of a siege, conquered it decisively (2 Kgs 17:1–6).

To make matters worse, Assyria brought groups of people from many of its other conquered nations, to resettle the former Northern Kingdom. Because of the common ancient belief that gods had control of particular geographical areas, Assyria sent back an Israelite priest to teach the new immigrants how to worship Israel's god, the LORD. Yet these peoples also continued the religious practices of their home countries and their own gods (2 Kgs 17:24–34).

Meanwhile, Judah hung on. Home of David's royal city of Jerusalem— where Solomon's glorious Temple to the LORD stood—Judah seemed to have remained relatively more loyal to the LORD's covenant than in the north. The traditions as we have inherited them in the present texts attribute Judah's survival to its king Hezekiah. He is remembered as being faithful to the LORD "just as his ancestor David" (2 Kgs 18:3), a phrase expressing the highest of compliments. Hezekiah got rid of objects of worship and sacrifice that were being used for other gods, and even destroyed the bronze serpent from Moses' day, since it was being worshipped, too. Early in his twenty-nine-year reign, Hezekiah also resisted the Assyrian empire. As the years went by, however, the Assyrian army was getting harder to keep at bay. A number of Judah's cities were captured by Assyria as the result of a new campaign. The stage was set for some high-stakes drama (2 Kgs 18:1–13).

> *The Assyrian king laid siege to the northern capital and conquered it after three years.*

Hezekiah sent a message to King Sennacherib of Assyria, offering to pay whatever tribute he asked, if the imperial army would withdraw. Sennacherib called for a large amount of silver and gold, which Hezekiah procured by cleaning out the temple and the royal treasury. The imperial army then marched to Jerusalem and waited as three of Sennacherib's top aides asked to speak to Hezekiah. Instead, the king of Judah sent out three of his own top aides. A verbal standoff of sorts ensued, as Sennacherib's representatives gave reasons why Judah should give up, and Hezekiah's representatives asked for them to speak in Aramaic, not Hebrew (the latter which all the Jerusalem residents who were watching would understand easily and hence become quickly intimidated) (2 Kgs 18:14–25; Isa 36:1–12).

Sennacherib's envoy spoke confidently of Judah's impending disastrous fate and then addressed them all in Hebrew anyway. He told all of Jerusalem to ignore what Hezekiah promised, to give up easily so that they could be removed by the army to a comfortable place where they would live. The envoy, speaking for Sennacherib, rhetorically asked if any of the gods of the other conquered nations had spared them from Assyria. At that point, no one responded, since Hezekiah had told them not to do so. Instead, his three representatives brought Hezekiah back the message, whereupon the threatened king ripped his garments, put on sackcloth, and went to the temple in great distress. Then he instructed two of the three to visit a prophet: his name was Isaiah (2 Kgs 18:26—19:2; Isa 36:13—37:1).

Clearly, Hezekiah trusted Isaiah's vocation as a prophet of the LORD. The king's messengers painted an appropriately gloomy picture of the situation with Sennacherib and asked for Isaiah's help. Isaiah replied that Hezekiah had nothing to fear: the LORD promised safety and an end to Sennacherib's threat. By this time, the Assyrian king had moved his army to fight against a Canaanite city. He then sent Hezekiah a letter this time, basically repeating the earlier argument that no gods had saved any of the other conquered peoples. Hezekiah took this letter with him to the temple, opened it out in full, and then prayed to the LORD. In that prayer, he acknowledged God's great glory, he pointed out Sennacherib's mockery of the LORD and destruction of neighboring lands, he denied that these other gods had any divine status—and then asked for the LORD to save Judah. Why should the LORD do so? It was, Hezekiah concluded, to demonstrate to every nation in the world that there is only one God, who is the LORD (2 Kgs 19:3–19; Isa 37:2–20).

Because of King Hezekiah's trust in the LORD,
Jerusalem was spared conquest by Assyria.

Isaiah replied, in vivid and sometimes harsh poetic language, as though the LORD were speaking to Sennacherib himself. These words affirmed that nothing of the Assyrian king's achievements had occurred outside of the LORD's jurisdiction. Further, Sennacherib's conceit would lead to his own slave-like departure from Judah. The LORD would deliver Jerusalem, "for my own sake and for the sake of my servant David" (2 Kgs 19:33c). In other words, the faithfulness of the beloved shepherd-king, reflected also in Hezekiah's life and reign, continued at that time as a key part of the covenant formula between the LORD and this fickle, undeserving People (2 Kgs 19:20–33; Isa 37:21–35).

> **Pause to Reflect**
> Is prayer similar to magic? If not, do you think
> that prayer can improve outcomes? In what way?
> If prayer and magic are similar, what would be
> any difference between priests and witches?

Once again, the traditions responsible for the texts as we have them include a dramatic, divine, saving intervention on behalf of the chosen ones. This episode is concisely recorded, almost anticlimactically so: at night, a messenger from God wiped out the huge Assyrian army, so King Sennacherib withdrew and returned home (2 Kgs 19:35–37; Isa 37:36–38). In at least one other place in this siege account, however, hints of other explanations for Jerusalem's survival can be spotted. One appears in Isaiah's first reply to Hezekiah; there, Sennacherib would leave Jerusalem alone because of a "spirit" that the LORD would put in him, causing the dangerous king to "hear a rumor, and return to his own land" (2 Kgs 19:7). Either way, the overall driving purpose of the outcome is clear: the LORD, the God of this People, remained faithful to the covenant and spared them from conquest. Judah would live to see another day as its own state, ruled by its own king, in the line of David.

THE DANGER OF SELF-DECEPTION

We will see in chapter 7 that Judah's well-being as a nation-state could not be taken for granted. Tragically—as the traditions that we are following here make clear—the subsequent kings and their subjects suffered from an odd kind of amnesia, not to mention their itchy ears. The LORD had saved them, once again! How could they not remember and remain loyal to their covenant? Throughout these long, painful generations, The Story relied primarily on the prophets to bring its message in contemporary circumstances to the beloved Judah. Chapter 7 will walk us through the main trajectory of the prophetic witness to The Story. Before doing so, however, we will pause for a moment, to catch a glimpse of how The Story made its way into the worship life of This People. The collection of poetry that tradition calls "the Psalms" reveals ways in which The One Great Story was rehearsed and reclaimed during the era of the great temple. These psalms remind us that, even back then, our spiritual ancestors understood—at least some of the time and to some degree—the essential value of remembering from whence they came and whose they were.

FOR THE READER

1. The great King Solomon was remembered for many things. On the one hand, the traditions recall two key moments where he prayed to the LORD with great devotion (1 Kgs 3:3–15, 8:22–61) and was promised wisdom and great riches (1 Kgs 3:11–13; compare 9:1–5, 4:29–34). On the other hand, the traditions recall that he built huge, expensive structures with forced Israelite labor (see 1 Kgs 5:13–16) and kept hundreds of wives, many from nations with whom Israel had fought many times (1 Kgs 11:1–3). Because of them, later in life, Solomon also worshipped gods of these other nations (1 Kgs 11:4–8). How do the biblical traditions come to terms with these contrasting behaviors?

2. What might be the most compelling reasons why the northern tribes found it so easy to split away and create their own kingdom, independent of Jerusalem?

3. Why was it so important to those who passed on these royal traditions to point out what any particular king did or did not do about "high places," altars to Baal, and "sacred poles (see, for example, 1 Kgs 14:23; 2 Kgs 3:2, 12:3)?"

4. If prophetic ministries—like Elijah's and Elisha's—were like walking a tightrope, what were the two sides to which the tightrope was fastened?

5. How easy do you think it was for Hezekiah to believe that Jerusalem would be spared Assyria's onslaught?

SUGGESTED ACTIVITIES

- Go online and search the topic, "Solomon's Temple," and look at some of the renderings of what the original structure might have looked like, inside and out. How might a rural peasant of the time (that is, from the majority of the population) have thought and felt about this promise to King David being realized?

- Go online again and find a map of the Ancient Near East, including Egypt to the southwest, the eastern Mediterranean Sea to the west, the Arabian Desert to the east, and present-day Turkey to the north. Locating the area where the two kingdoms had been situated, what was the people of Israel's primary challenge to being its own political entity, its own nation-state?

- Read 1 Kgs 19:1–18 with a friend. Talk together about what this episode of Elijah in the wilderness implies about how those traditions understood the LORD and the work of a prophet.

Chapter 6

The Story Claimed as the People Worship

"The princes of the peoples gather as the people of the God of Abraham."

—Ps 47:9

My home church met in a building that had been constructed with a full daylight basement situated underneath a simple, traditional sanctuary. Instead of a small set of steps dropping down into that lower level, the concrete-and-tiled floor, at the double-doored building entrance facing the two sets of steps rising to the narthex, sloped gently from the left, straight but downward. Besides the large open room, where we gathered on Sunday mornings for "opening exercises," the basement included a good-sized kitchen, separate classroom, boiler room, bathroom, and janitor's closet. That basement level was where my Christian education began, as a young child participating in Sunday school.

My earliest memory there is of sitting in that classroom right off the basement hallway, on one of those tiny oak chairs, surrounded by children who mostly seemed older than me. There was a low wooden table or two as well, with things like construction paper and crayons placed on them— and medium-sized posters on the walls, with drawings and simple prints of people in Bible times. The room felt quietly inviting, no doubt in part because of the genuine smile on the face of the woman who seemed to be in charge. We all knew her as "Mrs. Smith." Years later, a still-cheerful Elizabeth Smith helped to organize the reception for my ordination but, on that day, in that room, she served as our Sunday-school teacher.

> **Pause to Reflect**
> If you went to Sunday school as a child, how was the Bible made part of your experience there? Did you ever memorize any passages? What did they mean to you then? How do you understand them now?

MEMORIZE—AND THEN WHAT?

Along with snatches of images, people, remarks (by teachers and students), and the like, I look back now and realize that some of my experiences from Sunday school are deeply planted in my recall. In other words, I memorized some things, as a child, in Sunday school, growing up. In particular, I know that I memorized a couple of psalms, along with my classmates. We learned them together, line by line:

> Make a joyful noise unto the LORD, all ye lands;
> Serve the LORD with gladness, come into his presence with singing.
> Know ye that the LORD is God; it is he that made us, and not we ourselves.
> We are his people, and the sheep of his pasture . . . (Ps 100:1–3)

And so on to the last verse, ending with, "and his faithfulness to all generations," Psalm 100 was the first biblical passage that I learned, and Psalm 23 probably was the second. Mrs. Smith, and other adults who helped out with the classes, would say a line or phrase, and we would repeat it back, in a chanting style, raising the pitch of our voices a little at the beginning of each phrase, then dropping them down at the end. Each phrase was intoned the same, regardless of its length or actual text. And—we never talked about any of it. I have no memory ever of hearing an explanation, interpretation, exegesis, or even application of any of the passages that we memorized in Sunday school. We simply learned how to say the words.

My experience with "learning Scripture" in those days was fairly typical. It is not hard to find church traditions that hold the Bible in such high regard that any part of it is treated implicitly as needing no explanation.

That is, its understanding is taken for granted: hearing and remembering become almost ends in themselves.

Memorizing biblical passages can be a useful tool,
when linked with other spiritual practices.

This particular attitude about the Bible as Scripture is not mine now. Memorizing biblical passages can be a useful tool for religious nurture, but only when linked with other practices for strengthening one's faith. The same, hence, can be said for any religious practice. Within the biblical traditions themselves—yes, specifically within The One Great Story—we detect plenty of evidence that allegiance to God involves more than rote memorization, ritual, and ceremony.

WHEN RECITING IS REMEMBERING

Perhaps nowhere is this theme more consistently and dramatically evident than in the collection of poetry that is known as "the Psalms." Expressing a wide range of circumstance, feeling, purpose, and hope, the Psalms represent the long life of a community that gathered before its God. Although a number of these expressive songs and poems bear attributions to King David, it is virtually impossible—as is usually the case in biblical writings—to know exactly who was responsible for creating them or putting them into written form. Careful reading of the collection as a whole suggests that its present form grew out of generations of development and use, across periods of significant change for the People and their religious expression. Some of these songs sound intensely personal; others almost roar with the voices of the People gathered in the Temple. There are prayers by individuals, asking God for help (more than any other type) and some giving thanks; there are prayers by the community seeking divine favor; there are songs praising God for being the Creator of all and/or for wondrous deeds on behalf of the People; and there are a number of psalms that aim to encourage, instruct, or otherwise offer astute advice to the faithful.[11]

The Psalms as a collection developed across
periods of significant change.

11. For an overview of issues related to the Psalms—composition, history, collection, varieties, and theology—see Mays, *Psalms*, 1–39.

It is likely, however, that we miss some of the richness and meaning of psalms, when we don't give attention to the contexts to which they speak. Concerning this point, the Psalms certainly contribute to our exploration of The One Great Story. Here and there, we find scattered clues that The Story indeed informed the Chosen People's worship. As a young reader of the Bible, I missed virtually all of these clues, because I didn't know their reference points or what to make of them. Consequently, I could not benefit from appreciating the ways by which our spiritual ancestors were guided in worship by their Story.

> *The One Great Story was claimed by the*
> *people of Israel as they worshipped.*

In this chapter, therefore, we will interrupt our pursuit of The Story itself, in order to see how This Story influenced Israel's expressions of faith over many generations. The One Great Story was claimed by this People as they worshipped, and the Psalms provide an insightful, instructive compilation of evidence to that end.

THE HEROES AND THE VILLAINS

It is not a matter of seeing clues to The Story in every single psalm, but rather of paying attention to what and where the clues themselves appear. The most obvious of these clues are names, names of persons and places that play some significant role in one of The Story's many episodes. Abraham, Jacob, Moses, Joseph, Egypt, David, Israel, Canaan, and Zion all are mentioned in one psalm or another. How they are used within the particular psalm reveals a particular understanding about how those persons and places spoke to the People in later generations.

For instance, the verse that opens this chapter mentions *Abraham*: "The princes of the peoples gather as the people of the God of Abraham" (Ps 47:9a). This sentence comes in the last verse of a psalm that declares the LORD as god of all nations and peoples, not just of Israel. When we reflect upon the many parts of The Story that involve other national and tribal groups—such as "the Amorites, the Perizzites, the Canaanites, the Hittites, the Girgashites, the Hivites, and the Jebusites" (Josh 24:11)—the emphasis of this psalm and its final verse takes on a noteworthy meaning. Those descendants of Abram and Sarai, the couple who began a journey for blessing to "all the families of the earth" (Gen 12:3c), affirmed many centuries later that their God will draw heads of state from beyond Israel to worship and follow the Only One.

The name "*Jacob*" appears thirty-four times in the Psalms, sometimes more than once in the same psalm. This name, which began as the given name of one of Isaac's twin sons, alludes in many of the Psalms to that historical figure:

- "The name of the God of Jacob protect you!" (Ps 20:1)
- "the God of Jacob is our refuge." (Ps 46:7)
- "I will sing praises to the God of Jacob"; (Ps 75:9)
- "O offspring of his servant Abraham, children of Jacob, his chosen ones" (Ps 105:6)
- "the Mighty One of Jacob" (Ps 132:2, 5)

Other times, the references seem directed more to the People as a nation, as the descendants of Jacob:

- "When the LORD restores the fortunes of his people, Jacob will rejoice; . . . " (Ps 14:7)
- "You are my King and my God; you command victories for Jacob." (Ps 44:4)
- "Then it will be known to the ends of the earth that God rules over Jacob." (Ps 59:13)
- " . . . he brought him [David] to be the shepherd of his people Jacob, . . . " (Ps 78:71)
- "When Israel went out from Egypt, the house of Jacob from a people of strange language," (Ps 114:1)
- "He declares his word to Jacob, his statues and ordinances to Israel." (Ps 147:19)

It is clear from these and the other references to Jacob that the worshipping community is to remember its ancestor's lineage, its narrative, its dependence on the LORD from the very beginning.

The worshipping community is to remember its ancestor's lineage, its narrative, its dependence on the LORD from the very beginning.

Jacob's eleventh son, *Joseph*, also shows up in the Psalms, in five different places. His name appears once with Jacob's, in a passage recalling "the deeds of the LORD, . . . your wonders of old" (Ps 77:11). Here, the psalmist pledges to ponder "your mighty deeds" (Ps 77:12b):

"You are the God who works wonders; you have displayed your might among the peoples. With your strong arm you redeemed your people, the descendants of Jacob and Joseph." (Ps 77:14–15)

Images in this psalm of the escape from Egypt through the Red Sea refer to nature's mighty display, opening up an escape route through such an unlikely, forbidding obstacle: "Your way was through the sea, your path, through the mighty waters . . ." (Ps 77:19ab).

In another place, God is called "O Shepherd of Israel, you who lead Joseph like a flock!" (Ps 80:1). The LORD's rescue and protection of the People's ancestors appears again with Joseph's name (Ps 81:5).

Indeed, references to *Egypt* turn up—either explicitly or otherwise—in the Psalms in a number of places. The name "Egypt" appears fifteen times, occasionally in a neutral way ("Then Israel came to Egypt" [Ps 105:23a]), but more often in the context of oppression and escape:

- "You brought a vine out of Egypt; you drove out the nations and planted it." (Ps 80:8)

- "I am the LORD your God, who brought you up out of the land of Egypt." (Ps 81:10ab)

- "When Israel went out from Egypt, the house of Jacob from a people of strange language," (Ps 114:1)

- "[God] sent signs and wonders into your midst, O Egypt, against Pharaoh and all his servants." (Ps 135:9)

- "who struck Egypt through their firstborn, . . . " (Ps 136:10a)

As we will see below, Egypt is one of several key names that are employed by a certain grouping of psalms that go beyond mere "name-dropping."

> **Pause to Reflect**
> Who is one of your heroes? What has she or he done
> to attract your high regard? Are there any "negative"
> aspects about them that you overlook or explain away?

One of the central characters in and around the story of Egypt is *Moses*, and yet his name appears in psalms only seven times. A few times, Moses is mentioned together with *Aaron*: once, as the two who "led your people like a flock" (Ps 77:20); again, as some of the LORD's priests (Ps 99:6a); yet again, as two who were chosen to carry out signs from the LORD in the presence of the people (Ps 105:26–27); in another place, in a reference to the people's lack of trust while wandering in the wilderness—here, Aaron is called "the holy one of the LORD" (Ps 106:16). Elsewhere, another psalm affirms that God "made known [God's] ways to Moses" (Ps 103:7a).

A couple more names that appear in the Psalms merit particular attention. Remember that the patriarch Jacob received a new name after wrestling with a divine being, who named him "*Israel*" (Gen 32:28). This designation for the man, and later for his descendants and people, became one of the most prevalent names in the Old Testament. It appears there more than 2,500 times—incredibly, in thirty-four of the Protestant version's thirty-nine Old Testament books! In the Psalms alone, the name "Israel" appears sixty-one times, mostly referring to the chosen community rather than to its progenitor Jacob. This name is included in prayers for deliverance of the people (e.g., Pss 14:7, 25:22,), calls for praise and blessing of the LORD (e.g., Pss 22:23, 41:13, 72:18), calls by God against the people (Pss 50:7, 81:8), identification of the LORD's relationship to the People (Ps 68:8), and affirmations of God's longstanding loyalty to the People (Ps 98:3). It is almost impossible to underestimate the weight that the name "Israel" carries within The One Great Story: it encapsulates the meaning of this People's identity and purpose.

The name "Israel" appears sixty-one times in the Psalms, encapsulating the meaning of This People's identity and purpose.

The other name to note at this point is that of the beloved king, *David*. Although his name appears only thirteen times within the verses of a psalm (e.g., Pss 18:50, 72:20, 89:3, 122:5, 132:11, 144:10), David's legend and legacy pervade this collection of songs and prayers. Of the first seventy psalms, fifty-five of them appear with David's name, as part of notes attached at the top of each psalm—and, in the final eighty psalms, only seventeen times. These notes to the worship leader certainly demonstrate the high regard with which the shepherd-king was held, far beyond his lifetime. Indeed, David's story as a shepherd-turned-king is recounted in one psalm:

> "[God] chose [t]his servant David, and took him from the sheepfolds;
> . . . to be the shepherd of [t]his people Jacob, . . .
> With upright heart he tended them, and guided them with skillful hand." (Ps 78:70–72)

David's unique role in The Story is affirmed in Ps 89, in which David is specifically named four times, as the psalm declares God's purpose for him:

> [God] said, I have made a covenant with my chosen one,
> I have sworn to my servant David:
> 'I will establish your descendants forever,

and build your throne for all generations.' (Ps 89:3–4)

David's unique place in The Story is affirmed frequently in the Psalms.

Verses 19–37 elaborate upon this divine promise to the youngest son of Jesse. In another psalm, David's royal lineage is linked to the holy city, Jerusalem, and its well-being (Ps 122). David's promise to build a house for the LORD (2 Sam 7) is celebrated in conjunction, once again, with an affirmation of David's lineage, this time reminding worshippers of the conditions by which the LORD will honor this covenant (Ps 132, see vss 3–5, 11–12).

THE STORY IN WORSHIP

The presence of the term *covenant* in the Psalms not only relates to David's legacy and stature but also to the broader theme of the LORD's initiative in relationship with this People. We have seen, in episodes with Noah, Abraham, Moses, and Joshua, how the LORD initiated special arrangements with them that served as key turning points. These arrangements involved a solemn pledge from God, as well as calling for whole-hearted allegiance from human parties.

> **Pause to Reflect**
> Who in your family tells its stories, warts and all? Is it done more "under the radar" or more publicly? How do family members respond? What do you get out of these stories?

Here are some of the points about covenant that appear in various psalms:

- *God does not forget this pledge* ("[God] provides food for those who fear [God]; [God] is ever mindful of [t]his covenant." [Ps. 111:5])
- *It will remain in force for all time* ("[God] sent redemption to [t]his people; [God] has commanded [t]his covenant forever." [Ps 111:9])
- *The LORD will uphold its terms* ("I will not violate my covenant, or alter the word that went forth from my lips." [Ps 89:34])
- *It expects something from the People* ("All the paths of the LORD are steadfast love and faithfulness, for those who keep [t]his covenant and [these] decrees." [Ps 25:10])

- *The People appeal to it when conditions are threatening* ("Have regard for your covenant, for the dark places of the land are full of the haunts of violence." [Ps 74:20])
- *Wrongdoing practically cancels one's entitlement to it* ("But to the wicked God says, 'What right have you to recite my statutes, or take my covenant on your lips?'" [Ps 50:16])

In these and similar verses, echoes of Moses, Mt. Sinai, and the Ten Words reverberate poetically and dramatically. They remind worshippers from later times of their identity and function as the Chosen People, being rooted many generations ago in earlier episodes of their Story.

> *This worshipping community was reminded*
> *often of its covenant with the LORD.*

Most of the references to The Story mentioned up to this point appear individually—that is, the name or term used as a sort of passing nod to something significant from the narrative overall. Within the vast collection of these hymns, songs, and prayers, however, a handful of the psalms go into much greater detail. This small set of psalms stands out from the others, in the way that they recite several of The Story's major episodes. In this way, they serve as liturgical declarations and theological ruminations, demonstrating how those episodes—and, certainly, the entire Story itself—call for remembering, claiming, and asserting their authority in every generation.

These five psalms are 78, 105, 106, 135, and 136; they share some features in common, while each one also expresses something distinctive. For one thing, these five tend to be longer than many other psalms: they contain seventy-two, forty-five, forty-eight, twenty-one, and twenty-six verses respectively. For another thing, they recite long stretches of The Story, from the patriarchs (Abraham, Isaac, and/or Jacob) through the settling of the land and subsequent lapses of faith. Both 135 and 136 even begin at the beginning, that is, by affirming that the LORD is the One who is above all things—who created the heavens, the earth, and the seas (Pss 135:5-7, 136:5-9).

> *Five specific psalms witness to The Story by extensive*
> *recitation, with individual emphasis.*

Psalm 78 is the longest of these five and the most detailed with elements of The Story line. Its tone is instructive, like that of a wise sage who "will utter dark sayings from of old, . . . that our ancestors have told us"

(78:2b, 3b). In response, the worshippers early on pledge to pass on to "their children . . . the coming generation . . ." what they themselves have received concerning the LORD's amazing exploits (78:4). Although beginning with establishment of "a law (78:5)," the way of life for the People to follow and pass on, this psalm spends a lot of time recounting their ancestors' lack of trust. References to the escape from Egypt ("[God] divided the sea and let them pass through it [78:13]"), divine guidance through the wilderness (78:14–16), and provision of the manna (78:23–25) and quail ("winged birds") to eat during their journey (78:26–29), are woven together with comments on the People's lack of gratitude:

> "In spite of all this they still sinned;
> they did not believe in [God's] wonders." (Ps 78:32)

> **Pause to Reflect**
> What kind of music inspires you? What lyrics to a favorite
> song lift you up? What is it about that musical piece and
> those lyrics that affect you in such a positive way?

Later, more references to the time in Egypt identify several of the plagues that finally led to the Israelites' escape (78:43–53). One verse (78:54) summarizes the accounts from Joshua's era, of taking control of the land that the LORD promised and establishing all the tribes in it. Yet this psalm also continues to rail against the People's rebellion and neglect of God's ways, all of which led to unpleasant consequences. Ending on an upbeat tone, however, Psalm 78 reminds worshippers of King David's selection as the People's "shepherd," one who was favored by God, serving them righteously and effectively (78:70–72).

As we can see, this psalm would not be what it is without The One Great Story. It uses that Story as a sober reminder of what God expects of the People in any generation—because this God, the LORD, is proven worthy of such loyalty and obedience.

Psalm 105 moves more simply and directly as a worshipful, praise-driven recitation of The Story. It specifically mentions Abraham and the covenant (105:9a), the promise to Isaac and Jacob of Canaan "'for an inheritance'" (105:9b–11), Joseph's role in bringing the family to safety in Egypt (105:16–24), Moses' (and Aaron's) part in Israel's escape—plagues and all (105:26–38), the ways that the LORD guided and sustained the People in the wilderness (105:39–42), and God's giving of the land and its abundance to them (105:44). One of The Story's central themes punctuates this psalm's conclusion. The LORD's purpose in all this deliverance, protection, and provision of a home was to develop in the People everlasting allegiance and grateful obedience (105:45):

> "For [God] remembered [the] holy promise,
> and Abraham, [God's] servant." (Ps 105:42)

Psalm 106 is similar in theme and style to Psalm 78. Graphic images from early episodes of The Story serve as a testimony to consequences of the People's lack of faithfulness. Here, the psalmist begins by acknowledging the LORD's goodness and greatness and by reminding worshippers that following justice and righteousness brings blessing (106:2–3). Before reciting parts of The Story, the psalmist prays to see the People flourish, even in spite of their sin (106:5–6). Familiar details of being in Egypt, of the Red Sea, of desert wanderings, of the golden calf, of unacceptable worship practices borrowed from other nations' religions, fill most of the psalm's forty-eight verses. Yet this psalm ends on hope, as The Story witnesses to it:

> . . . but they were rebellious in their purposes,
> and were brought low through their iniquity.
> Nevertheless [God] regarded their distress when [God] heard their cry.
> For their sake [God] remembered [t]his covenant,
> And showed compassion according to the abundance of [God's] steadfast love. (Ps 106:43–45)

This psalm ends with a prayer for salvation of the scattered People ("gather us from among the nations" [106:47b]) and a benediction punctuated with "And let all the people say, 'Amen.' Praise the LORD!" (106:48b).

Graphic images from The Story testify to
The People's lack of faithfulness.

Psalm 135 summarizes The Story in five brief verses (135:8–12), mentioning the Egyptian plagues ("signs and wonders into your midst, O Egypt" [135:9a]) and the defeat of other nations in fulfilling the promise of land "as a heritage, a heritage to [t]his people Israel" (135:12). Also framing this psalm of praise is another theme from The Story—namely, that the gods of other nations are nothing but human fabrications—voiceless, blind, deaf, and lifeless (135:15–17):

> "Those who make them, and all who trust them, shall become
> like them." (Ps 135:18)

As a climax of praise, the psalm calls for the People to bless the LORD by using familiar names—Aaron, Levi, Zion, Jerusalem (135:19–21). It becomes a rousing affirmation of the One who remains the central and strategically necessary figure throughout the entire sweep of The Story's reach.

Finally, *Psalm 136* takes the form of a litany, as it concisely recites vivid images and dramatic actions from The Story. The phrase, "for [God's] steadfast love endures forever" is repeated in the second half of every verse—twenty-six times. Here, The Story echoes Gen 1 as it begins with acts of creation—the heavens, earth's waters, and the sun, moon, and stars (136:5–9). Then (136:10–22) its rhythm works in the episodes about the Exodus, the Red Sea, wilderness wanderings, conquest of kings in claiming "their land as a heritage" (136:21).

> "It is [God] who remembered us in our low estate." (Ps 136:23a)

This psalm begins (136:1–3) and ends (136:26) with exhortations to thanksgiving, naming the People's God as "the LORD" (136:1), "the God of gods" (136:2), "the LORD of lords" (136:3), and "the God of heaven" (136:26). In tone, Psalm 136 is the most upbeat of these five Story-telling psalms.

CLAIMING—AND BEING CLAIMED

Taken together, these five psalms clearly draw upon many episodes and images from The One Great Story. These episodes and images define, through recitation and repetition, the People's reason for coming into being and claim upon their life as a community. It is a reason and claim that consistently carries both good news and bad news. The good news emerges out of the LORD God's decision to create a community that would become a witness to the rest of the world of who this LORD is and what this God expects and hopes. As such, this covenant requires agreement and obedience. The bad news emerges out of this community's rather persistent failure to keep up its end of the covenant bargain.

Through the Psalms, these traditions remain vibrant: they breathe purpose and life into the People every time they gather.

We have seen these key elements of The Story already play out, again and again. Here, in the five "Story-telling" psalms especially, the People weave these elements honestly into their public devotional practices. For them, what happened in their past calls for recognition and response in each present moment. Who Israel is to be flows out of where it has been. Worship—whether praising, confessing, lamenting or otherwise acknowledging the LORD in creation and human events—arises from an embrace of the persons, places, events, and basic themes that constitute Their Story. In this way, those traditions remain alive: far from a sterile recounting, they breathe purpose and life into the People every time they gather. They are not merely words that bear remembering but meaning that calls for response.[12]

Pause to Reflect
Recall an experience from earlier in your life that was very significant for you. Why was it so? How does that experience influence you today? In what way might it serve as a positive influence on you in the future?

When we possess a sense of the overall movement of This Story, reading the psalms today can become a fascinating experience. It helps us get a closer feel for what it must have been like for the ancient Israelites and Jews to gather together and pray these holy poems. It demonstrates how the psalms were created in particular places and circumstances; they came from somewhere, not just anywhere. To affirm its identity as People of The Story, the community evoked the memories and narratives of the ancestors—Abraham, Isaac, Jacob, Joseph, Moses, Aaron, Joshua, David. The community would not forget Egypt, Canaan, Judah, Zion. It gradually would assert that the LORD is not merely a god among many but The God of all the world, to whom every people are summoned to worship. It is true that many psalms contain scant mention of The Story. Yet, this collection would not hold near the power that it does without those many phrases and verses, scattered here and there, that evoke both the glory and the pain of what it meant to be claimed by The One Great Story.

12. For elaboration of these points, see Mays, *Psalms*, 257–58, 338–42, 416–21.

FOR THE READER

1. With Moses being such a major figure in early episodes of The One Great Story, why do you think his name shows up only seven times in the Psalms? What does David's frequent reference in the Psalms's worship notes imply about his place in the development of Israel's traditions of worship?

2. In reading the six bullet points in this chapter about the concept of "covenant," of which characters, events, and places from The Story are you reminded? How might those characters, events, and places be utilized in a psalm to make a particular point?

SUGGESTED ACTIVITIES

- Select one of the shorter psalms and use the melody line from one of your favorite pieces of music to sing it aloud. What is this experience like? How do you "hear" the psalm differently?

- Select one of the "story" psalms (i.e., 78, 105, 106, 135, or 136) and read through it slowly. Which elements of The Story that are mentioned there catch your attention? What "feel" does this psalm have? How might this psalm have been used as a part of worship during or after the period of the kings?

- Invite a friend to read a psalm of their selection to you and tell you why they chose it. Then share with your friend a couple of your main impressions from this chapter about The Story's presence in the Psalms. Where are there points that overlap between the two of you? What are the differences? What do all of these points suggest to you about the potential value of the Psalms today?

Chapter 7

The Story Begins to Echo

Prophecy, Exile, and Rebuilding

"make yourselves clean; . . .cease to do evil, learn to do good; seek justice,
rescue the oppressed, defend the orphan, plead for the widow."

—Isa 1:16–17

When the Assyrian army disappeared from its positions around the holy
city of Jerusalem, the entire city must have exalted and exulted. Those
troops easily could have overwhelmed Judah; the residents within the gates
who had had the nerve to observe might have felt on the losing end of a
cat-and-mouse game. Assyria's ruler, Sennacherib, had offered Judah's king,
Hezekiah, a deal that seemed merciful. Yet when Hezekiah consulted with
the prophet Isaiah, after praying fervently to the LORD for rescue, the word
was "courage." Judah did not have to fight or surrender: Sennacherib's troops
inexplicably withdrew—and Hezekiah knew that it was the LORD's doing.

During the period of history from the time of two kingdoms onward,
the People of the Promise heard the word from God most vividly from persons whom we know as "prophets." As we have seen already in chapter 5,
this era saw the rise of Israel as a nation with its own monarchy, but that
rise did not last. This People's worldly success, in political and economic

terms, was not accompanied by an equal measure of spiritual and religious faithfulness. In the Bible, we find the friction during this time between politics, economics, status, international relations, religion, and ethics most painfully articulated among the testimony associated with the ministries of prophets. Their witness to the conditions of the day, in light of God's expectations for the People, expresses a mature and courageous faith. In all their testimony, too, we can discover the engagement by these prophets with The One Great Story.

This chapter picks up where chapter 5 left off, with the conquest of the Northern Kingdom, Israel, and the sparing of the Southern Kingdom, Judah. Here, we first will look at ways in which certain prophets from those days—Isaiah, Micah, and Amos—echoed and drew upon the earlier traditions during these dire circumstances. Then we will watch Jerusalem gradually fall, while Jeremiah bore witness during those years to the LORD's ways. The period of exile eventually led to a period of rebuilding in Jerusalem, under the guidance of two faithful persons—Ezra and Nehemiah. Mixed into this late biblical era are two other characters whose historical presence is less reliable but whose stories represent the kind of integrity and hope that certainly must have flickered among the remnant that sought to recover their faith and rediscover their place in The Story. Our closing comments will reflect on how these echoes rooted in The Story sound here at this point, and where The Story leaves its followers, as the canon of the Hebrew Bible closes.

A TRAIN WRECK—IN SLOW MOTION

One of the interesting special effects that motion picture technology has developed is the slow-motion sequence. Before the invention of movies, everything that anyone ever saw was either a still (drawings, sculpture, paintings, then photography) or in real time. Once motion picture engineers figured out a way to slow down the projection of a filmed sequence, we were able to witness an event, not as it actually occurred, but as a drawn-out, deliberate version of it. This effect has been used many times for raising the dramatic feel of a scene. Not infrequently, that dramatic feel intensifies a dangerous, harmful incident: we jump in our seats when we see it, or take a deep breath, or cry out with surprise and fear.

Those prophets who spoke against the faithlessness and foolishness of Israel and Judah many centuries ago must have felt like they were foreseeing something that we today might call a train wreck in slow motion. It was as though the path on which the nation and its king were traveling was like a certain set of train tracks, with no switching station up ahead. The prophets could see where the country was headed: in their mind's spiritual eye, they must have viewed the upcoming disaster the way that we watch a slow-motion disaster play out on a movie screen.

As we noted at the beginning of this chapter, however, Judah saw the switching station and traveled onto a different set of tracks. Remember the episode from the end of chapter 5, when *Hezekiah* prayed to the LORD, after his envoys reported the conversation with Sennacherib's representatives (Isa 36–37)? Hezekiah's appeal in his prayer was not about saving his own bacon. Instead, it was so that the Assyrians—and the rest of the world—would know that the LORD was the only true god. As this episode played out, the humbled king's appeal is what got Judah onto another track, away from the almost-inevitable train wreck.

> *Throughout his ministry of prophetic utterances,*
> *Micah was informed by The Story.*

If only every biblical king had heeded the words of these true prophets! Before the fall of the North, a prophet named *Micah* spoke of impending doom for both Samaria (Mic 1:2–7) and Judah (Mic 1:8–16). He railed against unjust practices among the People (Mic 2:1–11) and called out wicked behavior by those in positions of responsibility (Mic 3:1–12). As most prophets did, Micah also saw an eventual restoring of the Promise, but not until disaster would strike (Mic 4). Throughout his ministry of prophetic utterances, Micah was informed by The Story. In the final verse of his collection of sayings, Micah hearkened back about as far as The Story goes, invoking names from the first generations of their heritage. Boldly, Micah speaks to the LORD:

> You will show faithfulness to Jacob,
> and unswerving loyalty to Abraham,
> as you have sworn to our ancestors
> from the days of old. (Mic 7:20)

The name "Jacob" is mentioned ten other times in Micah's short collection of seven chapters (1:5 twice; 2:7, 12; 3:1, 8, 9; 4:2; 5:7, 8), the name "Israel" twelve times, often in concert with "Jacob" (1:5, 13, 14, 15; 2:12; 3:1, 8, 9; 5:1, 2, 3; 6:2). The Egyptian exodus and leadership become the LORD's first item of evidence in what reads like a staged court appearance for the People:

Rise, plead your case before the mountains,
. . . O my people, what have I done to you?
. . . Answer me!
For I brought you up from the house of Egypt,
. . . and I sent before you Moses, Aaron, and Miriam. (Mic 6:1b, 3ac;
4; see also 7:15)

Lesser-known names and places also are mentioned in this call—like King Balak of Moab and Balaam son of Beor (Mic 6:5ab), who figured largely in a dramatic series of events while the wandering Israelites were protected by the LORD from threatening neighbors (Num 22–24). God's call for the People to speak ends with a clause reminiscent of many like it in The Story:

". . . that you may know the saving acts of the LORD." (Mic 6:5d)

Once again, the People hear that God has been taking care of them for a long time—so why are they so faithless?

Another prophet from the days of the North's descent into decimation was *Amos.* This prophet also expressed a keen sense of the North's failure to live out its covenant with the LORD. Amos articulated oppressive behaviors that he apparently observed—taking advantage of poor and needy people (Amos 2:6–7; 5:11), hating to hear the truth (Amos 5:10), relishing lavish lifestyles while their nation was crumbling (Amos 6:4–7). Amos's ministry threatened the king, Jeroboam, who asked him to leave their country and go back to the south (Judah) to prophesy (Amos 7:10–13)! Amos did not back down, instead speaking of doom, death, loss, and exile for the king, his family, and his nation.

Amos was courageous in speaking the word of the LORD. In one of the prophet's utterances, God asked rhetorically whether or not it was God who delivered the People from Egypt (Amos 9:7). In an earlier oracle, the LORD reminded them of that rescue and their forty-year journey (Amos 2:1). Egypt is also mentioned negatively, reminding Israel that its faithlessness resulted in disasters similar to those that befell their ancient oppressors (Amos 4:10). Other names from the distant past appear here and there: Sodom and Gomorrah (Amos 4:11); Isaac (Amos 7:9, 16), Jacob (Amos 3:13; 6:8; 7:2; 5; 8:7, 9:8), and even King David. First, the beloved king is remembered for his musical creativity in a passage that condemns "the revelry of the loungers" (Amos 6:5b, 7b). Toward the end of the Amos collection, the former shepherd's memory is invoked with promise:

"On that day I will raise up the booth of David that is fallen,
. . . and rebuild it as in the days of old." (Amos 9:11)

Pause to Reflect
Have you ever tried to warn someone of the dangers
of what they were doing? What was it like for you to
get ready to warn them? What did you risk? What
was their response? For what had you hoped?

Just as striking and powerful a prophetic voice during the time of Israel's disintegration is found within the incisive, eloquent, and poignant sayings compiled under the name of Isaiah. In this lengthy collection, covering Jerusalem from the time before the North's (Samaria's) fall until the time of the return of (Southern Judah) exiles from Babylon, echoes of The One Great Story reverberate all over. Space does not permit a thorough summary of this tradition's theological interpretations, especially in comparing one era to another (that is, Jerusalem's rescue from Assyrian domination, Jerusalem's eventual destruction and exile to Babylon, and the return of exiles to rebuild Jerusalem). What we can appreciate here is a similar prophetic use of terms and images drawn from earlier episodes in The Story.

For instance, the name of *Abraham* is linked with Jacob, in reminding Isaiah's audience that the LORD "redeemed Abraham" and will take away Jacob's (that is, the chosen people's) shame (Isa 29:22). *Jacob* is mentioned a whopping forty-two times in Isaiah, in phrases like

- "the house of the God of Jacob" (Isa 2:3c)
- "the house of Jacob" (Isa 8:17b; 10:20; 14:1c)
- "the remnant of Jacob" (Isa 10:21)
- "the glory of Jacob" (Isa 17:4a)
- "the guilt of Jacob" (Isa 27:9a)
- "you worm Jacob" (Isa 41:14a)
- "the King of Jacob" (Isa 41:21b)
- "O Jacob my servant" (Isa 44:1a; 45:4a)
- "the tribes of Jacob" (Isa 49:6b)
- "the Mighty One of Jacob" (Isa 49:26d; 60:16d)

The variety of images that these various phrases evoke suggests how fundamental Jacob was to this prophetic tradition's understanding of its heritage and its responsibility. Similarly, the name "*David*" conjures up a variety of images that affirm a major place for the popular king's chapters in The Story:

- "the house of David" (Isa 7:2; 7:13; 22:22)
- "the throne of David" (Isa 9:7)
- "the tent of David" (Isa 16:5)
- "the city of David" (Isa 22:9; 29:1)
- "my servant David" (Isa 37:35)
- "the god of David your father" (Isa 38:5)
- "my steadfast, sure love for David" (Isa 55:3)

In Isaiah, prophetic insight looks at the People's past not only to interpret and justify circumstances of the impending present, but also to reaffirm Promise for the future. Isaiah's prophetic legacy connects Israel's creation and eventual restoration to The Story's most seminal claim—that this People will be a blessing to all. In two places, the LORD declares that the People are given "as a light to the nations" (Isa 42:6c; 49:6c). God's purpose in this gifting is for bringing release (Isa 49:7bc) and healing (Isa 42:7a, 49:6d) "to the ends of the earth" (Isa 49:6d). Echoes of the LORD's promise to Abraham (Gen 12:3) are hard to miss here.

> *In Isaiah, prophetic insight looks at the People's past not only to interpret and justify circumstances of the impending present, but also to reaffirm Promise for the future.*

Thus we have seen, as in chapter 5, that the prophets were right about the Northern Kingdom: it indeed was conquered by Assyria and gradually lost its identity as part of the continuing Story. While Judah in the South was spared the same fate at the time, it did not remain safe and free in the long run. Danger built gradually, from within and without, and then caught up with David's line and its seemingly impervious guarantee.

THE OTHER (UNEXPECTED?) TRAIN WRECK

Even with the many reforms that Josiah instituted during his thirty-one-year reign (2 Kgs 22—23:30), more of Judah's kings turned away from the LORD's covenant than followed it. Other empires rose and fell; more than a century after Samaria's fall, Judah was caught in a squeeze between competing empires. Josiah's son Jehoahaz followed his father to the throne, but he was removed by the Egyptian Pharaoh, who extracted heavy taxes on Judah and replaced Jehoahaz with his brother, Jehoiakim (2 Kgs 23:31–35).

Then another emperor, this one from the East, came into the picture, Nebuchadnezzar of Babylon, having conquered large sections of what had been in Egypt's control. After a few years of serving this emperor, Jehoiakim tried to get out from under his rule. Nebuchadnezzar responded with troops from some of his vassal states. During this period of harassment, Jehoiakim died and was succeeded by his son, Jehoiachin. Perhaps Nebuchadnezzar got word of the new, young (eighteen years of age) king, because the emperor came to meet his troops near Jerusalem. The new king surrendered. Nebuchadnezzar then cleaned house: he took virtually all of Jerusalem's population to Babylon—royal court and family, servants, officials, skilled craftspeople, thousands of able-bodied men, leaving only "the poorest people of the land" (2 Kgs 24:14e). Next, the emperor set up Jehoiachin's uncle, Zedekiah, as the puppet king (2 Kgs 24).

After several years, the political buzz in Jerusalem must have emboldened Zedekiah. He tried to break free from Babylon's rule. The effort didn't work: Babylon's army appeared in all its strength and barricaded Jerusalem inside itself. After eighteen months, the food shortage was so great that Zedekiah tried a desperate move—punching a hole in a city wall and trying to sneak out at night with his soldiers. When Nebuchadnezzar's mercenaries caught up with him, Zedekiah's troops took off on their own, leaving their king defenseless. The hapless monarch then had to watch his own sons killed by the emperor's troops before losing his eyesight at the hands of his captors and being taken in chains to Babylon (2 Kgs 25:1–7).

In the meantime, Jerusalem was destroyed. The palace, the Temple, and every "great house" in the city were burned down. All the walls that had been protecting the city were knocked down. All the beautiful, precious items that had been lovingly and carefully crafted for use in worship and ceremonies, all the bronze and gold and silver—carried off to Babylon. A number of religious and military officials were executed. The only people allowed to remain were "some of the poorest people of the land" (2 Kgs 25:12), who were given the responsibilities of farming and caring for the vineyards. Finally, Nebuchadnezzar appointed a governor in his stead, who encouraged his fellow Judahites to go along with the situation, so that things would be fine. But he was murdered several months later by a relative of the king, and the rest of the population escaped to Egypt in fear (2 Kgs 25:8–26).

Pause to Reflect

As a child, did you have stories that you enjoyed
hearing, because they helped you feel better? What
were the characters like, the story line, the ending?
How do you look at those stories today?

The Chosen People's life under kings had come to a disastrous end. Following a rocky beginning, first with Saul and then the beloved David, the monarchy and its nation had achieved what would be its pinnacle of earthly accomplishments under David's son Solomon. After Solomon's death, tensions that had been under the surface between northern and southern loyalties led to a split. The North claimed its own king and set up its own capital. For about two hundred years, with nineteen kings, Israel existed as its own country. Six of its monarchs were murdered, usually by conspiracy. The traditions as we have inherited them do not look favorably upon the kings of Israel: thirteen of them are explicitly judged as having done "what is evil in the sight of the LORD."

The Chosen People's life under kings came to a disastrous end.

Judah, in the south, where Jerusalem—the city of David—was located, survived the Assyrian threat that overtook their cousin state, Israel. Some in Judah concluded that David's lineage was so favored by God that nothing ever could happen to their country. The traditions as we have inherited them do look more favorably upon Judah's monarchs: only eight of them "did what was evil," whereas six "did what was right" in the sight of the LORD. Still, the geographical factors that have influenced this part of the world for many centuries would work, in the long run, against a peaceful, stable Judah. Egypt and Assyria were not the only empires to threaten Judah's existence within that small strip of valleys and mountains along the eastern Mediterranean. I suppose we could say that history was not Judah's friend.

However, in this era of the People's Story, external forces do not receive the primary blame for the People's fortunes. Just as in the earlier episodes, here during the era of the monarchy, the traditions maintain a consistent theme. To remain in faithful covenant with the LORD, the god who created and sustained them—indeed, the only god there is!—continues even here as the primary theme and trajectory. The prophetic tradition echoes this trajectory, often in startling images that contrast divine judgment with divine hope.

JEREMIAH'S WITNESS

Nowhere are these contrasts more painstakingly explored than in the literary traditions that surround the prophet *Jeremiah.* Throughout his long years in delivering the word of the LORD, Jeremiah never beat around the bush; the purpose of his call was remembered in this way:

Then the LORD put out his hand and touched my mouth;
and the LORD said to me,
'Now I have put my words in your mouth.
See, today I appoint you over nations and over kingdoms,
to pluck up and to pull down,
to destroy and to overthrow,
to build and to plant.' (Jer 1:9–10)

As he heard God speak to the political and religious crises of his day, Jeremiah spared no tough language or jarring images:

Declare this in the house of Jacob,
proclaim it in Judah:
Hear this, O foolish and senseless people,
who have eyes, but do not see,
who have ears, but do not hear.
Do you not fear me? says the LORD.
Do you not tremble before me? (Jer 5:20–22a)

Often, these words and images were drawn from The Story. At the end of a passage that affirms the cherished promise made to King *David*, Jeremiah heard this:

Thus says the LORD:
Only if I had not established my covenant with day and night
and the ordinances of heaven and earth,
would I reject the offspring of Jacob and of my servant David
and not choose any of his descendants
as rulers over the offspring of *Abraham*, *Isaac*, and *Jacob*.
For I will restore their fortunes,
and will have mercy on them. (Jer 33:25–26)

In supporting its claim to trustworthiness, this oracle pulls out all the stops: not only does it name the first three generations of "patriarchs" from The Story, it also appeals to the LORD's role in *creation*—"my covenant with day and night and the ordinances of heaven and earth." Although the presentation of this argument is concise, it would have packed a wallop of a message nonetheless. The god who made a covenant with the People's ancestors swears by [his] status as the Creator of heaven and earth that the People will have a future of blessing.

Like all the true prophets, Jeremiah never beat around the bush.

Indeed, the Jeremiah tradition hearkens to the shepherd-king "*David*" a total of fourteen times (Jer 17:25; 21:12; 22:2, 4, 30; 23:5; 29:16; 30:9; 33:15, 17, 21, 22, 26; 36:30) and to the older patriarch "*Jacob*" thirteen times (Jer 2:4, 5:20; 10:16, 25; 30:7, 10, 18; 31:7, 11; 33:26; 46:27, 28; 51:9). The monarchical line that began with David will be restored ("the throne of David" [Jer 17:25; 22:2, 4, 30; 29:16; 36:30]). That lineage is inextricably woven into the fabric that is the People's ancestry; as Jeremiah spoke of the coming restoration:

> "Alas! that day is so great there is none like it;
> it is a time of distress for Jacob; yet he shall be rescued from it." (Jer 30:7)

> "Thus says the LORD: I am going to restore the fortunes of the tents of Jacob,
> and have compassion on his dwellings; . . ." (Jer 30:18)

In a passage that warned of impending destruction to Judah, Jeremiah heard a reference to two other earlier leaders of the People:

> "Then the LORD said to me: Though Moses and Samuel stood before me,
> yet my heart would not turn toward this people." (Jer 15:1)

The "wilderness" also becomes a reminder of those episodes with Moses:

> "Thus says the LORD: I remember the devotion of your youth,
> your love as a bride,
> how you followed me in the wilderness, . . ." (Jer 2:2b)

> "They did not say, 'Where is the LORD
> who brought us up from the land of Egypt,
> who led us in the wilderness, . . . ?'" (Jer 2:6ab)

Pause to Reflect
What is your first memory of realizing that your
actions had consequences? What was the occasion?
What kind of consequences were you facing?
Were they "good" ones or "bad" ones?

References to *Egypt* in Jeremiah are numerous—that nation is mentioned by name sixty-two times! Many of those references are to contemporary circumstances, namely, in opposing the People's hope during the Babylonian threat to Jerusalem that Egypt would serve as a safe haven (see, for instance, Jer 2:18 and 42:13–17). However, in a number of passages,

"Egypt" is used to recall their ancestors' slavery and exodus. The above quotation, that includes the word "wilderness," also includes a phrase about escaping Egypt that is used in a number of places within the literary traditions. Versions of this phrase, "brought them up out of the land of Egypt," appear several other times in Jeremiah (7:22, 25; 11:4, 7; 16:14; 23:7; 31:32; 32:20, 21; 34:13). Surely, some of the hearers of both uses of the name "Egypt" in the Jeremiah tradition would have recognized a deep irony—that descendants of those who escaped oppression by Pharaoh were willing to return to his land, thinking that they would be safe there!

Jeremiah's witness, as with other prophets, also linked the People's decisions and consequences to their ancient *covenant* with the LORD. Four different times, this tradition recalls Jeremiah's delivery of divine messages, laden as they are with concern for the People's long-standing deal with God. In one case, Jeremiah's generation was reminded that the covenant made with their ancestors still applied to them:

> For I solemnly warned your ancestors
> when I brought them up out of the land of Egypt,
> warning them persistently, even to this day,
> saying, Obey my voice. . . .
> I brought upon them all the words of this covenant,
> which I commanded them to do, but they did not. (Jer 11:7–8)

Another time, in a passage quoted above, Jeremiah's generation was reminded that their covenant with the LORD encompassed not only David's legacy, but also God's role as Creator (see again Jer 33:25–26; also 33:20–21). In a third case, Jeremiah's generation is reminded of the covenant from the wilderness years, after the People first agreed to a release of their own enslaved Judeans (that is, their own kinfolk) and then reneged on the agreement:

> Thus says the LORD, the God of Israel:
> I myself made a covenant with your ancestors
> when I brought them out of the land of Egypt,
> out of the house of slavery, saying,
> 'Every seventh year each of you must set free
> any Hebrews who have been sold to you
> and have served you six years;
> you must set them free from your service.' (Jer 34:13–14)

The LORD in this passage speaks harsh words against the People, for backing out of their own covenant with their own people: "You have not obeyed me by granting a release to your neighbors and friends" (Jer 34:17b).

Jeremiah's generation was reminded that their covenant with the LORD encompassed not only David's legacy, but also God's role as Creator.

Of all the covenant references in this particular prophetic tradition, probably none is more well-known in Christian circles than the one that contrasts the ancient covenant with the promise of something "new":

> The days are surely coming, says the LORD, when I will make a new covenant with the house of Israel and the house of Judah. It will not be like the covenant that I made with their ancestors when I took them by the hand to bring them out of the land of Egypt—a covenant that they broke, though I was their husband, says the LORD. But this is the covenant that I will make with the house of Israel after those days, says the LORD: I will put my law within them, and I will write it on their hearts; and I will be their God, and they shall be my people. (Jer 33:31–33)

The tone behind this passage sounds like it hails from the time of exile, after Jerusalem has been destroyed by Babylonian forces and hopes for David's royal lineage there have been mutilated. Over the centuries, Christian theology has found it easy to link this promise of a new covenant to the coming of Jesus; such an interpretation is understandable, even though it extends beyond what the oracle seems to be saying to its exiled audience. Whether today's reader draws a straight line to Jesus, or understands the "new" here as more closely related to traditions and theology of the time, we will not attempt to explore here. What we do acknowledge is the strength of the covenant tradition for Jeremiah as a prophet—so powerful as an appeal that it continued to pertain to the People when they languished in exile.

LIFE IN EXILE: STORIES OF FAITH AND HOPE

As we have seen, The Story comes to a crashing low point. Judah, the surviving kingdom, finally fell to an empire. Its delusion of divine privilege could not protect it from the vagaries of conquest. Jerusalem was torn apart, and anyone who cared about its beauty, its Temple, its history—and even the Promise that brought it all into existence—surely felt the weight of devastation. The People of this Promise had been soundly defeated and scattered. Their next, clearly undesired, episode in The Story began, and it carried little hope for a favorable outcome.

From within the fog and mist of this period in exile appeared two characters—one, a man and the other, a woman—whose stories exhibit the skill and power of ancient, oral legend. Even if evidence is murky on the matter of their historical presence, both Daniel and Esther play a significant role in the movement of The One Great Story. They display the creative imagination of a community coming to terms with its dispersed condition and still managing to construct meaning and purpose in it.

THE LEGENDARY DANIEL

Daniel's narrative is set within the royal court of Babylon, Judah's conqueror. It begins with a group of young men from the defeated nation's elite, selected to be trained for service to Nebuchadnezzar the king. Daniel was one of four of these men who proved themselves far and away superior in their training, even beyond the king's native sages (Dan 1). Not long afterward, the narrative continues, Nebuchadnezzar became troubled by some dreams that he was having. He expected his sages first to tell him what the dreams were and then interpret them.

When none of the king's men would attempt such a difficult task, Daniel stepped forward to do so. He credited his knowledge of the dreams and their interpretation to "the God of heaven" (Dan 2:18a) who gave Daniel a vision revealing them to him at night (Dan 2:19). When Daniel stood before Nebuchadnezzar, he began by claiming that "there is a God in heaven who reveals mysteries" (Dan 2:28a). After hearing Daniel's report, the king praised Daniel, acknowledged Daniel's God, lavished Daniel with gifts, and raised him up to a position of tremendous authority and responsibility (Dan 2:46–49). At this point, the outline of this tale contains many parallels to that of Joseph, from more than a thousand years earlier.

As the narrative continued, Daniel's fortunes went up and down dramatically. His friends would not worship a huge golden statue that King Nebuchadnezzar ordered built. The king—who is portrayed, with a sense of almost fairy-tale exaggeration, as having a hot temper—blew his stack and commanded that Daniel's three friends be burned alive in an overheated furnace. When they were not harmed by the blaze and heat, the king (again) praised their God and gave the three men promotions (Dan 3). Daniel again interpreted another one of the king's dreams, in this case advising the king on how to avoid its negative consequences. Once again, the king gave great praise to "the Most High" (Dan 4:34c), honoring "the King of heaven" (Dan 4:37a) for truth and justice.

Eventually, Nebuchadnezzar's son, Belshazzar, succeeded his father as king. He once arranged a huge banquet, where he drank quite a bit of wine (using gold and silver vessels that had been removed by his father from the Temple in Jerusalem) and became tipsy. As Belshazzar and his party were reveling, a finger appeared from nowhere and began writing on the wall. The king became quite afraid, especially because no one at the banquet could read the writing. His queen mentioned Daniel, "found to have enlightenment, understanding, and wisdom like the wisdom of gods" (Dan 5:11c). The young man then was brought to the king and readily explained the writing, which told of a coming division and loss of the king's land. Belshazzar promoted Daniel on the spot but then he died that night, and a ruler from another kingdom took over Belshazzar's land (Dan 5).

The last episode in the legends about Daniel recounts a tale that sounds as fantastic as the three of Daniel's friends in the furnace. This time, our hero Daniel was facing a plot against himself. A bunch of the royal officials approached Darius, the new king, and urged him to sign a document declaring that the penalty for praying to anyone except the king himself would be to be thrown into a den of lions. These officials saw how much Darius favored Daniel as one of the king's appointed high officials and knew that Daniel was faithful to "his God." As expected, the schemers found Daniel praying as he always did and hence reported him to Darius. The king, bound by his own edict, sent Daniel to the lion's den, in much anguish, hoping for Daniel's divine rescue (Dan 6:1–18).

When dawn arrived, Darius went quickly and nervously to the den. There, he found Daniel alive and well, the young man crediting God with his safety. The king was overjoyed and ordered Daniel released. Then he punished Daniel's plotters and issued a statement, written in "every language throughout the whole world" (Dan 6:25), commanding that all peoples under Darius's rule will worship Daniel's God. The words of praise attributed to Darius here sound like one of the biblical psalms (Dan 6:19–27)! Daniel's legend would have encouraged the People to remain faithful and above reproach, even under the restraints of empire.

Daniel's legend would have encouraged the People to remain faithful and above reproach, even under the restraints of empire.

THE UNEXPECTED QUEEN

With some similar patterns, the story of *Esther* demonstrates the exiled People's hope of survival. It does so in an unusual way: there are no explicit references to God, or to religious practices, anywhere in the story. Yet, Esther's character comes to stand at the center of a narrative that became cherished with community pride—and driven at points by humor and irony.

As this story goes, Esther was a Jewish orphan living with her uncle, Mordecai, in the Persian Empire. When King Ahasuerus's wife—the queen—refused to join him at a banquet, where he wished to show her off, he became enraged and issued a pronouncement against her and against wives not honoring their husbands. Then, with great care, the royal court went about an elaborate process of helping the king select for himself a new queen. Because of her beauty, Esther became one of the many young "contestants" for the king. Once all the "tryouts" had been completed, King Ahasuerus selected Esther and threw a huge banquet. No one in the royal court, however, knew that she was a Jew, from the conquered Israelite nation (Esth 1–2).

Time went by. Esther's uncle, Mordecai, apparently held a low-level position with the court and was able to thwart an assassination plot against the king. Ahasuerus appointed a new second-in-command, a fellow named Haman, who was supposed to receive great deference from everyone. Mordecai would not do so, which inflamed Haman. Discovering Mordecai's ethnic background, Haman decided to annihilate Mordecai and all Jews in the empire. He persuaded the king of his intent, by misrepresenting the Jews and their behavior. Ahasuerus granted Haman's request, sending out a letter of command to all of his provinces (Esth 3).

> **Pause to Reflect**
> In your experience, what kind of risks do women have
> to take to achieve what they hope for? How might
> these risks be different than for men/ How do these
> differences affect the way that you read the Bible?

Meanwhile, Mordecai became quite distressed about this development and went to Queen Esther, urging her to do something. She put a plan in motion, in which she risked her favor with the king. By getting the king to agree to join her at a banquet, with Haman, Esther set up a situation by which the king had to agree to join her at a second banquet and then consent to her request. Meanwhile, Haman tried to put in motion his own plan—to have Mordecai hanged. The king, however, found out about Mordecai's earlier loyalty over the assassination plot; Haman, who wanted the Jewish servant dead, ended up having to carry out Ahasuerus's orders, which were to honor Mordecai in the public square (Esth 4–6)!

In Esther's legend, the Jewish orphan-become-queen used her
position and wiles to save the People from destruction.

Haman's days as a favored royal official were coming to a swift end. At her second banquet with the king and Haman, Esther revealed that Haman was behind the plan to wipe out all of the Jews. Ahasuerus then ordered Haman to be hung on the gallows that Haman had prepared for Mordecai. Esther then begged the king to repeal the annihilation order; Ahasuerus then authorized the queen and her uncle to act on his behalf in the matter. Thus, more letters went out with the king's seal to the entire empire, permitting Jews to defend themselves against any attacks against them. Celebration followed in the city and beyond, with a great festive spirit, Mordecai himself dressed in splendid royal garb, Jews rejoicing and some of the empire's peoples themselves converting to the faith. Esther (with help from her uncle) had saved her people from destruction (Esth 7–8)!

RETURN AND REBUILDING

The stories about Daniel and Esther must have been well-liked by the People, which would help to explain their preservation and eventual inclusion in the Hebrew Bible. They symbolized how the People, under the conditions of exile, could cope and hope—and even find ways to laugh and snicker about their conquerors. Otherwise, for those who remembered and cherished The Story, life in exile would have felt aimless, empty, and uncertain.

Historically, what is much more certain are the episodes recorded about returning to Jerusalem and rebuilding the Temple. After a couple of generations, Babylon had fallen to the Persian emperor Cyrus, who rather quickly announced that he would allow the People to return to their favorite city, Jerusalem, and rebuild its Temple. Cyrus was even generous enough to release to them all of the Temple bowls, basins, and knives that Nebuchadnezzar had removed during his conquest of Jerusalem and transported back to Babylon (Ezra 1).

Their journey of return was remembered in great detail, more by which descendants returned than by anything else. The record is precise—42,360 persons, categorized by family and city names, by priestly and Levitical lineage, by temple service and (last of all) by being singers. Oh, yes, the list also counts horses, mules, donkeys, and camels—hundreds and thousands of them (Ezra 2)! Once getting settled back into their precious homeland, the People then assembled in Jerusalem and began worshipping there. The next year, they began the Temple reconstruction, by laying a new foundation; the completion of this step was celebrated with pomp, instruments, and "a great shout." Older members, who could remember the Temple before it had been destroyed, wept loudly, so that sounds of weeping and of joy blended almost without distinction (Ezra 3).

Not everyone who was part of the Promise liked this idea, however. After a period of time, in which intimidation, accusations, and imperial politics all came into play (Ezra 4), work on the Temple resumed. It eventually took a declaration by the new king, Darius, to clear the way for the Temple to be completed. Then the People again held a great celebration, with offerings and sacrifices, followed by an observance of the Passover—that is, a ceremony marking their ancestors' escape from Egypt, led by Moses (Ezra 5–6).

Time passed once again. A new king now was in charge of Persia, the empire that continued to control many lands, including Jerusalem and Judah. The Story picks up again when a new figure, another descendant of the exiles, returned to Jerusalem. His name was *Ezra*, known as a "scribe," that is, one who was well-versed in the People's ancient written traditions ("skilled in the law of Moses that the LORD the God of Israel had given" [Ezra 7:6b]). Ezra carried with him a letter from the new king, Artaxerxes, in which Ezra was granted funds and latitude to appoint officials who would provide religious instruction and judicial authority. Although much smaller by count, Ezra's companions were counted like those of the first return, by family connections. This group journeyed back to Jerusalem without military protection, fasting and praying to God for safe passage. Once they arrived, they delivered other items for the Temple and offered sacrifices (Ezra 7–8).

What Ezra found when he had arrived among the People troubled his religious sensibilities. Many of them, including top officials, had married persons who were not part of the Israelite/Jewish community. Ezra saw this as a sign that the People had lost faith, once again, in the God who had created them and brought them back to their land. Ezra's prayers and display of distress over the People prompted a large group of them to come before him with intense weeping on their own part. One member of the crowd then spoke to Ezra, confessing their lack of faith in God and calling for a return to their ancient precepts. Ezra fasted and mourned for three days, until an announcement concerning the matter could reach all the villages (Ezra 9—10:8).

What Ezra found in Jerusalem among the People
troubled his religious sensibilities.

Rain was falling hard that day, when "all the people of Judah and Benjamin" (remember, these were the two original tribes who constituted the Davidic, southern kingdom) gathered before the Temple with trepida-tion. Ezra spoke to the crowd, declaring that marriage to women outside of their ancient lineage was a violation that "increased the guilt of Israel." He called on them to "separate yourselves" from them and from those in the land who were not considered part of their community heritage. The crowd agreed to do so; Ezra then set up a process for determining which of the men, in every town, had alien wives. Three months later, the task was finished, and more than one hundred men were found to be in violation (Ezra 10:9–44).

On the surface, this episode might seem strange—if not narrowly restrictive—to a twenty-first-century American reader. What difference would it make whether the returning exiles married women of their own background or chose instead to wed those of other nations? This kind of question, arising as it does from our own reading of a biblical episode, is a fair one—yet it also gives us a chance to remind ourselves of something very basic, something that is easy to forget. We are reading and listening to stories of events and characters that took place in a faraway place and ancient times. Our first task as a faithful listener to The Story is to seek to understand, as best as is possible, how the episode would have been heard and interpreted by its earliest audiences. To do so, we become aware of how different are our social, economic, cultural, political—and even religious—practices from those represented in the Bible. Thus, we try to understand what these obvious differences likely meant in their place and time.

In the case of Ezra confronting families with "foreign wives," perhaps our best clue is found in the prayer that the tradition remembered Ezra praying (Ezra 9:6–15). In that prayer, Ezra recalled that "From the days of our ancestors to this day we have been deep in guilt," which finally led to the People's captivity and shame (Ezra 9:7). Ezra also recalled from early episodes of The Story the promise from God of the People possessing a land. Yet (as readers will recall) that land had been populated by other groups and nations, whose ways of life were not consistent with the type of community that the LORD sought to create through the People. The practices of these other "peoples of the land" were considered unclean and "abominations." Ezra recalled the tradition that the LORD aimed for the land to be a prosperous place for the People, who—by maintaining their own identity and remaining faithful—would pass on this blessed habita-tion to their descendants for all time. Living with, and like, those other na-tions compromised the People's ability to fulfill their part of this wonderful covenant with God.

Pause to Reflect
What do you think of your society today? Is it
"better" or "worse" than generations gone by?
What standards guide your perspective?

How vividly do we hear echoes of The Story in this episode about Ezra and the mixed marriages! It was a time of re-establishing the People's identity, by re-affirming practices that easily could have disappeared throughout the period of exile. During those shaky years, as People of the Promise were allowed to return to their homeland, restoration of one kind or another was on their minds. Some of that restoration focused outwardly, as we have seen with rebuilding the Temple—and will see more soon—but for figures like Ezra, the restoration of physical structures represented something deeper, and perhaps even more elemental, for the People and their faith.

It was a time of re-establishing the People's identity,
by re-affirming practices that easily could have
disappeared throughout the period of exile.

We detect this same outward-inward restoration theme as The Story opens its episode with *Nehemiah*. Nehemiah held a trusted position in the Persian royal court, selecting the king's wine and tasting it for possible poison. He received a report from his brother that things in their homeland were in bad shape. Like Ezra, Nehemiah asked for Artaxerxes's permission to return to Jerusalem to help with restoration—in his case, to reconstruct the city walls. Like Ezra, Nehemiah carried letters from the king with him during his journey. Unlike Ezra, Nehemiah had a military escort. When he arrived in Jerusalem, Nehemiah looked over the damaged walls at night and then brought in the local Jewish officials to his mission. He persuaded them of the Persian king's support and of his confidence in God for the project (Neh 1–2).

Work on the walls involved many men from many families. Several towers and gates were carefully reconstructed and the details recorded. Opposition to the project became known, however, from officials in neighboring lands, who were upset with the prospect of a stronger Jerusalem. Nehemiah then set up a schedule, so that some workers stayed on their projects while other workers took turns guarding the workers with weapons of war (Neh 3–4).

To make the situation even more trying, some of Jerusalem's Jewish residents complained that they could not get food; others were putting their families and lands in economic jeopardy to richer residents, just to get by. Nehemiah was upset by these reports, but he took some time before responding. Then he called together the upper crust of Jerusalem society and accused them of taking advantage of their own kin, by charging interest. Nehemiah's words were true and received no rebuttal; he told them to stop the practice, and they promised to do so. Their promise was kept. By the time the wall was finished, Nehemiah had had to maneuver skillfully when Jerusalem's local adversaries tried to accuse him of rebellion (Neh 5–6).

Nehemiah became the governor of Judah, an appointment from the Persian king, and held the post for twelve years. However, he did not use the position to his advantage, but shared his governor's food with dozens of other people; neither did he gain any property due to his position. Rather, he was conscious of how hard the rest of his community had to work to get by, and he trusted in God (Neh 5:14–19).

Not long after the wall was completed, the People assembled in an open space outside the Temple and asked the priest/scribe Ezra to do something. At their request, Ezra brought out one of the ancient written documents, one that they knew to be "the book of the law of Moses." For several hours, Ezra read from this document, while the people—both men and women—listened intently. It was a very solemn occasion, as several Levites explained to the crowd what the readings meant. The People bowed in worship, and even wept, as they listened. Finally, Nehemiah dismissed the crowd with encouraging words, telling them that this was a holy day for celebration. From there, they all went home "to eat and drink and . . . to make great rejoicing" (Neh 8:1–12).

The next day, some of the family leaders met with religious officials to continue studying the law of Moses. There, they discovered a commandment about details for a festival commemorating the period of wandering in the wilderness after escaping from Egypt and its Pharaoh. It was the time of year for this festival, so the people prepared for it and celebrated, for seven days, continuing to listen to Ezra as he read from the book. This festival was followed by fasting and public confession, which also included more reading of the book of the law. Ezra led the people in a prayer that touched on the earliest episodes of The One Great Story (Neh 9:6–31):

- Abram's call and name change
- Abraham's covenant with the LORD
- the trials in Egypt and escape through the Red Sea
- the manna, the pillar of cloud by day and pillar of fire by night
- the giving of the Ten Words from Mt. Sinai

- the years of wilderness wanderings and the calf they made to worship
- settling the land, which was rich and filled with good things
- the People's cycle of disobedience, suffering, cries for help, and gracious divine deliverance

Ezra closed the prayer, acknowledging the People's current condition of servitude to Persia but also repeatedly affirming God's mercy, grace, and justice. In response, a sealed document was drawn up, with the names of Nehemiah, twenty-two priests, three Levites and fourteen of their associates, and forty-four "leaders of the people." They, along with all the other people and civil and religious officials, vowed "to walk in God's law, which was given by Moses the servant of God" (Neh 10:29b). A number of the details of this vow were spelled out, mostly having to do with support of the Temple (Neh 9–10).

> *As governor, Nehemiah continued to initiate*
> *reforms in Jerusalem and Judah.*

Nehemiah also was instrumental in the official dedication of Jerusalem's rebuilt wall. Priests, Levites, other officials, and groups of singers all prepared for the big event. Nehemiah divided them up with the people into two parties, one processing to the right on the wall, and the other party to the left with Nehemiah. They met up at the Temple, singing and offering sacrifices; even the women and children participated! It surely was a day to remember, "for God had made them rejoice with great joy . . . The joy of Jerusalem was heard far away" (Neh 12:27–43).

Life in a (relatively) restored Jerusalem and Judah had been given a fitting start and compass. As governor, Nehemiah continued to initiate reforms, mostly to do with appropriate activities in the Temple and with the people's Sabbath (day of rest) practices. He was seeking to follow all the commandments and ordinances of the ancient law associated with Moses, so that the people would live the kind of holy lives that would bring blessing to the nation. Nehemiah understood the ancient law's purpose to keep the people wholesome and clearly different from the other peoples; otherwise, they would not be able to fulfill God's hope for them. It was a purpose that Nehemiah took to heart, even when it meant telling people to stop doing things that they enjoyed and from which they benefitted (Neh 13).

Pause to Reflect
What influence do you think that elected officials
have today on the well-being of a nation?

WISHIN' AND HOPIN'

Let's pause for a few moments and reflect on the journey that we have witnessed here, and in chapter 5, concerning these particular episodes of The Story. Generations of royal intrigue and deceit, mixed with international shifts and threats, finally culminated in a tragic and devastating end to the Israelite experiment with monarchy. Along the way, the traditions that were passed down and recorded include harsh assessment of most of the kings, north and south, and negative consequences for the People. Centuries earlier, they had sought out status and (an appearance of) stability by asking Samuel—the last judge chosen by the LORD—to appoint for them a king (1 Sam 8). In spite of David's wild popularity, and Solomon's power, wealth, and wisdom, monarchy proved to be an elusive, and ultimately ineffective, means for Israel to fulfill its calling and covenant. Babylonian exile became a time for some members of this chosen community to look back and wonder what happened to their special place and mission, their covenant with the Holy One of Israel. What had happened to the Promise of blessing for the nations, through Abram and Sarai (Gen 12:1–3)? Especially by the time of figures like Ezra and Nehemiah, that covenant, its history and expectations, seems to have faded from most of The People's memory and concern.

Monarchy proved to be an elusive, and ultimately ineffective, means for Israel to fulfill its calling and covenant.

Those who did pay attention surely drew some hope from certain oracles out of the prophetic tradition. Yes, the prophets whose pronouncements survived spared no words when describing the sins of kings and the People and seeing what disastrous consequences were headed their way. Yet—as the section above regarding Jeremiah suggests—these same prophets also expressed an almost uncanny confidence that divine judgment for the People's abandoning of the covenant eventually would be overcome by divine mercy and grace. They perceived that there was something about the LORD that was tenacious and generous beyond human achievement and comprehension.

Perhaps nowhere else in these many difficult episodes in The Story do we find a more spectacular illustration of this theological theme than in the prophet *Ezekiel*'s vision of the valley of dry bones (Ezek 37:1–14). This prophet found himself "by the spirit of the LORD" standing in the midst of a valley that was covered with human bones. Ezekiel noted that the condition of those bones was "very dry," suggesting a situation of slain soldiers being dead for a very long time. The prophet remembered the LORD asking him whether the bones could come alive; in the context of Ezekiel's prophetic legacy (and later in this vision), it seems clear that the question has to do with the future of the people of Israel. Ezekiel would not give an answer, so God told him to speak to the bones, in order that they indeed would live (Ezek 37:1–6).

Ezekiel did as the LORD instructed, and, before his eyes, the bones took on all the fleshy features that they had lost in death—even then, however, none of the bodies were breathing. Then the LORD instructed Ezekiel to call the "wind" or ("spirit") to give them life. Ezekiel obeyed, the breath/wind came, and all of the "vast multitude" stood up. God then named the bones "the house of Israel," the people of exile who felt abandoned without hope. The LORD then gave Ezekiel one more instruction—to tell the bones that God would raise them out of their graves, take them back to their land, and live with God's spirit in them. This last prophetic instruction in the vision reaffirms the LORD's own unbroken bond to them, in the phrase, "O my people," that is used twice. The vision ends with the assertions that the People will recognize their God, because their God will accomplish what the prophetic word says (Ezek 37:11–14).

In the vision of the dry bones, the phrase "O my people"
reaffirms the LORD's own unbroken bond to them.

The two stories of Daniel and Esther illustrate how the exiled People could cope imaginatively with their captivity. The prophets were clear that something had been lost along the way: Israel's lack of commitment to its faithful, gracious God led to the destruction of its monarchy and land. The ministries of Ezra and Nehemiah linked the restoration of Jerusalem with a return, not merely to their place of Promise, but also to their ancestral covenant life with the LORD. As the valley of dry bones vision shows, sensitive and faithful persons who spoke God's word could see beyond devastation and oppression, to a hope that God would keep the Promise. What would that look like? How long would the People have to wait? What would they have to do to prepare for its coming?

As we read a little between the lines of the episodes in this chapter, we can detect these kinds of questions. At this point, The Story seems somewhat in a holding pattern. What finally happens next is both expected and unexpected.

FOR THE READER

1. Judah's eventual conquest, with Jerusalem's destruction, occurred following years of internal and external pressures. What do you think that life would have been like during that time for the common person? How might their daily and weekly routines have been affected? What did they worry about? hope for?

2. How do the prophets mentioned in this chapter (Amos, Micah, Isaiah, Jeremiah) draw upon The One Great Story to pronounce the LORD's judgment on The People? to declare hope for The People's future?

3. What parallels and comparisons do you see between Daniel's story and that of Joseph (Gen 37, 39–50, esp. 39–41)? What do these comparisons suggest about biblical storytelling? about The Story's understanding of what it means to live in faith?

4. Esther's story gives more attention to one female character than just about any other woman in the Bible. How do you think Jewish women after the exile would have thought about her character and story?

5. How would you describe the motivations that drove Ezra and Nehemiah in their efforts to rebuild Jerusalem? What do the traditions suggest about how the two of them understood the purpose for rebuilding the Temple and renewing the ancient covenant?

SUGGESTED ACTIVITIES

- Read the Book of Micah all the way through in one sitting (seven chapters, six pages), while you make a list of all names, phrases, and images that you recognize so far from The One Great Story. Which ones of those that you identify caught your attention? Of those, how is Micah using them—for judgment, or for hope (or, sometimes, for both)?

- As first suggested at the end of chapter 5, go online again and locate a map of the Ancient Near East—this time one that includes Babylonia and especially Persia. Note the locations and sizes of the respective empires, including Egypt, where the two Israelite kingdoms had been situated, and so forth. If you were an adviser to governor Nehemiah (or his successors), what advice would you have given him about Jerusalem's and Judah's future? What would be your reasoning?

- Share with a friend your notes and thoughts from having read through Micah. What comments or questions does your friend pose? How might discussion from this chapter speak to any of those comments or questions?

Chapter 8

The Story Revived Through Jesus

"And the Word became flesh and lived among us,
and we have seen his glory, . . ."

—JOHN 1:14A

Almost everywhere that one goes today, life moves at a fast pace. For the past century or so, air travel, the telephone, motion pictures, television—and certainly the Internet and social media—have done more than shrink our perception of our planetary home. These technologies have contributed to a widespread sense that things must be done faster, and more of them in one day or week or month, than ever before. Instant coffee and microwaved meals are not enough; now, we are expected to "multi-task" to be successful. This mindset about speed and accomplishment has become so pervasive that, in countries and small towns where life still preserves a measure of sane rhythm to a day, those who don't welcome high velocity are considered suspect. If it can't be ready "right now," something is wrong.

Consequently, those of us who read the Bible in the context of a "now, now, now!" world find it strange, and even irritating, that life there moves at a very different pace. Abram and Sarai were given a divine promise but never came close to seeing it realized. Jacob had to work for his father-in-law for fourteen years before he could marry the wife that he wanted, Rachel. Moses and the Israelites wandered through the wilderness for forty years, the traditions say. Generations came and generations went, often with little change of scenery and much of the "same old same old," no matter who claimed to be in charge.

"HOW LONG, O LORD?"

Yet, even with a less-hurried view of time and life, surely the People of The One Great Story felt some frustration and irritation about their future after monarchy and exile. Yes, it was the case that (at least some of) the exiles returned to Jerusalem and Judah, to resettle, rebuild, and restore their nation. They were quite aware that life there and then was not the same; the People now existed as subjects of first one empire and then another. Many "Jews"—as they came to be called—simply got on with their daily lives, giving little thought about the prophetic promises that spoke of restoration, or a new covenant, or some other way of giving hope. During these generations, faithful scribes assembled, maintained, and searched through written versions of the People's traditions—not just the Law, but also the Writings and the Prophets. It probably is not a coincidence that the last verses in this large collection of writings speak of a coming "day of the LORD," in which the prophet Elijah will return, and for those "who revere my name the sun of righteousness shall rise, with healing in its wings" (Mal 4:2–5). In this final word of encouragement, the People were urged to follow what "my servant Moses" taught them (Mal 4:4). Expectancy, waiting, discouragement, impatience, falling away: the long period after return from exile revealed many emotions and attitudes. It seemed like The Story was stalled and had nowhere else to go.

AND THEN, SEEMINGLY OUT OF NOWHERE . . .

If we were reading a biography or history book, we would expect that the author would begin a chapter by letting the reader know where things left off in the previous chapter. We might assume that any gaps in the story line, lapse of time, or sequence of things would become clear, at some point: an author who wants to keep readers interested and following the story will think about these things. Concerning the Bible, however, we are dealing with a different kind of animal—remember, it is a library, an assortment of records and texts across many centuries and with many, mostly unknown, storytellers, scribes, authors, and editors. Consequently, moving from one set of documents to another does not necessarily presume any obvious continuity. And it certainly does not presume that the lapse of time from one period to the next one is short or easy to figure out.

When they get to the end of the Hebrew Bible, readers
are supposed to feel like they are left hanging.

When they get to the end of the Hebrew Bible (the Old Testament), I think that readers are supposed to feel like they are left hanging. Something has not been resolved yet, something really important—yes, even at the heart of the entire story line. How will it get settled, come to fruition? It sort of feels like being in the bottom of the ninth inning, with two outs and no one on base, and the home team needs some runs to win.

> **Pause to Reflect**
> What is something in your life for which you
> waited a long time? What was the waiting like?
> How did it feel when the waiting was finally over?
> In what ways was it "worth the wait"—or not?

Reading the Christian Bible means that, when we get to the end of the Old Testament, we turn another page and discover that Its Story does indeed continue. Turning this one page, from the end of Malachi to the beginning of Matthew, seems both like stepping over a puddle and traveling across an ocean. What we read from here on out seems different, even while it rings familiar. This is certainly the case, because The One Great Story becomes revived, through the presence of a single person, from whom The Story pivots and moves. That person, of course, is Jesus of Nazareth. Here, a fresh generation of witnesses stands behind yet another set of documents that came to be known as "the New Testament." The fact that the term "testament" is used to refer to both parts of the Bible provides a big clue to how these two groupings of ancient works are related. This somewhat old-fashioned term, "testament," refers to things like "being a witness" or "giving testimony"—ideas that we today associate perhaps most readily with a court of law. For the earliest compilers of biblical materials, their task indeed was to be witnesses, to provide evidence that The Story was worth remembering. For the New Testament, the testimony of evidence claims that it picks up where the older texts of testimony leave off.

The One Great Story becomes revived and more fully realized, through
the presence of a single person, from whom The Story pivots and moves.

QUADRAPHONIC SOUND

So here we are now, ready to discover how elements of The Story both inform and are extended by the testimonies about Jesus. Ironically—perhaps—in terms of sheer volume, there is no comparison: the Old Testament is about three-and-a-half times longer than the New Testament. In terms of significance to the Story line, though, the New Testament cannot be underestimated. Another way of making this point is to say that The Story becomes more fully realized through the New Testament. I say "*more* fully" here, because (as we will find out) there is something about the "end" of The Story that remains unfinished. For now, there is a lot of ground to cover—and it begins with four distinct versions of the next big episode.

Our purpose here, however, is not to provide summaries or outlines of these four Gospels, expounding on their similarities and differences. Instead, we are following That One Great Story, as That Story becomes retold, expanded, and interpreted through the witness of Jesus of Nazareth. A number of the names and events that we have heard and witnessed in earlier chapters of this book we will find in these Gospels—and, with even more of them, in other New Testament locations. In doing so, we will discover in what ways That Story informs—and is utilized by—each one of the four. The best place to begin this discovery probably is not with the document that appears first in the collection—that is, Matthew—but with the one that is the shortest in length and most likely the earliest to be put in its final form—Mark.

THE GOSPEL IN A HURRY

To the writer responsible for the book that we know as "Mark," telling the story of Jesus meant keeping up a fast pace. It is illuminating to note that one form of the Greek word for fast pace, *euthus*, "immediately," appears in Mark's sixteen chapters thirty-four times, nine of those in the first chapter alone. Compare this frequency to all other translations of "immediately" in the other three Gospels—twenty-eight. Clearly, the Gospel that we know as Mark presents an interpretation of Jesus that carries in it a sense of urgency. Graphic, busy, hands-on in style, this Gospel moves!

Make no mistake: in spite of its tempo, Mark displays a defined understanding of Jesus' place in The Story, and he does so "immediately"! Its second verse introduces a quotation with sources in Isaiah and another prophet:

> See, I am sending my messenger ahead of you,
> who will prepare your way;
> the voice of one crying out in the wilderness:

'Prepare the way of the Lord, make his paths straight.' (Mark 1:2–3)

The "messenger" then is announced as "John the baptizer" or "John the Baptist." John came out of the badlands (that is, "the wilderness"—for antiquity, a very dangerous place) to preach and baptize. His message was for the people of Judea to confess, repent, be baptized, and prepare for someone else who would follow John. In his preaching style, appearance, and diet (camel's hair, leather belt, locusts, and wild honey), John seems to have been understood as a prophetic figure, such as those in the Old Testament. So begins Mark's rapid, tightly told story about Jesus.

One of the ways in which the Jesus-Story connects readily with The One Great Story is through some symbolism that would not have been lost on any descendant of Abraham, Isaac, and Jacob. In Mark—as in all four of the Jesus-Story documents—Jesus designated, from among his followers, twelve men to be his inner circle (Mark 3:13–19; compare Matt 10:1–4; Luke 6:12–16; and John 6:67–71). These twelve apparently traveled with Jesus wherever he went and, at times, were given special tasks (see, for example, Mark 6:6–13, 30–44). Does that number "twelve" ring a bell? It is the same number as the tribes of Israel, each tribe descending from one of Jacob's sons—Jacob, whose name was changed to "Israel" after a midnight wrestling match with an angel (Gen 32:22–32). Thus, Jesus' twelve appear to represent some kind of re-establishment of the People and their age-old Promise: that long-standing covenant with the LORD somehow would find continuity through Jesus. This particular connection is subtle, not ever spelled out directly in the four Jesus-Stories, but it also is hard to overlook.

Jesus' ministry was challenged by Jewish officials who believed that he was violating their cherished religious traditions.

Other evidence of continuity seems more intentional. There are thirteen places in Mark where the form of the text directly or indirectly refers to a passage from the Old Testament. Of those references, five of them echo something from The One Great Story. The first of these five appears early, as Jesus has begun his ministry with some preaching and healing. Mark relates a story (2:23–28) in which Jesus and some of his followers were traveling on the Sabbath and picked heads of grain in a field, to have something to eat. When questioned by some religious officials (Pharisees) about their action being forbidden, Jesus answered by recalling a story from the life of the beloved David. David and his entourage had been running from King Saul, who was out to get the popular, young upstart. In that situation, David persuaded the high priest to allow him and his men to eat bread from the altar—forbidden to anyone but priests (1 Sam 21:1–6). Jesus concluded his recounting of the story by claiming that the Sabbath—with its religious rules—was designed for the benefit of people, not the other way around. Extending the point, Jesus also claimed that he, as "the Son of Man" had authority over the Sabbath.

> **Pause to Reflect**
> Have you ever met someone and then found out later
> that they were much more impressive than you realized?
> How did you react to your new awareness about them?
> What did you wonder about yourself as a result?

A second obvious appeal in Mark to The Story shows up in the middle of the document (7:1–13). As we just saw above, Jesus' ministry was challenged by Jewish officials who believed that he was violating their cherished religious traditions. In one such standoff, some of these officials saw that some of Jesus' followers did not follow certain laws concerning food and eating. Jesus replied to these officials first by quoting from Isaiah (29:13), bluntly calling them "hypocrites" who talk as though they follow God but whose "hearts are far from" God. Then Jesus quoted from The Ten Words (in Exod 20:12) and another ancient source in referring to Moses. It is clear from Jesus' words here that, by appealing to the status of Moses as receiver of the LORD's law, Jesus was criticizing those scribes and Pharisees. He said that they were "making void the word of God through your tradition" (Mark 7:13a).

Moses appears again in Mark's story, this time with another famous figure from the earlier episodes of The Story, Elijah (Mark 9:2–13). Jesus had taken three of his chosen followers on a trip up a tall mountain. In this episode, Jesus was remembered to have changed form—that is, to have "transfigured" (Mark 9:2c), with his garments giving off an intensely bleached look. Jesus' three companions—Peter, James, and John—then saw that Jesus had company there: Moses and Elijah were talking with him. The episode includes an honest comment about what surely would have been the companions' reaction to this unexpected moment: they were petrified and nearly struck dumb (Mark 9:6)!

It is not surprising that we would see Moses in this episode with Jesus, for he casts a long, imposing shadow on many parts of The Story that we have heard already. Perhaps, then, we are puzzled about Elijah, a famed prophet during the divided kingdoms who was taken up into heaven after passing on his ministry to Elisha (2 Kgs 2:1–12). Why would he appear with Moses, to meet and talk with a transfigured Jesus?

An answer to this question is implied by the conversation that Jesus and his companions had a little later, as they left the mountain and Jesus told them to keep it to themselves for the time being. They talked about Elijah's place in the People's hope for the LORD to "restore all things" (Mark 9:12a). It was not a fantastic speculation on their part; remember—mentioned at the beginning of this chapter—the prophetic word that closes the Hebrew Bible? That word promises that the LORD would send Elijah back to the earth, to prepare everyone for God's "great and terrible day" (Mal 4:5). Centuries later, Jesus' generation was still speculating on this promise. Jesus' last comment about Elijah in this episode (Mark 9:13) implies that Jesus saw John the Baptist as the returning Elijah. King Herod—the regional Jewish official overseeing this part of the Eastern Mediterranean for the Roman Empire—had beheaded John, as a result of some internal family issues and to save face before local persons of influence (Mark 6:14–29). John's death in this manner seems to emphasize here, for Jesus, the rejection by the People of the purpose of Elijah's return.

In one episode, a lowly, disabled beggar recognized that Jesus was someone special.

In a fourth echo from The Story, Mark included a healing episode in which a blind man in a crowd called out to Jesus for mercy (Mark 10:46–52). The episode implies that the man already had heard about Jesus, for he hollered Jesus' name and then used a particular designation, "Son of David" (Mark 10:47, 48). The term itself hailed back hundreds of years, understandably used at first to refer to the popular king's own male offspring (as in 2 Chr 11:18, 13:6). Later, "Son of David" came to be associated with the promise of one who would come to restore God's purposes for The People. That promise had been associated for centuries with the covenant that the LORD had established with David as chosen king (2 Sam 7:4–17). This recognition by a lowly, disabled beggar—that Jesus was someone special—in the divinely based hopes of The People, surely carried a dramatic effect for the earliest audiences of the episode.

Lastly, the figure of Elijah shows up once more in Mark, this time during Jesus' crucifixion (Mark 15:33–39). The tradition passing on this dark and dramatic episode remembers Jesus calling out loudly from the cross, recording what most likely were the actual Aramaic words that Jesus used, "*Eloi, Eloi, lema sabach-thani,*" followed by a translation in Greek. The words themselves come from Ps 22:1, but Mark's telling of this episode shows that some onlookers thought that he was speaking the ancient prophet Elijah's name ("Eloi" could sound like "Elijah," especially when hearing it from a distance). According to the account, one of those persons even urged the others to watch, in case "Elijah will come to take him down" (Mark 15:36c).

At this point, those reading this Markan Jesus-Story know that Elijah/John the Baptist was dead; yet, the onlooker's statement suggests a tradition in Judaism that wondrous acts could be anticipated in Elijah's name. In their eyes, the guy still had a lot of mojo left!

Mark's compact, straightforward testimony to Jesus expresses a deliberate effort to weave Jesus as Messiah into The Story of the People of God. We will see later in this chapter some ways in which Mark compares with the other three Gospel storytellers.

JESUS AND TORAH

Another one of the Jesus-Story documents in the New Testament develops its case for continuing The Story right out of the starting blocks. This one, known as Matthew, pulls out lots of stops to show how Jesus was part of the direct lineage of the People's ancestors. In its very first sentence, Matthew makes it clear that—not only was he the "Messiah" (or "Christ" in Greek)— this Jesus character was descended from David and from Abraham as well. The book opens with a genealogy that begins with Abraham, naming men (and a few women!) who have appeared in what we have seen up to this point (and some who did not), and ending with "Joseph the husband of Mary, of whom Jesus was born, who is called the Messiah" (Matt 1:16). Abraham and David serve as linchpins in the trajectory that leads to Jesus (Matt 1:17), thus underscoring his authority. Whether the details of this genealogy correspond fully with what can be ascertained from earlier sources is less important than Matthew's emphasis on Jesus' role in God's longstanding purposes. As the "Anointed One"—the Christ—Jesus will accomplish the fulness of what God intends, for the People and for the world.

> **Pause to Reflect**
> Have you ever "broken a rule" for what you thought
> was a good reason? How did you decide to do it? How
> did it feel when you did so? What was the outcome?
> Would you do it again? Why or why not?

Matthew continues its claim of continuity with The Story early on by introducing some key episodes that present striking, unexpected, and even gruesome events. To those of us who grew up in Sunday school, these episodes of Joseph being told in a dream to marry his pregnant fiancée, of the baby Jesus being born, of the visit from the magi, of their escape and return to Egypt, were recited and imparted with a dutiful, benign mood. A more careful reading betrays such an innocent sentiment! These early vignettes surrounding the special child (Matt 1:18—2:23) crackle with social impropriety, international implications, political deception, outright slaughter, and temporary exile (the young family's escape to Egypt seems to parallel the ancient episodes of Jacob's son Joseph, sold by his brothers, ending up in Egypt, yet eventually saving his entire family [Gen 37–50]). There is nothing mellow in this series that provides background to the adult Jesus; more likely, we are to understand these circumstances as foreshadowing the rest of the story line. What stands out among them, though, is the quiet acceptance and obedience of the main character to this point—Joseph (not the baby Jesus). His openness to the guidance of the angelic dreams surely resonates with many characters whom we have encountered in The Story already.

> *Matthew presents Jesus as a teacher, in the way that*
> *traditions after Moses remember him as the "lawgiver."*

There are some structural and stylistic clues in Matthew that point to this Jesus-Story's particular appropriation of The One Great Story. Besides including the genealogy (like those found in several places in the Hebrew Bible), Matthew presents Jesus as a teacher, in the way that traditions after Moses remember him as the "lawgiver." When Jesus got started with his ministry of preaching and healing, he was attracting "great crowds" (Matt 4:25a). In this setting, Matthew presents Jesus giving a long discourse, a series of teachings about many subjects (e.g., anger, adultery, divorce, retaliation, enemies, fasting, etc.). This teaching moment (Matt 5–7) is popularly known as "the Sermon on the Mount," in which Jesus sat down on a mountain and taught the people. There are four more teaching sections in Matthew (chaps 10, 13, 18, 24–25), giving this book the feel of Jesus as a new Moses.

The Jesus-as-Moses motif is underscored, yet given a spin, in the Sermon on the Mount. On the one hand, Jesus is remembered as having said that his ministry was "not to abolish but to fulfill [the law and the prophets]" (Matt 5:17). Certainly, this statement would have been understood as emphasizing Jesus as one who maintains The Story and its covenantal expectations. On the other hand, the Sermon on the Mount also depicts Jesus appearing to argue with some of the oldest elements of The Story's ethical injunctions. In six consecutive passages, Jesus uses a formula, "You have heard that it was said [to those of ancient times], . . . but I say to you, . . . " (Matt 5:21–22, 27–28, 31–32, 33–34, 38–39, and 43–44). These passages cover the topics of anger, adultery, divorce, oaths, retaliation, and enemies.

At first, it might seem that Jesus was contradicting each one of the verses that he quoted from the Jews' cherished scriptures. Reading more carefully, though, we realize that he was taking the task of "fulfilling the law and the prophets" to another level. For instance, in reference to oaths ("vows" and "swearing"), Jesus said not to do it at all. Instead, Jesus explained, "let your word be 'Yes, Yes' or 'No, No'" (Matt 5:37a). Similarly, in speaking of retaliation ("an eye for an eye and a tooth for a tooth"), Jesus went so far as to tell his audience never to fight back: "turn the other cheek; . . . give your cloak as well; . . . go also the second mile" (Matt 5:39–41). These "decrees" from the mouth of Jesus in the Sermon on the Mount imply that simply following the letter of a law does not get at the heart of its purpose. What God expects of the People who are called to be a blessing goes beyond mere adherence to stiffly interpreted commandments.

Matthew, then, construes Jesus' relationship to The Story with both nuance and intricacy. Even further, Matthew is the book among the four in the New Testament that conveys the strongest ties to the traditions of The Story. The more that we know about the Hebrew Bible, the more that we think of Matthew's earliest audience as those who would identify as legitimate People of the Promise. Throughout the book, we run into one citation after another that is attributed to Jewish scriptures. A dozen of these citations—from chapter 1 to chapter 26—state directly, or indicate, fulfillment of a prophetic word from of old. These citations include the promise of Jesus' birth (Matt 1:22–23), the appearance of John the Baptizer as preparing the way (Matt 3:1–3), Jesus quoting scripture back to the devil (Matt 4:4, 7), the significance of Jesus making his home in Capernaum (Matt 4:12–16), Jesus quoting the same verse on two different occasions (Matt 9:13, 12:7), the reason for Jesus asking the crowds not to speak about him (Matt 12:15–21), Jesus' ride into Jerusalem on a donkey (Matt 21:1–5), and so on. Several of these citations come from Isaiah, and many of the rest from other prophets. The summary effect of these several citations weaves a picture of Jewish Christians who find in Matthew a compelling rationale for Jesus realizing God's ancient objective—to bless all nations through the descendants of Abraham and Sarah.

THE WORD "PITCHED A TENT"

Both Mark and Matthew tell the Jesus-Story in their own distinctive ways, and yet they share many episodes, sayings, and vignettes in common. For a long time, biblical scholars have studied this common material (and their variations) and have argued for assorted explanations of their origins.[13]

13. Like many discussions in biblical studies, this one goes back many generations

What adds to the challenges in such a comparative study is that the fourth "Jesus" document in the New Testament is, in certain ways, quite different than the other three.

The fourth Gospel articulates the Jesus-Story with a distinctive structure and tone.

This fourth "Gospel," identified by early tradition as "John," conveys the Jesus-Story with a distinctive tone and mood, using a completely different structure to the story line and very little of the same material. For instance, the only "sign and wonder" story that the four share is Jesus feeding five thousand (or more) people (John 6:1–14; Matt 14:13–21; Mark 6:30–44; Luke 9:10–17).

Of the thirty-nine places where the four Gospels display either common material or a similar theme, John's version of the episode typically reads very differently—and half of them (twenty-one) appear in the sequence of events that occurs from the night of Jesus' arrest up to the empty-tomb episode.[14] Most of John's material is unique, consisting of long sections of narrative, occasionally drifting off into theological reflection, as well as a five-chapter section in the middle (John 13–17) almost entirely comprised of monologues by Jesus. At the Passover meal (the night of his arrest), Jesus does not institute the Lord's Supper as he does in the other three Gospels; instead, he washes the feet of his disciples (John 13:1–15).

Overall, the structure of this Gospel moves in its first half through seven "signs," beginning with turning water into wine at a wedding (John 2:1–12), building in "wonder" until the seventh and final one, raising a friend who had been dead for four days (John 11:1–44). John also employs a unique literary device, in which a few key terms—"believe," "truth," "light," "life," and "spirit"—appear a number of times at key points in the narration or in Jesus' mouth. Based on all this internal evidence, John seems to have been written for a very distinctive audience, unlike those of the other three Gospels. In spite of all its singular qualities, though, we discover a number of details and images out of The One Great Story that this fourth Gospel effectively employs.

---

and is filled with theories. For summaries of the longstanding approaches that assume literary origins, see Neirynck, "Q" and "Synoptic Problem," 715–16 and 845–48. For scholarly explorations into oral tradition, its ancient character, and how it reframes our understanding of these earliest sources about Jesus, see, for instance, Kelber, *The Oral and the Written Gospel*, esp. chaps. 2 and 5; see also Horsley, *Jesus in Context*, Part II, "Oral Performance," and Part IV, ch. 10.

14. These observations were calculated based upon Sparks, *The Johannine Synopsis of the Gospels*, Introduction and Table of Contents.

John does not ignore the historical or religious context of the Jesus-Story: he does, however, handle it as one who is addressing an audience unfamiliar with first-century Judaism, its history and its customs. There are regular references in John to geographical locations, religious officials, or ritual practices; sometimes, these references come with a parenthetical explanation, like during a conversation between Jesus and a Samaritan woman (John 4:4-9). To those who are familiar with The Story, though, the fourth Gospel grabs their attention with its very first words: "In the beginning." Sound familiar? It is the exact same phrase that begins the first book of the Hebrew Bible (Gen 1:1a).

In fact, the Greek version of the Hebrew Bible uses the same Greek words as appear here in John: *en arché*. This Gospel proclaims from the start that the active presence of God at creation ("the Word") is the same active presence that "became flesh" (John 1:14a) in Jesus. John does not name him, though, until the seventeenth verse of the book's introduction. There, the Gospel contrasts "grace and truth through Jesus Christ" with "the law" that "was given through Moses" (John 1:17). Grounding this telling of the Jesus-Story in creation itself, the fourth Gospel affirms its place in The Story, while also telegraphing to its audience that the Jesus-Story puts a new spin on The Story's interpretation. There will be something about "grace and truth" that adds to how the fourth Gospel understands "the law"—which, if you remember, is more than rules and regulations, rather also including the entire narrative dealing with slavery, exodus, and covenant.

This Gospel proclaims from the start that the active
presence of God at creation ("the Word") is the same active
presence that "became flesh" in Jesus. (John 1:14a)

We do not conclude, therefore, that John treats The Story dismissively. In chapter 1 alone:

- John the Baptist quotes Isaiah, in referring to himself (1:22-23).

- Some Jewish officials ask the Baptist about his purpose, since he does not claim to be "Elijah, nor the prophet" (1:24-25).

- The Baptist refers to Jesus as "the Lamb of God who takes away the sin of the world" (1:29), an exclamation that he repeats the next day as well (1:35-36).

- One of the men whom Jesus calls to follow him (Philip) told someone (Nathanael) that "We have found him about whom Moses in the law and also the prophets wrote" (1:43-45).

- Nathanael addresses Jesus as "the Son of God . . . the King of Israel" (1:49)

From these several references (including "In the beginning"), it is clear that the fourth Gospel takes The One Great Story seriously. We saw in chapter 3 of this book the key role that *Moses* played in the People's escape from Egypt and receiving of the covenant with its Ten Words; Moses' name is mentioned in John thirteen times, more than in any of the four Gospels. In using the term, "*the Lamb of God,*" John hearkens to the moment in the Israelites' exodus plan in which a lamb was sacrificed, to use its blood as a sign of protection for their escape from Egypt (Exod 12:1–13). *Elijah's* name held a special place in Jewish anticipation of the next action of God on behalf of The People. References to, and quotations from, the traditions of *Isaiah* appear in all four Gospels and two other New Testament documents (Acts and Romans). Of course, too, in addressing Jesus as "the king of Israel," Nathanael expressed the long-standing hope that God would send someone to reinstate the monarchy.

One of the fourth Gospel's uses of a reference to Moses illustrates two valuable points about reading the New Testament—one, to appreciate how echoes of The Story are understood; and, two, to be careful about how we can take something out of context and thus misinterpret it. In John 3, Jesus had an "after-hours" conversation with a Pharisee named Nicodemus. Like other conversations in this Gospel, this one feathers off into a monologue by Jesus, which touches on several theological concepts that are important in this document (spirit, light, darkness, believe, and so on). During the monologue, we run across what is perhaps the most well-known verse in the New Testament, at least among Protestants—John 3:16.

What is often neglected when this verse ("For God so loved the world . . . ") is recited are the two verses that come just before it. John 3:14–15 reads as follows:

> "And just as Moses lifted up the serpent in the wilderness,
> so must the Son of Man be lifted up,
> that whoever believes in him may have eternal life."

Pause to Reflect

Have you ever listened to a song many times and finally realized that you had been misunderstanding some of its lyrics? What did that new insight do to your sense about the meaning of that song? What was that "Now I get it!" moment like for you?

Right away, we can tell that John's Jesus is using an episode from the Moses part of The Story to make a point. In that episode (Num 21:4–9), the People were dying as a result of their complaints against God and Moses: poisonous snakes were biting them. The People then confessed to Moses and asked for rescue, so Moses prayed for them. The LORD instructed Moses to fashion a snake of bronze and mount it on a pole. Moses did so, and when someone was bitten by a snake, by gazing at the bronze serpent, he or she would not die.

Jesus, as "the Son of Man," is compared to the bronze serpent that Moses made for saving the People. As first-time hearers or readers of the fourth Gospel, we would not know yet what is going to happen to Jesus—so this is a hint of it. What the Gospel wants to emphasize here, however, is how this one part of the Ancient Story provides a symbol of what is to come with Jesus. Whoever trusts in the Lifted-Up One will live (just like the sinning Israelites lived by looking at the bronze serpent). The act of being "lifted up"—both of the bronze serpent and of Jesus—occurs at the instigation of God; by these divine actions, people live.

Secondly, the common use of this brief passage reminds us how easy it can be to misread something in the Bible. The beginning of the famous verse 16 is often understood as meaning, "God loved the world *so much.*" Yet, when we read all three verses carefully (and the others that follow it), we realize that the point in verse 16 is not about the *intensity* of God's love but in the *manner* in which God is willing to act, in order to rescue humanity. The English word "so" appearing in verses 14 and 16—translating the Greek word *outos*—means "in this way" or "thus." In other words, God loved the world *in this way*, as One who will give life to those who turned away and then admitted to the error of their ways. This emphasis continues in the following verses (John 3:17–18), claiming that the purpose of Jesus (like the purpose of the bronze serpent) is not to condemn. The fourth Gospel tips off its listeners: Jesus the Messiah will be lifted up, in order to bring healing and life. So, here in these few verses, we see John's creative theological application of a Moses episode—and we remind ourselves to read carefully, in order that the intention of the text can speak with authenticity and vigor.

The act of being "lifted up"—both of the bronze serpent and of Jesus— occurs at the instigation of God; by these divine actions, people live.

Not every reference in the fourth Gospel to The Story carries quite as much punch as this section of chapter 3. In the following chapter, for instance, the narrator notes that Jesus stopped one day at a location "near the plot of ground that Jacob had given to his son Joseph. Jacob's well was there" (John 4:5b; see Gen 33:19). There are references in John to Jewish festivals (John 2:23; 7:2; 10:22; 13:1) and to Jerusalem (John 7:25; 11:18) that do not necessarily serve as major elements of a story line. Still, a watchful reader will detect fingerprints, shadows, and echoes of The Story throughout this document. Mention of "prophet" or "the prophets" appears in several places (e.g., John 1:21; 4:19; 6:45; 7:40; 9:17; 8:52). Abraham was the subject of one of Jesus' livelier conversations (John 8:31–59). Mention of "scripture" or "the scriptures" appears eleven times, four of which occur during the crucifixion chapter.

> **Pause to Reflect**
> Have you ever witnessed an unexpected, dramatic event in the company of other people? What was it like to talk with them about what they saw happen? Did everyone emphasize the same details? If not, what do you suppose would account for the variations?

DARKNESS—AND THEN LIGHT

Indeed, it is in the telling of the events of Jesus' final meal, betrayal, arrest, trial, crucifixion, burial, and the empty-tomb scene that the fourth Gospel shares more with the other three Gospels than anywhere else. John still tends to narrate these events in its own particular way, however, showing much less reliance on a common source than the other three. It is impossible to understand the gravity and significance of Jesus as Messiah to The One Great Story without considering these recalled events. Let us therefore take a look at the sweep of them in Mark, Matthew, and John (Mark 14–16; Matt 26–28; John 18–20).

For one thing, these scenes and actions in all three move in a similar pattern. Jesus and his closest followers (including the twelve) shared the Passover meal together at night. From there, they went to a garden where, in the other two versions, Jesus prayed while the disciples couldn't stay awake. Then Judas—one of Jesus' inner circle of twelve—showed up there, accompanied by soldiers and Jewish officials. Jesus was arrested in that garden and taken to the Jewish high priest. Another one of Jesus' inner circle, Peter, was shadowing the movements of the throng and got caught in a situation where he denied, in the presence of others, that he knew Jesus. After being grilled and beaten in the presence of the high priest, Jesus was sent to Pilate, the head Roman official for the area.

Pilate found himself in a tough spot. According to the accounts, Jewish officials accused Jesus of stirring up trouble among the People, including a claim to be a king. Pilate seemed reluctant to authorize this request for Jesus' execution, since he could see no reason to do so. Instead, the Roman procurator put the question to the crowd that had gathered, since it was customary for him during Passover to set free one of their own from prison. Stirred up by their own officials, the crowd asked for someone else and for Pilate to put Jesus to death. Caught in a squeeze play, the vexed imperial administrator yielded to their wishes. Jesus was crucified between two thieves and, when he died, his body was claimed by someone named Joseph, who had the body entombed and the tomb sealed with a large boulder. It was Friday night, the beginning of the Jewish Sabbath observance.

Initially, all the Gospels continue following a similar narrative, in their telling of what the earliest Christian traditions remembered about the days *after* Jesus' crucifixion. Early Sunday morning (after Sabbath had passed), some of the women who were part of Jesus' entourage arrived at Jesus' tomb, apparently to complete the burial process for Jesus' body. They were stunned to find that Jesus was not there. The versions vary in detail, with messengers reporting that Jesus was alive, and giving instructions about where to meet him. From there, the versions display even more variation:

- *Mark's* shorter ending (16:1–8) has the women leaving in dumbfounded silence; then its longer ending briefly mentions some appearances of Jesus to disbelieving followers before Jesus tells them to "proclaim the good news to the whole creation" (16:15).

- *Matthew* tells of a deal made by Jewish officials to report the empty tomb as a case of body snatching (28:11–15); in the final episode, Jesus meets the eleven (Judas was out of the picture by then, although only Matthew mentions his demise [27:3–10]) and authorizes them to preach, teach, and baptize to "all nations" (28:16–20).

- *John's* telling is more elaborate: after appearing to Mary during her second morning visit to the empty tomb, Jesus appeared that night among his followers in a closed room; he "breathed on them" to receive the Holy Spirit (20:22–23); a week later, he appeared there again and showed "doubting Thomas" his crucifixion scars: "You believe because you have seen me? Blessed are those who have not seen and yet have come to believe" (20:29). Following a short paragraph that feels like an ending, chapter 21 adds three more scenes, all set on the beach of Lake Tiberias—the fishing disciples, following Jesus' suggestion, hauling in a huge catch, then eating breakfast with him (21:1–14); Jesus giving Peter instructions to "feed my sheep" (21:15–20); and some final comments about Peter and another disciple (21: 21–23).

In these final chapters of the fourth Gospel, we can see a few more echoes and images from the Hebrew Bible. Most of them are linked to specific moments that John sees as "fulfilling" the specific reference (19:24 quotes Ps 22:18; 19:28–29 refers to Ps 69:21; 19:36 could refer to Exod 12:46; 19:37 quotes part of Zech 12:10). As with other Hebrew Bible quotations or allusions in the other Gospels, these few "proof texts" add credence to John's overall, initial claim—namely, that

> And the Word became flesh and lived among us,
> and we have seen his glory (John 1:14ab) [so that]
> . . . to all who received him, who believed his name,
> [God] gave power to become children of God, . . . (John 1:12)

This unique recounting of Jesus' life, ministry, death, and resurrection accomplishes what each one of the other three Gospel accounts accomplishes: it testifies to the realization of divine purpose, one that opens up a new era of God's way with humanity. The One Great Story arrives at a watershed moment. All four Gospels argue, in their own ways, that the ancient Promise of People, covenant, land, and blessing reaches a turning point because of Jesus. What all of this Promise now will look like receives clues at the end of each Gospel; they are clues that depend on following the call of the One who is now known as Savior.

All four Gospels argue, in their own ways, that the
ancient Promise of People, covenant, land, and blessing
reaches a turning point because of Jesus.

But wait! We have referred at times in this chapter to four Gospels, yet we have considered only three of them. What about the other one—what about Luke?

In the next chapter, we will begin by hearing a summary of Luke's "take" on the Jesus-Story. What makes Luke particularly unique is that, in all likelihood, it was put together by the same author/editor who is responsible for another unique New Testament document. The book known as "The

Acts of the Apostles" clearly picks up where Luke leaves off, as it provides an energetic and dramatic recounting of life in The Story after Jesus. From here, The Story spreads in a new way, with joys, challenges, and threats. Let's see how Luke-Acts helps us get inside this major transition.

FOR THE READER

1. Why do you think Mark's account about Jesus moves so quickly? Why does it show Jesus telling people not to speak of declarations about himself (3:12, 8:30) or healings that Jesus performed (5:43, 7:36, 9:9)?

2. How would Matthew's indirect association of Jesus with Moses have appealed to early generations of Jesus who listened to Matthew's account?

3. Why would the creator of the fourth Gospel be so interested in making considerable use of the Hebrew Bible if the document's primary audience is Gentile (that is, non-Jewish)?

4. How do Mark, Matthew, and John handle Jesus' resurrection as part of continuing The One Great Story? What do variations in their tellings suggest about what they were interested in emphasizing?

SUGGESTED ACTIVITIES

- Read the Gospel of Mark in one sitting (45–60 minutes) and jot down notes on anything that catches your attention. What impression does Mark give you of Jesus? How does Jesus appear to deal with the traditions of his people?

- Imagine that you were one of Jesus' followers, had watched his crucifixion, then heard about his resurrection. How might you have reacted to the news? What might you have done to help "get the word out"?

- Invite a friend to share with you what she or he knows about Jesus from Mark, Matthew, or John. How does the idea that Jesus "fulfilled prophecy" help, or maybe hinder, an understanding of his role in The One Great Story?

Chapter 9

The Story Spreads

From Jesus to the Earliest Churches

"I too decided,... to write an orderly account for you,... so that you may
know the truth ..."

—LUKE 1:3–4

For a long time now in today's world, we have gotten used to knowing who
wrote what. People who write things usually get their name directly associated with those words; books and articles inevitably come with bylines, and
those who write them typically get paid for their work; the legal world recognizes the concept of "intellectual property"; tens of thousands of books
are published in the United States each year, on subjects both familiar and
eccentric. It would be almost unthinkable for a book to become a best seller
today, if the author or authors were completely unknown to the public.

You know by now that, when considering origins of the books of the
Bible, we are dealing almost entirely with sources and individuals that remain anonymous. This reality is due in no small part to the limited role in
antiquity of writing, compared with the dominance of—and dependence
upon—the spoken word. Most of the books in the Bible include no attribu-
tion of a specific author. Names that are associated with particular books

(for instance, Moses, Samuel, Isaiah, and the four Gospels) tend to reflect more of memory and honor to key figures than to authorship as we know it in our own era. Even named books that include sections of what one particular person was reported to have *said* (like Jeremiah or any one of the Gospels) bear little internal evidence that (especially in the case of the Gospels) the main character actually *wrote down* those words. Not even all the letters that include Paul's name as author are universally accepted as having been dictated by the famous apostle (yes, Paul used scribes for composing his epistles—see Rom 16:22; and compare 2 Thess 3:17).

> *Luke and Acts tell two parts of One Story—first, of the Jesus-Story, and then, of the beginning of the Christian Story.*

When looking at the two New Testament documents under consideration in this chapter, we face a different kind of issue about authorship. There is no way to know for sure who was responsible for these two "books" in the form in which we have inherited them, but there is little doubt that it was the same person. The most obvious (although not the only) reason to come to this conclusion greets the reader at the beginning of the second document; it reads as follows:

> "In the first book, Theophilus, I wrote about all that Jesus did
> and taught from the beginning until the day when he was taken
> up to heaven, . . . "(Acts 1:1–2a)

Who is Theophilus? Again, we don't know, either whether he was an actual person or a general name that the author gave to the readers/listeners to this document. We do know, however, that this name, "Theophilus," appears in another New Testament document—in the introduction to the Gospel that tradition calls "Luke":

> "I too decided, after investigating everything carefully from the
> very first, to write an orderly account for you, most excellent
> Theophilus, so that you may know the truth concerning the
> things about which you have been instructed." (Luke 1:3–4)

This name, "Theophilus," literally means "God-friend." These are the only two places in the Bible—Hebrew or New Testament—where this name is used. It seems pretty clear, then, that both of these documents have a common origin, a link that is flagged by this unusual but fitting name. Luke and Acts tell two parts of One Story—first, of the Jesus-Story, and then, of the beginning of the Christian Story. One unnamed author brought together all the details of this pivotal sweep: now, The One Great Story speaks not only of Promise accomplished, but also of that Promise continuing. How Luke tells the Jesus-Story leaves a trail of clues and a theme that reaches clarity in the second document, the one that tradition named "The Acts of the Apostles." We don't know who is responsible for these two documents; nonetheless, they provide absorbing justification that This Story indeed continued.

> **Pause to Reflect**
> What is the most surprising, life-changing message
> that you ever received? Could you have seen it coming?
> How did it change your life? Beyond yourself, what
> other consequences resulted from this message?

TOPSY-TURVY GOSPEL

If Matthew comes across as a book by a Jewish Christian written primarily for Jews and other Jewish Christians, then Luke conveys the flavor of a non-Jewish writer speaking to a wider audience. This distinction does not imply, however, that the content and tone of Luke's version of the Jesus-Story diminishes any possible connections to The One Great Story. Far from it! Even accounting for all the episodes and vignettes that Matthew and Luke share in common (depending on how they are counted, about sixty-one of them), Luke expresses a distinct slant on Jesus and his significance, both to the heirs of Israel and to the world. This distinct slant picks up at the very beginning, after an introduction that reads like histories and biographies of the time, and yet it provides no clues to its topic, let alone its main figure.[15]

What Luke presents immediately following its foreword sets the tenor for the entire book. Characters are introduced who remind us of common, genuinely pious characters in the Old Testament—characters like Abraham and Sarah (as, for instance, Gen 18), as well as Elkanah and Hannah (1 Sam 1–2). Yet, as common as they might have been, these particular men and women displayed a willing, accepting faith; through them, God's aims could be realized. Like Abraham and Sarah, Zechariah and Elizabeth were old and childless. Like Abraham, Zechariah was visited by a divine messenger and given a promise of a son, who would play a special part in the Divine Promise—"to make ready a people prepared for the Lord" (Luke 1:17c). This son would be John the baptizer, and his mother, Elizabeth, happens (in Luke's telling) to be an older cousin of a young woman named Mary (Luke 1:5–26).

---

15. See Culpepper, "Luke," 39.

Several months later, Mary herself also was visited by a divine messenger and given a promise of a son. According to the messenger, this child's eventual role in the purposes of God would be even more dramatic than John's:

> He will be great, and will be called the Son of the Most High,
> And the Lord God will give to him the throne of this ancestor David.
> He will reign over the house of Jacob forever,
> And of his kingdom there will be no end. (Luke 1:32–33)

Like Hannah centuries before her ("Let your servant find favor in your sight." [1 Sam 1:18a]), Mary yielded to this message ("Here I am, the servant of the Lord; let it be with me according to your word." [Luke 1:38]). Soon after, Mary traveled to see her cousin Elizabeth. The older woman blessed Mary when she arrived, whereupon Mary spoke eloquently, in words that seem deliberately to echo those of Hannah. Consider, for instance, how both songs begin:

> "My heart exults in the Lord;
> my strength is exalted in my God."—Hannah (1 Sam 2:1)
> "My soul magnifies the Lord,
> and my spirit rejoices in God my Savior."—Mary (Luke 1:46b–47)

A little later:

> "Talk no more so very proudly,
> let not arrogance come from your mouth."—Hannah (1 Sam 2:3ab)
> "[The Mighty One] has scattered the proud
> in the thoughts of their hearts."—Mary (Luke 1:51b)

In a verse that affirms God's concern for those in need:

> "those who were hungry are fat with spoil."—Hannah (1 Sam 2:5b)
> "[God] has filled the hungry with good things."—Mary (Luke 1:53a)

Then, in a parallel that begins to highlight—by a contrast—one of Luke's major themes:

> "[The LORD] raises up the poor from the dust;
> [and] lifts the needy from the ash heap,
> to make them sit with princes,
> and inherit a seat of honor."—Hannah (1 Sam 2:8)
> "[God] has brought down the powerful from their thrones,
> and lifted up the lowly, . . . and sent the rich empty away."—Mary (Luke 1:52, 53b)

The themes and language between Hannah's and Mary's songs show a theological affinity to which Luke seems to point—that God will take care of those in society who struggle the most (the poor and lowly). Yet in this final pair of quotations above, Hannah's song suggests no criticism of royal politics, whereas Mary's seems pretty clear that it does. Still, Mary's song concludes by remembering—even claiming—the old, old pledge that anchors the Hebrew Bible:

> "[God] has helped [this] servant Israel,
> in remembrance of [God's] mercy,
> according to the promise [God] made to our ancestors,
> to Abraham and to his descendants forever." (Luke 1:54–55)

God's great goal for the world will become possible because of ordinary, everyday people who demonstrate faithful willingness to God.

This contrast between the Promise and "the powerful/their thrones" tips off the reader of Luke to where this telling of the Jesus-Story is headed. What God is going to do through Jesus will have the effect—even the purpose—of reversing what the world values about status and power. The blessing to all nations that had been promised a very long time ago (Gen 12:1–3; 17:1–22) will not be established through—or benefit—human institutions of power and might; rather, God's great goal for the world will become possible because of ordinary, everyday people who demonstrate faithful willingness to God. This point is expressed even more surprisingly through women characters: we saw some of them in early episodes of The Story (like Rahab, Ruth, and Hannah), and now we are introduced to later ones—Elizabeth and Mary. In the male-dominated world of antiquity, this aspect of these vignettes was not lost on their early audiences!

THE STORY THROUGHOUT LUKE

Luke's early scenes also indicate that this action of God-in-Jesus would flow right out of the ancient Promise that traces all the way back to Abraham. By the time that this Gospel tells of John the Baptizer's birth (Luke 1:57–66), of his father Zechariah's prophetic song (Luke 1:67–79), of Jesus' birth and announcement by shepherds (Luke 2:1–20), of his presentation as a baby in the Jerusalem Temple (Luke 2:22–38), and of his parents' scare when the twelve-year-old Jesus stayed behind in the Temple after Passover (Luke 2:41–51), the stage had been set. God's ancient covenant would be maintained, its blessing was coming—in a way that would startle perhaps everyone and certainly disgruntle many.

Like Matthew, Luke is much longer than Mark and contains many images, phrases, and quotations from the Hebrew Bible. One of the more prominent of these quotations appears at the beginning of Jesus' ministry and sets the stage for the tension that he experienced throughout it. Jesus attended the synagogue one Sabbath in his hometown (Nazareth) and was given a scroll from which to read. Luke says that Jesus found a particular passage, read it aloud, rolled up the scroll, and sat down (Luke 4:16–21). The passage was from Isaiah (as Luke indicates), and it speaks of someone who will bear the LORD's Spirit, to bring healing and release for impoverished and browbeaten people. When Jesus started to explain that those words were coming to pass, the people there responded favorably to him.

However, when they started asking about his family ties, Jesus didn't leave well enough alone. He reminded them of a couple of episodes from The Story, first during Elijah's ministry, at a time of great famine. In spite of all the need among his own people, Elijah "was sent to none of them" but instead to a non-Israelite, and a widow to boot (Luke 4:25–26)! Similarly, Jesus continued, Elijah's successor Elisha could have healed many leprous Israelites but instead healed a Syrian military officer (Luke 4:27). These comments infuriated everyone in the synagogue, who then ran Jesus out and were preparing to throw him off a cliff (Luke 4:28)!

As you might guess, Jesus escaped safely from the mob, but this scene (along with the birth-childhood scenes) served to put Luke's readers on notice. Not only was Jesus a unique person with a mission that linked him to the ancient covenant Promise; Jesus also understood The Story well and was not afraid to tell even the parts of it that his own people might not have wanted to hear. Luke emphasizes that Jesus continued a preaching ministry throughout his Jewish homeland (Luke 4:42–44). Yet his ministry ruffled feathers among religious officials of his people—as evidenced by Jesus' encounter with Pharisees and teachers over forgiveness and healing of a paralyzed man (Luke 5:17–26) and his healing of a crippled woman on the Sabbath (Luke 13:10–17). As part of his appeal for the legitimacy of healing the crippled woman, Jesus called her "a daughter of Abraham."

Jesus' appropriation in Luke of his People's Story also can be found woven into his parables. Luke recorded that Jesus once told a story about a rich man and a poor, sick man, both of whom died. The poor man, Lazarus, "was carried away by the angels to be with Abraham" (Luke 16:22a), whereas the rich man ended up in the anguish of Hades. That rich man then pleaded with Abraham for mercy, but the patriarch reminded the rich man that his request was not possible. Then the rich man asked Abraham to send Lazarus to alert his five brothers: " . . . if someone goes to them from the dead, they will repent" (Luke 16:30). Abraham's reply to the rich man's plea both echoes traditions from Their Story and anticipates where the story of Jesus was going: "If they do not listen to Moses and the prophets, neither will they be convinced even if someone rises from the dead" (Luke 16:31).

> *Jesus' appropriation in Luke of his People's Story*
> *also can be found woven into his parables.*

To its very end, the Gospel of Luke connects Jesus to The Story. After Jesus was executed and buried, some of his female followers showed up at his tomb but discovered with great fright that Jesus was not there (Luke 24:1–12). The risen Jesus' first appearance in Luke occurred later that day, on a road outside Jerusalem, as two of his followers were walking to a village known as Emmaus (Luke 24:13–27). Jesus approached them but was not recognized as the three traveled and talked about the events that began that morning with the women at the tomb. Remaining incognito, Jesus eventually spoke to them, as though they already should have figured things out. Patiently, however, Jesus explained it all to them: "Then beginning with Moses and all the prophets, he interpreted to them the things about himself in all the scriptures" (Luke 24:27).

> **Pause to Reflect**
> See if you can recall something that you understood a certain
> way when you were younger, and now you understand it
> differently. What changed, that led to your new awareness?
> How has this new understanding affected your life?

Note here the word "interpreted." It is an unusual verb for the New Testament, *diermeneuo*, used only five times—once here in Luke and four times in one of Paul's letters. There, the apostle was addressing questions in a congregation about certain worship practices—namely, that some worshippers would be moved to "speak in tongues," that is, utter sounds in the form of speech but were unintelligible. Paul emphasized that, when this kind of speaking occurred, someone needed to "interpret" what was said, to explain its meaning (1 Cor 14:5–27).

This emphasis upon the need for explanation also comes through in the road to Emmaus story, although the subject of the explanation clearly is different. For Jesus in Luke, the issue centered on understanding where—and how—in the Hebrew Bible his coming and mission was anticipated. Those connections were there, Luke's Jesus claims, and he chided his traveling companions for not seeing them: "O how foolish you are, and how slow of heart to believe all that the prophets declared" (Luke 24:25)! He had to *interpret* it for them, *explain* how The Story leads up to him.

With Mark, this Gospel shares reporting an event that sets the stage for answering the big question, "Now what?" That event has been known for centuries as "the ascension" since, in Mark, Jesus left the earth to join God:

> So then the Lord Jesus, after he had spoken to them,
> was taken up into heaven and sat down at the right hand of God.
> (Mark 16:19)

In certain of the earliest versions of Luke also, Jesus also "ascends" into heaven (Luke 24:51), although no details are provided here or in Mark. What makes Luke even more noteworthy, however, are its many connections to the book that tradition named The Acts of the Apostles. One of those connections is a second report of Jesus' ascension which, here, includes his unexpected appearance in the midst of his apostles, with "two men in white robes" asking them what they are doing, staring up into the sky (Acts 1:9–11a). This version of the ascension incident follows a brief summary explaining that Jesus hung around with his apostles for a period of time, performing "many convincing proofs" and talking about God's realm (Acts 1:3).

So, now what? Well, Luke set the stage for answering this palpable question even before mentioning Jesus' ascension. During his days with the apostles after his resurrection, Jesus hinted that something exceptional would occur soon—so they needed to stay in Jerusalem to wait for it (Acts 1:4–5). What would it be? The answer: a gift, from above, Jesus said—a gift implied to be greater than the baptism of John the Baptist (Acts 1:5).

TURNING UP THE ENERGY

It is at this point, as the Luke-Acts tradition begins to continue The One Great Story beyond Jesus of Nazareth, that an element of That Story moves from just inside its perimeter to center stage. We have seen, over and over again, how the People had been claimed by a Divine Presence that they came to know as "the LORD (*YHWH*: 'I will be who I will be')." As the generations and centuries passed, the People's telling of their Story gradually—unevenly, even subtly—expresses an awareness of this Presence as more than one deity among many. By the time that prophets during the monarchy and exile spoke, this Presence began to be affirmed, not just as their local god, but as the Creator God. Surely, we see this shift in the first two chapters of Genesis, during the creation accounts. There and afterward, furthermore, one of the ways in which the Story refers to how this God is active is by using a specialized term, "spirit."

One of the ways in which the Story refers to how this God is active is by using a specialized term, "spirit."

When it is capitalized in English translations, the word "spirit" (*ruach* in Hebrew, *pneuma* in Greek) alludes to the energy of God that makes divine deeds and actions possible. At creation, "a wind from God" or "a spirit of God" moved over "the face of the waters" (Gen 1:2b). When Moses was on the mountain receiving the Ten Words and other instructions, the LORD appointed a fellow named Bezalel to work with another craftsman to construct the vessel to hold the tablets of stone. This Bezalel was "filled . . . with divine spirit (or 'the spirit of God')" (Exod 31:1–2). As was noted in chapter 4, the People's judges were recognized through their deeds as having "the Spirit of the LORD" come upon them (as Judg 3:10), sometimes "taking possession" of the person (as Judg 6:34), sometimes "rushing on" the person (as Judg 14:6, 19; 15:14).

This tradition of recognizing God's Spirit at work in particular people continued through the generations of the monarchy (see 1 Sam 10:10, 16:13, 19:20; 1 Kgs 22:24; 2 Kgs 2:16), including the prophets who spoke of national doom and calling for a return of trusting only in the LORD (as Isa 11:2, 40:13, 61:1). During the exile, the tradition surrounding the prophet Ezekiel is permeated by "spirit" language, both of human and divine. For Ezekiel, the message has become far-reaching: it is the Spirit of the LORD that will bring life back to a People who have all but died (see, for instance, Ezek 37:1–14); indeed, in this collection of oracles and visions, divine spirit is mentioned fourteen times. Other prophets echo Ezekiel's conviction (see Joel 2:28; Mic 3:8; Hag 2:5; Zech 4:6).

Now, as we consider how The Story develops through the testimony of the Acts of the Apostles, we discover "the Spirit" at every turn. Some even might argue that this ancient document would be more accurately named, "the Acts of the Holy Spirit"—since use of the word "spirit" for God appears in the Acts a whopping fifty-seven times, an average of twice every single chapter! For this writer, what makes possible the continuation of The Story in the absence of a physical Jesus is the dynamic presence of God's Spirit among the Messiah's followers. By themselves, ancient instruction, law, and ritual—although understood as having divine purpose on behalf of the People's covenant with the LORD—are incomplete, apart from recognizing and accepting the presence and activity of the Spirit. It is not too much to say that this is one of the Acts of the Apostles's major contributions to The Story: through Jesus the Messiah, God's Spirit becomes the dynamic companion of those who follow Jesus.

> *Through Jesus the Messiah, God's Spirit becomes the*
> *dynamic companion of those who follow Jesus.*

Acts makes this point early in the book, as Jesus' followers do what Jesus told them, by staying and waiting in Jerusalem for "the promise of the Father" (Acts 1:4b). First, though, the remaining eleven men whom Jesus had chosen early in his ministry as his inner circle cast lots to replace Judas Iscariot, the one from among the twelve who had betrayed Jesus to the officials (Acts 1:21–26). The number twelve remained a significant symbol from the early episodes of The Story: Jacob/Israel's twelve sons create the twelve tribes of the Promise. Once Jesus' remaining eleven made the selection, the stage was set—and, once again, a very early episode echoes, this time turning on its head.

> **Pause to Reflect**
> What kind of special moment have you experienced,
> that you could call "spiritual?" What happened? How
> long did it last? Why would you consider it spiritual?
> What kind of lasting effects has it had on you?

Acts revs up The Story by telling how Jesus' followers received the Holy Spirit during a Jewish festival that drew Jews from all corners of the known world. If we focus only on what might appear strange to us—namely, that Jesus' followers began speaking in languages that they did not know—we likely will miss the point. Their sudden ability to "speak in other tongues" occurred in the hearing of people who spoke those languages in their own homelands. Too, what all of them heard, from these backwater Galileans, were proclamations of their God at work in the world, "speaking about God's deeds of power" (Acts 2:11b). This fully unexpected phenomenon grabbed the attention of these devout pilgrims and prompted what Acts presents as the first Christian sermon.

Before we consider how that sermon sets the stage in Acts for The One Great Story, do you remember another incident from farther back, in which the world's human population was scattered? The "Tower of Babel" episode (Gen 11:1–9) follows the dramatic sequence with Noah and the flood and then earth's resettlement. The people (here unnamed) started building a city and a tower, with lofty aspirations—in their minds, the sky was the limit! But the LORD did not like the looks of things, seeing that humans were seeking to reach beyond their place as creatures of God. So God sent them every which way, making it impossible for the various new groups of people to understand each other's languages. Being unable to communicate with each other serves as a biblical symbol of what went wrong with humanity a long time ago and of the consequences that seemed, over many centuries, impossible to overcome.

. . . and then there was the Day of Pentecost, in which the barriers of language were shattered and those who were scattered could share in a wondrous announcement. Acts now presents Simon Peter—who in the Gospels appeared impulsive and cowardly—as a confident, eloquent, learned preacher! Here, Peter (this name is based on the Greek word, *petros*, "rock"; see Luke 6:14) begins what will become for the rest of the New Testament a "connecting of dots," between The One Great Story that the People already know (as their heritage) and the witness of Jesus the Messiah.

"THE ROCK" BECOMES ONE

Peter began by assuring his audience that what they were hearing was prophesied centuries earlier, as a sign that the fullness of God's purposes for all of humanity would be coming to fruition:

> In the last days it will be, God declares,
> that I will pour out my Spirit on all flesh, . . .
> Then everyone who calls on the name of the Lord
> shall be saved. (Acts 2:17ab, 21, from Joel 2:28–32)

Then Peter quoted from three passages in the Psalms (16:8–11; 132:1; 110:1) to support his argument that Jesus' life, death, and resurrection has realized God's intentions for the long-chosen People. The apostle concluded his sermon without any ambiguity on this point:

> "Therefore let the entire house of Israel know with certainty
> that God has made him both Lord and Messiah, this Jesus . . ." (Acts 2:36)

From this point on, Peter serves as a central figure through the first half of Acts. He preached again to another crowd of Jews, apparently somewhere in Jerusalem, appealing to "the God of Abraham, the God of Isaac, and the God of Jacob, the god of our ancestors" (Acts 3:13). Peter also argued then that the "holy prophets" (Acts 3:21) anticipated the coming of the Messiah, that even Moses (Acts 3:22) and Samuel (Acts 3:24) spoke of his coming. The bold, new apostle included Abraham and the covenant of their ancestors, quoting a verse from the beginning of The Story that has guided our entire study in this book: "And in your descendants all the families of the earth shall be blessed" (Acts 3:25). This is more than an echo! It comes straight from the call of Abram, 'way back in Genesis—the episode that kicks off the journey leading all the way to Jesus and beyond.

Peter serves as a central figure through the first half of Acts.

Dramatic episodes continue in Acts with Peter and his entourage—for a while, anyway. He and a colleague named John healed a crippled man (Acts 3:1–10); the two apostles had an audience with the religious council in Jerusalem, after being arrested for teaching and preaching (Acts 4:1–22); he chastised a woman for lying—and she died! (Acts 5:1–11); he and John were sent to Samaria and prayed with new believers there (Acts 8:24); Peter himself traveled again, healing a paralyzed man in a town called Lydda (Acts 9:32–35) and then being called to nearby Joppa, where he raised a woman disciple from death (Acts 9:36–43).

After receiving a vision during prayer one day, Peter received a respectful summons from a centurion (that is, the officer in charge of a group of foot soldiers in the Roman army)[16] named Cornelius, who himself also had received a vision. Once the two met, Peter realized that the message of Jesus the Messiah was to be shared with Gentiles, too—that is, from nationalities who were not the People of The Story (Acts 10). Peter explained Jesus' life, ministry, crucifixion, and resurrection to Cornelius and his entourage, emphasizing that this message about the man from Nazareth had been anticipated by the biblical prophets (Acts 10:43). Much to the surprise of those in Peter's company, Cornelius's company received the message with great enthusiasm and then was baptized; Peter remained with them for a time (Acts 10:44–48).

When Peter returned to Jerusalem, his colleagues there (believers descended from The Story) had heard already what had happened and were not happy about it. Peter told them the episodes of the two men's visions and of the coming of the Spirit in their midst; then Peter's skeptics changed their minds, declaring praises: "Then God has given even to the Gentiles the repentance that leads to life" (Acts 11:1–18). Later, Peter was put in prison by King Herod, but he escaped at night with the help of a divine messenger

---

16. For a summary of the significant function and role of the centurion office in ancient Rome, see Gealy, "Centurion," 547–48.

and surprised his colleagues when he showed up while they were in a house praying (Acts 12:1–17).

> *The gift of the Holy Spirit, Peter argued, meant that God*
> *did not distinguish between Jews and Gentiles.*

Peter's last appearance in Acts comes during a big powwow that convened in Jerusalem, to discuss whether religious rules that the Jews had observed for centuries were required for Gentiles who followed Jesus (Acts 15). Following a lot of deliberation, Peter spoke to those assembled. He reminded them of the evidence that the Holy Spirit had come to Gentile believers, not just to those of Jewish descent. This gift, Peter argued, meant that God did not distinguish between Jews and Gentiles. The crux of his argument followed:

> "Now therefore why are you putting God to the test
> by placing on the neck of the disciples a yoke
> that neither our ancestors nor we have been able to bear?" (Acts 15:10)

Finally, a character who has been mentioned in Acts but not given much attention is the one who summarized this council's discussion and rendered a judgment. His name is James, and he drew his conclusions after quoting from the Hebrew Bible. According to James, two verses from the prophet Amos, with some massaging, supported the testimony at their council that the LORD of ancient days will make the Promise available to all nations (Jas 15:13–19). James then mentioned four details from the ancient law—things to avoid—that the council would require from Gentile believers (Jas 15:20–21). Through a small group of delegates, the council delivered a letter to the town of Antioch, where it was read to the church there, with a positive reception (Jas 15:22–33).

ELOQUENT MARTYR

As Peter fades from view, another character appears—from out of nowhere. We will follow this new character's activity in Acts in a little bit, but before we do so, we are going to backtrack first. The longest presentation of material in Acts that draws from The One Great Story occurs in an earlier episode, that—at its very end—introduces the man who dominates the second half of this book. This earlier episode centers around yet another character who is remembered for his active faith—and for his martyrdom. His name was Stephen, who was set up by some scheming religious leaders and forced to appear before its council on false charges (Acts 6:9–15).

Asked by the high priest to defend himself, Stephen recited an overview of The Story itself (Acts 7:2–51), beginning with Abraham leaving his home country and receiving "the covenant of circumcision" (Acts 7:8a) from God. Stephen then noted Isaac and Jacob, Jacob's sons, and Joseph's role in saving his family by bringing them to Egypt, the circumstances of Moses' birth and upbringing, Moses' murder of an Egyptian and flight to Midian, the burning bush call from God to return to Egypt, the People's escape from Egypt and the Red Sea and wilderness wanderings, the "living oracles" (Acts 7:38c) at Mount Sinai, the People's calf of gold and worship of idols, carrying "the tent of testimony" (Acts 7:44) with the Ten Words (the "living oracles") in it into the land that God gave them, and David's desire to build a temple that Solomon later built.

Stephen's speech ended with a critique of their ancestors, who Stephen claimed missed the point of their calling from God. He already had quoted from the prophet Amos a passage that criticized the People for worshipping things that are not God (Acts 7:42–43). As he prepared to call them a "stiff-necked people" (Acts 7:51a), Stephen first quoted from the Book of Isaiah to underscore the point that "the Most High does not dwell in houses made with human hands" (Acts 7:48). He went on to accuse them of being responsible for killing Jesus ("the Righteous One" [Acts 7:52b]) and finished by declaring, in no uncertain terms that

"You are the ones that received the law as ordained by angels,
and yet you have not kept it." (Acts 7:53)

Pause to Reflect
For what would you be willing to sacrifice
your life? To what purpose?

This was more than the religious authorities were willing to bear! They accosted Stephen, taking him outside the city walls, and stoned him to death (Acts 7:57–60). According to Acts, one of the witnesses to his stoning was "a young man named Saul" (Acts 7:58b). This "Saul" was a zealous Jew, a Pharisee and Roman citizen, whose own life was to change soon and dramatically. Saul was intent on finding and prosecuting Christians. On one of his travels to search for "any who belonged to the Way" (Acts 9:2b), he received a vision of Jesus as Lord and soon became one of his ardent followers (Acts 9:1–22). Before long, Saul returned to Jerusalem and met the apostles there, convincing them of his newfound zeal and mission for the Savior (Acts 9:26–28).

A SINGULAR CALLING

Saul's ministry as reported in the Acts is filled with much travel—hundreds of miles by sea and by land, across many parts of the Roman Empire. Saul became better known in Gentile circles by his Greek-style name, "Paul." He faced a number of challenging circumstances, such as physical harm, arrest, imprisonment, and dangerous traveling conditions. In the Acts, Paul comes across—in a manner similar to Peter in earlier chapters—as confident and eloquent. His longest recorded speech here addresses, as with Stephen, a Jewish audience—in this case, in a synagogue that was located hundreds of miles northwest of Judea, in Antioch of Pisidia, a Greco-Roman region. This location means that the Jews there had relocated generations earlier from their homeland.

Throughout his ministry, Paul traveled hundreds of miles by sea and by land, across many parts of the Roman Empire.

Like Stephen, Paul's speech to this particular group within the Diaspora (that is, Jewish communities that existed in other countries, mostly because of conquest)[17] drew upon key highlights from The Story. He began by referring to the divine selection of the People, of their time in Egypt and escape from it, and of their years in the wilderness (Acts 13:17–18). The land, judges, Samuel, the first King Saul, and then King David all are part of Paul's concise recitation (Acts 13:19–22). From there, Paul made two big moves in his speech, into new parts of The Story of which he had become a messenger. First, Paul claimed that Jesus was God's Savior who was promised long ago to come from David's lineage (Acts 13:23); second, he claimed (as do all four Gospels) that John the Baptist spoke during his own ministry of one coming who was greater than John (Acts 13:24–25). Paul spoke to his audience in the synagogue as "you descendants of Abraham's family" (Acts 13:26a) as he continued, stating that Jesus was unfairly treated, condemned, killed, taken "down from the tree" (Acts 13:29b), and laid to rest (Acts 13:27–29).

> **Pause to Reflect**
> Think about a time in your life when you were upset because someone who you didn't like got to be part of something that was important to you. How did they get "in" even though you had expected them to stay "out?" How did you respond? Did your mind ever change? Why or why not?

17 A brief but informative explanation of the Jewish "diaspora" can be found in Sanders, "Dispersion," 854–56.

Paul's connecting of Jesus to The Story did not stop there—as we might expect that it would not. He moved immediately to declare Jesus' resurrection and many appearances "from Galilee to Jerusalem" (Acts 13:31). This, Paul proclaimed to those in the synagogue, was not only "good news," it was good because it accomplished a promise that God had made to their ancestors. To support this grand assertion, the apostle quoted verses from two psalms (2:7, 16:10) and a prophetic book (Isa 55:3). As a result of what God did through Jesus, Paul then argued, descendants of The People were free from sin in a way that "the law of Moses" did not make possible. His speech ended with a warning to his listeners, that they not miss accepting the surprising act of God in Jesus—an act to which yet another prophetic verse spoke:

> "... for in your days I am doing a work,
> a work that you will never believe,
> even if someone tells you." (Hab 1:5)

Unlike with Stephen's experience, many of Paul's listeners (both Jewish and converts—that is, Gentile believers) responded positively, asking him to return and speak again the following week (Acts 13:42–43). When he did so—with his companion Barnabas—he was met with a jealous cadre of religious officials, who spoke against the two before the throngs. In response, Paul and Barnabas made a dramatic statement about who was to hear the message that they proclaimed. Clearly, most of the earliest believers in Jesus as Messiah, as followers of "the Way" (see Acts 9:2, 19:19, and 22:4) were Jewish—that is, inheritors of The Promise—but some were rebuffing the message. Paul and Barnabas took the opportunity to respond to the resistance of Antioch's religious authorities, by quoting a passage from Isaiah. They saw in this text an expectation of God reaching beyond the People themselves and into all the world:

> "I have set you to be a light for the Gentiles,
> so that you may bring salvation to the ends of the earth." (Isa 49:6)

Paul and Barnabas told the crowd that this centuries-old passage anticipated their mission: "we are now turning to the Gentiles" (Acts 13:46d). It was a word well-received by the non-Jews in the audience, as resistance by the authorities eventually led to the two missionaries leaving Pisidia (Acts 13:50).

The tide was turning. Paul and company dominate the rest of the Acts, as they visited one region after another, preaching, teaching, healing, and strengthening new assemblies of those who would follow Jesus. Most of their ministry, as the incident in Antioch reveals, was with Gentiles, communities of "nations" that were not part of the ancient Promise—in provinces like Pamphylia, Lycia, Mysia, Crete, Macedonia, and Achaia. Paul is remembered to have escaped from prison (Acts 16:16–40), debated with Greek philosophers (Acts 17:16–34), survived a riot (Acts 19:21–41), been arrested in the Jerusalem Temple (Acts 21:27–36), sent to first one—and then another—Roman regional ruler (Acts 23:23—24:23; 25:13—26:32), and held in custody for long periods of time.

On his way to Rome, under Roman guard, the ship on which Paul was traveling hit a storm and was wrecked, but with no loss of life (Acts 27). Later, when Paul finally arrived in Rome, he lived under house arrest, although persuading local Jewish officials to allow him to speak to them (Acts 28:16–22). He spent a long day with a large gathering, drawing upon both "the law of Moses and the prophets" to persuade them that Jesus was part of the Story of "the kingdom of God (Acts 28:23)." Their response was mixed; one more time, then, Paul quoted one of the ancient prophets (again, Isaiah) as he watched his visitors depart. His point in using the passage was the same as when Paul and Barnabas faced contentious religious officials in Antioch. Here is some of what he quoted to them in Rome:

> For this people's heart has grown dull, . . .
> and they have shut their eyes, so that they
> might not look . . . and listen . . . and understand . . .
> and turn—and I would heal them. (Acts 28:26–27)

His final comment to those religious officials that day was that Gentiles would receive word of the Promise—because the inheritors of that Promise would not listen and change their hearts (Acts 26–28:28).

TESTAMENT OF A BELIEVER

And so this striking and remarkable witness to the early movement that arose following Jesus' resurrection comes to an end. The author of these two documents that we know as "Luke" and "Acts of the Apostles" provided a carefully prepared testimony to what Christians see as two major chapters of The Story. When it comes to understanding the transition between the Old and New Testaments, we cannot underestimate the value of what these books contribute.

Unlike many of the other previous characters in The Story, Paul did not give a long speech and series of blessings on his deathbed and then give up the ghost. Instead, the Acts leaves Paul in Rome, busy, receiving visitors (still under house arrest), and doing what he seems to have loved doing most— "proclaiming the kingdom of God and teaching about the Lord Jesus Christ with all boldness and without hindrance" (Acts 28:30–31). It is an active, vigorous picture at the end of this unique narrative. Surely, one of its primary purposes was to demonstrate that The Story was continuing—perhaps at last fulfilling that oldest of calls, from Abram's days, to become a People from whom all peoples would live in the blessing of the Creator. Early hearers of the Acts very likely would have been startled by various elements of its accounts—which elements, depending on whether the particular listeners were descendants of The Promise or not. Ideological tension between long-established practices tied to the ancient covenant(s) and Paul's mission to Gentile communities remains to the very end of this ancient two-part document. That probably is not accidental, even though it could be possible to overlook evidence of that tension due to all the other, sometimes eye-popping, nail-biting, or mind-boggling incidents that occur throughout its chapters.

The People of the Promise had faced a number of significant shifts across the centuries. With Jesus and his followers, another shift began, another world of interpreting Their Story was opening up.

We would not be reading too much (if at all) into the encounters of Peter, Stephen, and Paul in Acts by saying that they saw something in The One Great Story that some persons in their own religious tradition did not see. When we look closely, it is almost always (as with Jesus in the Gospels) religious and civil officials who took issue with how these earliest of Christian missionaries connected dots between the People's Story and Jesus. Those who perceive that they might have the most to lose are likely to oppose something new. Still, we cannot escape the question of how The Story is to be interpreted from one era to another—or, for that matter, what constitutes a shift from one era to another. The People of the Promise had faced a number of significant shifts across the centuries. With Jesus and his followers, another shift began, another world of interpreting Their Story was opening up.

In the next chapter, we will consider how a few of the other writings in the New Testament deal with interpreting The Story in their own ways. Some of these writings seem to address audiences of People from the Covenant, while other writings imply a Greco-Roman audience. As this chapter shows, the world of the New Testament was dominated by an empire, this one based on Rome. Rome represented a complex culture that differed drastically from that of The People. Yet any appeal by the Messiah's followers—whether of the Covenant or of Rome—necessarily drew upon the resources of The Story. By now, we can appreciate that This Story continued to develop and speak a telling word to all kinds of communities, whatever their circumstances. Let us now listen to some of those witnesses.

FOR THE READER

1. Why do you think it was important to Luke that his audience hear in Mary's experience of divine promise some echoes of praise and hope from Hannah's ancient episode?

2. What does Luke's Jesus seem to be communicating about the nature and purpose of his tradition's Story?

3. How does Peter's experience with Cornelius the centurion foreshadow the rest of the Book of Acts?

4. What do Peter's, Stephen's, and Paul's speeches share in common from The One Great Story?

SUGGESTED ACTIVITIES

• Read 1 Sam 2:26 and 3:19–21 and then read Luke 1:80 (about John) and Luke 2:40 and 52 (about Jesus). Why do you think Luke hinted at parallels between the boy Samuel and the boy Jesus?

• Again using an edition of the Bible with maps, find the one that shows all the places that Paul traveled on his missionary voyages. There were three of them, plus his trip to Rome, the imperial capital. What do those distances and destinations suggest to you about Paul's motivation as an apostle?

• Read Stephen's speech in Acts 7:1–53. How fair do you think is Stephen's criticism of his ancestors' lack of faith? To what evidence would you point to support your answer?

• Ask a church-type friend what they can recall about the Book of Acts; then talk about what impressions you have about it from reading this chapter. See how your conversation develops—what kinds of insights and questions come up between you two?

Chapter 10

One Story, Many Audiences

"... so, you see, those who believe are the descendants of Abraham."

—GAL 3:7

Back in the day (not that very long ago!), there was no such thing as NetFlix, Twitter, YouTube, Facebook, smart phones, digital cameras, videotape recording, Polaroid pictures, television, celluloid motion pictures, radios, or telegrams. For even more perspective, consider this: the printing press was invented hardly more than 500 years ago; it made possible the mass publication of tracts, leaflets, books, journals, and magazines. Throughout most of human history, most people had basically only one way of conveying specific, detailed information—by speaking, talking, and telling (and its variations in poetry and music). Later, if your society had developed some version of writing, then this new form of communication would have been limited to only a very small percentage of people—usually those in charge of things.

Most writing in antiquity was not personal, but rather was used for economic, legal, and governmental purposes—edicts, property sales, judicial rulings, and the like. The ancient evidence for writing suggests that persons who were literate and could afford the materials for writing—or for hiring someone to take dictation—possessed some degree of standing in their communities. They would have had something that others in their world were expected to hear.

Obviously, by the time of Jesus, a large body of written material had been accumulated by those within the Hebrew/Israelite/Jewish tradition. We have seen in chapters 8 and 9 how, over time, a number of those writings had taken on a special status with the People of The Promise. These recognized writings became for the People *tas graphas* "the scriptures" (see, for example, Matt 21:42; Mark 12:24; Luke 24:27; John 5:39; Acts 17:2). The New Testament writers drew from what Christians call "the Old Testament" to relate their storytelling to That Greater Story which preceded, and now incorporated, theirs.

"DEAR _____; YOURS TRULY, _____"

There is something about the New Testament as a whole, however, that makes its storytelling more distinctive in style. The New Testament includes documents that take the form of a *letter*. We can tell that they are letters often from the introductions, in which the author usually identifies himself (it appears that they all were men) and then greets the audience, after identifying its location. Even more, the letter style is evident at the end of these documents, in which the author gives advice—traditionally termed "exhortations"—to the listeners about how they are to conduct themselves as believers. Thus, for the most part, the letters in the New Testament were intended to be read to a community of people, not only one person. For this reason, Christian tradition typically has used the term "epistle (from the Greek word *epistole*)" for these documents.[18] An epistle was a letter sent by a recognized spiritual leader, to a particular community, in order to encourage and strengthen its faith and witness.

An epistle was a letter sent by a spiritual leader, in order to strengthen and encourage the believing community.

As the earliest Christians began to make sense out of the dramatic, new twist to The One Great Story, no one was more prolific at writing letters about it than *the apostle Paul*. We met Paul in chapter 9, as the primary character in the second half of the Acts of the Apostles, which recounts Paul's

18. For a general explanation of biblical letters, see Seitz, "Letter," 113–15. More detail is available in Wall, "Introduction to Epistolary Literature," 369–91.

journeys into lands beyond, to "the Gentiles," all the nations that were not directly part of the ancient Promise. In Acts, Paul is shown to be drawing upon the Jewish biblical materials to make a case that The Story reaches out to all peoples. And this is only the beginning of what Paul had to say!

> **Pause to Reflect**
> Have you ever received a letter (email or otherwise)
> from someone who is part of a group that is important
> to you? What was the letter about? What was its
> main purpose and appeal? How did you respond?
> What difference did that letter make to you?

Paul the apostle brought what would have been impressive credentials to his ministry, although he was a late-bloomer. He once referred to himself in this way, as "one untimely born" (1 Cor 15:8), including himself at the end of a list of appearances by the post-resurrection Christ (1 Cor 15:3–9). This list itself is part of what sounds like an early Christian recitation, an extending of The Story:

> For I handed on to you as of first importance what I in turn had received: that Christ died for our sins in accordance with the scriptures, . . .
> (1 Cor 15:3)

In other places, Paul mentions that he is descended from the tribe of Benjamin (Jacob's youngest of his twelve sons and Joseph's younger brother) (Rom 11:1) and that he was a Pharisee (Phil 3:5). The latter title refers to a religious Jewish party, one that emerged during the exilic period, five centuries before Jesus. Pharisees were known to uphold strict interpretation of the Hebrew scriptures, to seek perfection in adhering to biblical statutes and ordinances. They also developed a high degree of political influence within ancient Jewish society—influence that always was tempered by, and negotiated with, the empire in charge at the time.[19]

Benjamite, Pharisee, and Roman citizen (see Acts 22), the man "Saul" who became "Paul" carried a status and authority that would have been easily recognized and acknowledged (even if grudgingly!) in his day. He knew that of which he spoke! and when he added "the least of all the apostles" (1 Cor 15:9a) to his résumé, Paul was in a unique position to weave Jesus as Savior into The One Great Story. His knowledge, tradition, and training were the foundation for continuing That Story through the ministry, crucifixion, and resurrection of Jesus of Nazareth.

19. See Black, "Pharisees," 774–81.

The apostle Paul was in a unique position to weave
Jesus as Savior into The One Great Story.

There are twenty-one epistles in the New Testament, of varying lengths and authorship, thirteen of these twenty-one connected to this roving apostle Paul. Scholars pretty much agree that Paul himself is directly responsible (that is, he tended to dictate rather than compose by hand) for Romans, 1 and 2 Corinthians, Galatians, Philippians, 1 and 2 Thessalonians, and Philemon. Five others sound like Paul but might have been written by his followers—Ephesians, Colossians, 1 and 2 Timothy, and Titus.[20] Regardless of one's conclusions about the nuances of authorship, the entire "Pauline corpus" is loaded with images, references, and echoes of The Story that were central to his earlier religious training. We also discover in Paul a few key ways in which elements of the fledgling Jesus-Story are employed as part of The Ancient Story itself—readily incorporated into its flow.

Ample evidence of Paul's appropriation of The Story appears in two of his most well-known (and longest!) missives: one was addressed to a congregation in the imperial capital and the other, his first letter to a congregation in the Greek city of Corinth.

IN THE CENTER OF EMPIRE

Shadows of empires cast broadly and imposingly over much of the history that the Bible covers, and the New Testament is no exception. Long before Jesus' time, the Roman Empire had dominated all of the Mediterranean region and, in places, far beyond it. Everyone who lived under its political organization and rule had to come to terms, in one way or another, with life as a Roman subject. Communities who claimed faith through a religion other than the official state Roman religion[21] took a big risk over their resources and very lives.

There is no clear direct evidence about who actually was part of the congregation in Rome to whom Paul wrote: were they all Gentiles, all Jews, or a mixture of persons from both backgrounds? The way in which Paul develops his theological argument implies that the congregation in the Empire's capital city included Christians who were both Gentiles and Jews. That alone would have created practical challenges concerning religious

20. A brief discussion of authorship among the New Testament epistles can be found in Wall, "Introduction to Epistolary Literature," 369–70.

21. A brief discussion of the development of religion before and during the Roman Empire is found in Grant, "Roman religion," 109–12.

practices, not even to mention the basic question about the value of Jewish texts and traditions, in light of Jesus.[22] If the promises of God are for "all the families of the earth" (as Gen 12:3), then what use are the sacred Jewish traditions, represented by the Hebrew scriptures, for everyone else?

Space here does not permit a detailed answer to this question, but we can be assured that Paul addresses it thoroughly, carefully, and affirmingly (in a qualified way) in his letter to the Roman congregation. Indeed, *Romans* is usually recognized as containing the longest sustained theological argument in the entire Bible. Furthermore, there would have been no way for Paul to mount this argument without drawing incisively upon The One Great Story. For our purposes, we are mainly interested in tracing how Paul pulls this off. In other words, we are not looking for just any Old Testament quotation or reference that Paul includes; instead, we seek to identify places in the letter where he appeals to some element of That Narrative, recalling it for a particular purpose in his line of thought.

GOD'S PURPOSES—AND ISRAEL'S PLACE

Typically, letters written in the Greco-Roman world of Paul's day began with three simple parts—the name of the one sending it, the name(s) of the one receiving it, and a short greeting. Paul often added a touch of his own to letters, a note of thanks, typically for the congregation receiving his letter.[23] However, in Romans, Paul sandwiches within the salutation formula itself a foreshadowing of his main purpose in writing. By briefly mentioning (Rom 1:2–6) the prophets, the holy scriptures, Jesus' lineage from King David, Jesus' status with God, Jesus' resurrection, Paul's own status as an apostle and his task thereof, Paul clearly sets the stage for the drama upon which he is about to expound. He refers to "Christ our Lord" (Rom 1:4c); he speaks of "the obedience of faith among all the Gentiles" (Rom 1:5b); and, when he finally gets to naming the recipients of this letter, he speaks of them as "all God's beloved in Rome" (Rom 1:7a). His use of "our" and "all" hints at Paul's thematic emphasis, namely that "the gospel of God" (Rom 1:1c) is a net that has been thrown widely. Both Jews and Gentiles (that is, the People inheriting the original Promise, as well as everyone else) are included in God's purposes.

22. See Wright, "The Letter to the Romans—Introduction," 395–412, esp. 406–08.
23. See Wall, "Introduction to Epistolary Literature," 380.

In Romans, Paul sandwiches within the salutation formula
itself, a foreshadowing of his main purpose for writing.

The reason for his audacious claim, Paul will contend, is that the heart of The Story always centers on faith, on trusting in the God who called and keeps calling. Believers are "justified by faith," not by following the Jewish "law," a particular set of rules elaborated upon throughout (and beyond!) the Hebrew Bible. To support this claim, Paul interprets the story of Abraham—one of the earliest episodes in The One Great Story—as being one that is fundamentally about faith and trust. It is this kind of faith and trust—in the God of The Story—that Paul sees possible even for people outside of the Israelite/Jewish orbit.

Paul goes to great lengths in his letter to Rome to show how Abraham serves as an exemplar of genuine faith, not of religious validation by deeds. Abraham was circumcised because of his faith, not to prove his loyalty (Rom 4:9-11). He trusted God's promise of his having descendants, even though he and Sarah were too old to have children (Rom 4:17-21). Because of this trust in God, Abraham was made good in God's eyes, that is, it was "reckoned to him as righteousness" (Rom 4:22). Following laws and rules were not what gave Abraham his standing with God; instead, it was faith, a faith that Paul says is available to anyone who believes in this same God, the God of the resurrected Jesus. Trust in Jesus as Lord is what vindicates people (Rom 4:23-25).

Although Paul leans a lot on Abraham, the apostle also finds plenty of ways to bolster his far-reaching claims with other elements of The Story. He contrasts Adam's disobedience and death with Christ's free gift of life (Rom 5:12-21). In emphasizing the distinction between natural descendants and children of promise, Paul cites characters (in addition to Abraham) such as Rebecca, Isaac, Esau, Moses, and even the Egyptian Pharaoh (Rom 9:4-14). Paul remembers Elijah's complaint about being the only faithful one remaining in Israel and God's reply that God still has faithful followers (Rom 11:2-4).

> **Pause to Reflect**
> What do you recognize as having authority over
> your life? Why do you accept it as such? What do
> you gain from it? What does it expect from you?

Besides retelling and interpreting certain scenes and episodes from The Story, Paul also quotes a number of times directly from the Hebrew Bible:

- In his mention of Abraham, "the father of many nations" verse from Gen 17:4–6 (Rom 4:17);

- The "your wife Sarah shall have a son" verse from Gen 18:10 (Rom 9:9);

- The "sand of the sea/remnant will return" verse from Isa 10:22 (Rom 9:27);

- The "stone in Zion that will make people stumble" verse from Isa 8:4–15 (Rom 9:33);

- "I will make you jealous of those who are not a nation" from Deut 32:21 (Rom 10:19);

- "I have been found by those who did not seek me" from Isa 65:1 (Rom 10:20);

- "I held out my hands to a disobedient people" from Isa 65:2 (Rom 10:21);

- "Let their table become a snare and a trap" from Ps 69:22–23 (Rom 11:9–10);

- "Out of Zion will come the Deliverer . . . this is my covenant with them, when I take away their sins" from Isa 59:20–21; 27:9 (Rom 11:26–27);

- "The root of Jesse shall come, the one who rises to rule the Gentiles; in him the Gentiles shall hope" from Isa 11:10 (Rom. 15:12).

Paul finds plenty of support in the Israelite scriptures: The gospel of Jesus the Savior extends and expands the Ancient Promise to which The One Great Story bears witness.

Taken as a whole, we can see from this quick list how Paul finds plenty of support in the Hebrew scriptures for his all-important claim: The gospel of Jesus the Savior extends and expands the Ancient Promise to which The One Great Story bears witness. Major moments and themes in The Story echo clearly from these quotations: Trust, not heritage or rules, is the key to participating with God in the purposes and hopes that God intends for this world. These divine purposes are not limited to the Chosen People; rather, that People's witness to God's ways opens the door for all human communities to share fully in divine mercy, grace, and life.

Understanding how The Story bears witness to this ancient Promise compelled Paul to travel all over the Roman world, to explain it to peoples outside his tradition, inviting them to become part of the new life that it offers.

BOTH JEW AND GREEK

Paul apparently spent a lot of time on ships! Accounts of his travels in service to his calling to the Gentiles (i.e., from Acts as well as Paul's own letters) provide evidence for three "missionary journeys" plus a trip to the imperial capital itself. All of these trips were undertaken over a fourteen-year period, during which he was on the move most of the time. Maps that biblical scholars have constructed to show all of his voyages reveal that he was on a ship about half of those thousands of miles. It is an impressive tour map, even by today's high-tech travel standards.

His final trek was his longest, taking Paul almost entirely by ship, from Caesarea in northern Judea across the Mediterranean and up to Rome. In the dozen or so years prior to visiting Rome, however, Paul journeyed to dozens of towns and cities in Asia Minor, around the Aegean Sea, and in Greece. One of those cities was striking enough in Paul's mind that he ended up writing them, not one, but two letters (or perhaps more than two!).[24] That city is Corinth, at the time a significant crossroads of commerce, cultural exchange, and religious variety.

Perusing the letter that we know as 1 Corinthians, we see that Paul tackles a number of issues in the fledgling Corinthian congregation over which he clearly was not satisfied. These issues included his concerns over division and unity, about social status and leadership, as well as questions about the nature of wisdom, discipline within the congregation, food and idols, dressing for worship, the Lord's Supper, and gifts of the Spirit. No long theological arguments appear here, as they do in Romans. Yet Paul still appealed to the Hebrew scriptures and The Story that runs through them, in seeking to teach and correct these new believers.

Use of The Story is not as extensive in 1 Corinthians as it is in Romans; the major source for it is in chapter 10 of the letter. Here, Paul creatively employs The Story's chapter in which the Israelites journey through the wilderness after their wondrous escape from Egypt's Pharaoh. In doing so, the apostle inserts into his recounting of those episodes imagery that interprets those ancient events through Christian eyes. For one thing, Paul speaks of the wandering Israelites as having been "baptized into Moses" (1 Cor 10:2). During that trying time, Paul continues, "our ancestors (here Paul is including his Greek/Gentile Christian audience)" (1 Cor 10:1b) were sustained by the Lord's Supper—"spiritual food . . . and . . . spiritual drink" (1 Cor 10:3–4a). To make his interpretation even more obvious, Paul claims

24. Most scholars concur that the letter known as "Second Corinthians" actually contains fragments of at least two letters; see Sampley, "The Second Letter to the Corinthians—Introduction," 5–10.

that "the rock" that the LORD had directed Moses to strike, for giving the wilderness people fresh water to drink (Exod 17:1–7), was the risen Savior whom Paul now proclaims—"the spiritual rock that followed them, and the rock was Christ" (1 Cor 10:4b).

Paul's theology here implies a similar note that we see more plainly articulated in the Fourth Gospel. Christ as "the Word" existed at the beginning with God, creating all things and being the source of life and true light (John 1:1–5, 14). It is not hard, then, for Paul to imagine the presence of the Word—Christ—in the ancient accounts of his ancestors' lives, challenges, blessings, and—yes—even faithlessness. It is not as much a "reading back into" the past episodes with something that was not there as it is reading the ancient text in light of a fresh understanding of the sweep of The Story. This might sound like a subtle or even forced distinction, but I think that it is more consistent with our view in this book—that The Story as presented through the Bible is organic in nature, a narrative that continues to move ahead toward the "not-yet" as it maintains essential relationships with its earlier episodes.

> **Pause to Reflect**
> In what area of life—at work, in your community,
> etc.—do you feel that you have some "authority"? How
> did you acquire it? In what ways do others acknowledge
> it? How do you feel when this authority of yours is
> not recognized? When it is not, what do you do?

Indeed, Paul continues to demonstrate this understanding of the flow of Sacred Narrative. In 1 Cor 10, he interprets for his listening audience more incidents from the wilderness wanderings, in particular some that show the Israelites at their worst. In spite of being protected and nourished, they still did not trust the LORD—so they paid the price, many being "struck down in the wilderness" (1 Cor 10:5b; see Num 14:16, 23). They violated moral standards; they complained about their circumstances; and they were punished for their lack of trust (1 Cor 10:8–10). For Paul, these stories from the wilderness function as cautionary tales for his contemporaries who follow Jesus: "These things happened to them to serve as an example, and they were written down to instruct us, . . ." (1 Cor 10:11ab). By locating his letter's audience with the Israelites in the scriptures, Paul wants the Corinthian congregation to identify with both the promise and the dangers of their spiritual ancestors' experience.

For Paul, these stories from the wilderness function as
cautionary tales for his contemporaries who follow Jesus.

There is more. At the end of his letter, Paul takes up a lot of space discussing a key claim of the Jesus continuation to The Story—that of resurrection. Here, he uses the figure of Adam—"the first [hu]man" (1 Cor 15:45a)—to illustrate an argument comparing flesh and spirit, earthly versus heavenly bodies. Because of Adam, Paul contends, death comes to flesh; but through the Savior ("Christ"), flesh is made alive through resurrection: "for as all die in Adam, so all will be made alive in Christ" (1 Cor 15:22). Paul refers to Christ here as "the last Adam" (1 Cor 15:45c) and "the second man" (1 Cor 15:47b), the "man of heaven" whose likeness will be seen in those who are raised with Christ (1 Cor 15:48b, 49).

If you are scratching your head a bit as you try to follow the intricacies of this discussion, you are in good company! He is utilizing a method of biblical interpretation known as "typology," in which a particular element of one scriptural tradition is correlated with another element from a different time period.[25] In this case, if we don't know much about the (prehistoric) Adam stories from Gen 2 and 3, Paul's argument could fall flat. Similarly, if we don't know much about the emerging, contemporary-to-Paul declarations about Jesus, it is hard to appreciate what Paul is doing here. The itinerant apostle is appealing to, and applying, the definitive character of Adam to a central Christian assertion, in a sort of "on the one hand, . . . on the other hand" contrasting style of argument. For our purposes, we want to recognize in 1 Cor 15 yet another way in which Paul is linking what he knows of his People's tradition with Jesus. Paul is convinced that, as the Christ, Jesus introduces a new, major development to those traditions. With Jesus as the Christ, any sense that The One Great Story had become stagnant had to be dismissed. For Paul, God is still on the move, and welcoming Gentiles into the Promise was perhaps Paul's most compelling confirmation of that assertion.

Paul is convinced that, with Jesus as the Christ, any sense that The
One Great Story had become stagnant had to be dismissed.

One last handful of references in this letter also indicates how Paul is swimming in streams that also carry Jesus chapters as part of The Story—streams that are corroborated by other New Testament documents. For

25. See Achtemeier, "Typology," 926–27.

instance, at one point, Paul mentions "the other apostles and the brothers of the Lord and Cephas," in appealing to the right of men traveling with him to have their own wives along with them (1 Cor 9:5). There is plenty of evidence of "the other apostles" in Matthew, Mark, Luke, and John; there is reference to Jesus' brothers in Matt 12:46–50 (as Mark 3:31–35 and Luke 8:19–21) and in John 2:12; and Cephas/Peter plays a prominent role, as one of the twelve called by Jesus, in all four Gospels. Also in 1 Corinthians, Paul discusses the Lord's Supper (11:23–26), not only concerning its proper observance, but also to defend his authority in receiving the story of how the practice originated. His account is faithful to those that appear in Matthew (26:26–29), Mark (14:22–25), and Luke (22:15–20).

Further, Paul's defense of his own apostolic authority includes—toward the end of this letter—an outline of the gospel proclamation, one of which he says "I handed on to you as of first importance what I in turn had received . . . " (1 Cor 15:3a). This proclamation contains several clauses, some of which summarize details that are cited elsewhere in the New Testament, too:

- Christ having died "for our sins" (1 Cor 15:3b); see the trial and crucifixion chapters in Matt 27, Mark 15, Luke 23, and John 19; see also Peter's speech in Acts 2, Stephen's speech in Acts 7 (esp. 7:51–53), Philip with the eunuch in Acts 8:26–39, Paul's speech in Acts 13 (esp. 13:16–31), and elsewhere in Acts.

- Jesus having been buried and then raised on the third day (1 Cor 15:4); see Matt 27:57—28:10; Mark 15:42—16:1–6; Luke 23:50—24:1–12; John 19:38—20:18; and locations in Acts.

- Jesus appearing to his followers and apostles (1 Cor 15:5–7); see Matt 28, Mark 16:1–8, Luke 24, John 20:11—21:14, and locations in Acts.

These details, being part of a very early Christian declaration,[26] tie Paul's telling of The (Jesus) Story, not only to other witnesses of his generation, but also to The One Great Story. Two times, this primal affirmation uses the phrase *kata tas graphas*, "according to the writings (scriptures)," to support its initial claims—that Christ died for human sin, that he was buried and then raised on the third day. In this way, Paul underscores what the creed itself avows: the story of Jesus of Nazareth flows out the Grand Narrative to which the Hebrew scriptures attest. Making sense out of Jesus is conceivable only through knowing and understanding the witness to God from the Law, the Prophets, and the Writings. Even more, for Paul,

---

26. A careful analysis of the this "formula" is undertaken in Conzelmann, *1 Corinthians*, 249–59.

explaining Jesus as Christ means a culmination of the call to Abram and Sarai, that through their faith in the LORD, all the nations of the earth will be blessed. For the mostly Gentile Corinthian congregation to hear this Jewish Pharisee draw the flaps of the gospel tent around them would have been a compelling, perhaps even overwhelming, experience!

OUTSIDE THE SHADOW OF THE APOSTLE PAUL

Paul's influence on Christian thinking and practice over the centuries cannot be overestimated. His reliance upon The Story for what he has to say is manifest and at the heart of his theological assertions, clearly evident even from this quick look at only two of his letters. Because so much of the New Testament includes writings by or attributed to Paul, it could be easy to regard the rest of the letters there (mostly much shorter) as of less value. If we did so, we would miss out on further angles and lenses through which The One Great Story (as it now includes Jesus) was claimed and utilized among the earliest Christian witnesses. While Paul's primary audience, and clearly the center of his theological appeal, was Gentile (that is, not Jewish by ancestry), there was a second audience—perhaps a more logical one—who might have been the main target for some of the other letters.

So, in order to broaden our appreciation of the letter-writing witness to The Story, we turn here to two short epistles that carry the name of an early, prominent character, one from within Jesus' own closest circle. *Peter*, the fisherman who (with his brother, Andrew) was called by Jesus to join Jesus in his ministry (see Matt 4:18–20), played a large part in that ministry. Known to Paul by the name "Cephas" (both names mean "rock"), Peter is also known by a Greek name, "Simon" (see, for example, Matt 4:18; Mark 3:16; Luke 5:8; John 13:6; and Acts 10:32).

Simon Peter was known to shoot off his mouth at times. When Jesus took Peter, James, and John up a mountain, and the teacher's appearance there glowed bright white while the three saw him talking with Moses and Elijah, Peter blathered something out loud, from sheer terror (see Mark 9:2–6). Peter's apparently impetuous personality is most dramatically evident, though, in a sequence at which he first pledged unwavering loyalty to Jesus (Mark 14:27–31) and then later denied three times that he even knew Jesus (Mark 14:66–72). This duplicity on Peter's part, however, did not disqualify him from becoming one of the leaders of the budding Jesus movement. As we saw in the previous chapter, Peter is remembered by Acts as giving the first speech/sermon to claim Jesus as the Messiah and tie him into The One Great Story (Acts 2:14–41).

It is not surprising, then, that an epistle or two from the early Christian years would have circulated with Peter's name on them, eventually being recognized as a faithful and authoritative witness to Messiah Jesus. Whether Peter himself is directly responsible for the composition of the two letters that bear his name as the author is less important to their authority than what they have to say. First and 2 Peter focus on holy living, personal discipline, and suffering and are packed with many exhortations and warnings to the audiences that are addressed.

> *It is not surprising that an epistle or two from the early Christian years would have circulated with Peter's name on them.*

There are at least forty-one direct and indirect biblical references in these two letters, seven of which are quotations—and some that refer to details in other New Testament documents! First Peter's audience, for example, hears the following:

- "You shall be holy, for I am holy" (1 Pet 1:16), from Lev 19:2, 11:44a, and 11:45b.

- "The stone that the builders rejected has become the very head of the corner" (1 Pet 2:7), from Ps 118:22.

- A longer quotation (1 Pet 3:10–12) from Ps 34:12–16a, about "Those who desire life and desire to see good days, . . . " (Ps 34:12)

- A quotation from Isaiah (1 Pet 1:24–25) that includes, "The grass withers, and the flower falls, but the word of the Lord endures forever" (Isa 40:6–8)

- Two other quotations from Isaiah (1 Pet 2:6, 8), not to mention several other places where the use of language evokes other references in the Psalms, Isaiah, and the Proverbs.

Again, however, our aim here is in tracing not simply the presence of earlier biblical material within the New Testament. Rather, it is to see how characters and events from previous episodes within The Story are brought to bear upon what New Testament documents testify about Jesus and his significance. Such use of earlier characters and previous events serve to substantiate the expansion of The Story, by integrating memories of, and reflections concerning, Jesus into the flow of the Hebrew scriptures.

TAKING IT ON THE CHIN

For instance, 1 Peter comments early on about the work of the biblical prophets (1:10–12). This author claims that prophets in the Hebrew scriptures understood that they were anticipating the Christ, the One coming to bring deliverance. According to "Peter," this prophetic anticipation included the suffering that the Messiah would endure, not just the splendor of the Messianic office. These prophets were inspired by the Holy Spirit, the same Spirit who sanctifies believers in Jesus the Savior, (the latter affirmation being emphasized at the beginning of the letter [1 Pet 1:2b]). As a result, 1 Peter provides a spiritual validation for the letter's audience concerning their suffering in faith: if our Savior suffered and the outcome was magnificent, then the suffering of the Savior's followers also serves a positive purpose.

Discussion in 1 Peter's opening chapter also implies a theological connection that carries practical encouragement to the letter's audience. It is that the Spirit, who was present long ago to inspire the prophets, also strengthened the Savior himself in his life, ministry, and struggles—especially during his trial and crucifixion. First Peter wants its listeners to recognize the presence of that same Spirit in their midst, too, strengthening them as Jesus himself was strengthened. God's Spirit, then, is present and active all throughout The Story, from ancient days, in Jesus the Christ, and with those who follow Jesus (see 1 Pet 1:10–21).

Pause to Reflect
How do you define "suffering"? What examples of suffering come to mind? What does suffering do to people? What would you say to someone who is suffering? What might you say to yourself?

Images from the Hebrew scriptures—and the episodes that they represent—appear in a number of places throughout 1 Peter. In one place, the letter applies language from ancient Israel to its audience of Jesus-followers. This audience is addressed as "a chosen race, a royal priesthood, a holy nation, God's own people" (1 Pet 2:9a) and later as "aliens and exiles (1 Pet 2:11a)." All of these terms hail back to olden episodes, to formative scenes from the Wondrous Drama, during which the Israelites were called, established, protected, rescued, and claimed by the LORD (see, for instance, Exod 19:3–6; 2 Kgs 24:8–16; Neh 1:2–3, 7:6; Isa 43:20–21; Jer 13:19, 29:1–7). Even more specifically, 1 Peter appeals to Abraham and Sarah in urging honorable relationships (1 Pet 3:6), as well as to the story of Noah and the flood. There, the letter recalls that eight people were saved on the ark from the deluge that came (1 Pet 3:20; see Gen 6–8.). Once again, 1 Peter connects the episode to something that is part of the Christian installment of The Story: the water of the flood anticipates, and perhaps contrasts with, the water of baptism.

First Peter wants its listeners to recognize the presence
of that same Spirit in their midst, too, strengthening
them as Jesus himself was strengthened.

YOU, TOO—BEWARE!

Similar treatments of material from The Story appear in the letter that follows, 2 Peter—along with a couple of surprises. Noah shows up again, as well as other names and events in Genesis, namely Sodom and Gomorrah and Lot, Abraham's nephew. Their inclusion builds a somewhat dreadful contrast between condemnation of "the ungodly" (see 2 Pet 2:5d and 2:6c) and rescue of righteous ones such as Lot (2 Pet 2:10). We easily recognize this theme, since it is treated in previous chapters of this book! Second Peter also refers to an even earlier episode from Genesis, namely creation itself (2 Pet 3:4–7). Here, the author sounds another cautionary note: the waters that were formed long ago were used later to flood the earth (another reference to Noah and the flood), as a consequence of "scoffers" (2 Pet 3:3) who—like the scoffers in 2 Peter's day—ignored God's ways and faced divine judgment.

One other cautionary tale (2 Peter seems to revel in them) from the Hebrew scriptures makes its point with a seemingly satirical flavor. Num 22 contains an unusual story about a man named Balaam who beat his donkey (ass) for turning aside, rather than continuing on their journey. The donkey had seen an angel of the LORD, who was blocking their passage because Balaam was not doing what the LORD had said to do. Finally, the donkey was given the power to speak, so she protested Balaam's beating and reminded Balaam of her longstanding loyalty to him. When Balaam acknowledged the donkey, he was able to see the angel there, who then chastised Balaam for his action. Balaam admitted his wrongdoing and promised to do what the LORD asked of him (Num 22:2–35).

The ancient story of Balaam and his talking donkey
become, in 2 Peter, a warning about getting off track
and acting dumber than a beast of burden!

With this ancient account, 2 Peter compares "false prophets" of their day to the actions of Balaam; they have "left the straight road and have gone astray" (2 Pet 2:15–16). The donkey had saved the day: "a speechless donkey spoke with a human voice and restrained the prophet's madness." It appears as though 2 Peter sees the trusty donkey as having more sense than her owner, who had been driven by the chance for gain. A mere domesticated creature, Balaam's ass was more reasonable, more judicious, than "these people," false teachers, to whom 2 Peter refers (among other terms) as "irrational animals" (2 Pet 22:12).[27]

STILL—HOPE AWAITS

Not all of 2 Peter's handling of elements from The Story carries such a stern tone, however. Some of it is more uplifting, as near the end of the letter, when it reads, "*we wait for new heavens and a new earth, where righteousness is at home*" (2 Pet 3:13). This phrase, "new heavens and a new earth," symbolizing a makeover of the created order, originates in the Book of Isaiah. There, the notion of God doing something radically new appears in several places ("See, the former things have come to pass, new things I now declare" [Isa 42:9]; "I am about to do a new thing; now it springs forth, do you not perceive it?" [Isa 43:18]; "for the heavens will vanish like smoke, the earth will wear out like a garment, . . . but my salvation will be forever" [Isa 51:6]). Here, 2 Peter is echoing two specific verses in Isaiah:

- "For I am about to create new heavens and a new earth; the former things shall not be remembered or come to mind" (Isa 65:17) and

- "For as the new heavens and the new earth, which I will make, shall remain before me, says the LORD; so shall your descendants and your name remain" (Isa 66:22).

This Christian letter-writer's hope for "the coming of the day of God" (2 Pet 3:12a) thus also echoes the same theological belief in God's dramatic impending action—this time, in the name of Jesus the Messiah, who is Lord and Savior.

Even more, 2 Peter is not the only place in the New Testament where this phrase, "new heavens and a new earth" appears. It also shows up (as we will see in the following chapter) in the last book of the Bible. With both 2 Peter and Revelation, "a new heaven and a new earth" (Rev 21:1) will emerge, following intense eradication of conditions in the world as it is

---

27. See Watson, "The Second Letter of Peter," 351.

now. These conditions reflect willful neglect of the ways of God and will be replaced, through God's initiative, with a glorious new universe. Ultimately, 2 Peter links judgment with coming splendor, both at the hands of God, associating scriptural promises from past centuries with the world and situation that the young Christian community faces.

> **Pause to Reflect**
> What do you see in today's world that is "new"? What makes it new? In what ways does this new thing make life better? What new thing would you choose, if you could?

In spite of these two short letters not being too popular today, they nonetheless include a couple of fascinating examples how the (new) Jesus-Story made its mark on those who linked it to The (ancient) One Great Story. Second Peter mentions in its opening chapter an incident from Jesus' life, a rare "outside" reference to an episode that is recorded in three of the Gospels. That is the episode known as "the transfiguration," which is mentioned briefly earlier in this chapter. There, Jesus has taken three of his inner circle—including Peter—to the top of a mountain, where he becomes almost glowing white and appears with Moses and Elijah (see Mark 9:2–6; Matt 17:1–8; and Luke 9:28–36). Second Peter even quotes the words that are recorded in the Gospels, from a voice out of heaven, "This is my Son, the Beloved, with whom I am well pleased" (2 Pet 1:17b). The author of this letter employs this dramatic moment in Jesus' life to undergird the authority of those who minister within the author's orbit:

> "We ourselves heard this voice come from heaven, while we were with him on the holy mountain. So we have the prophetic message more fully confirmed. You will do well to be attentive to this . . . " (2 Pet 1:18–19b)

Paul the apostle was not the only early Christian teacher who felt the need to bolster his authority! In this case, 2 Peter's theme of Christians being careful to listen to proper teaching and not "cleverly devised myths" (2 Pet 1:16a) includes a somewhat indirect defense of the author's own license and mandate. It would be hard to argue with someone who was "there" when the Messiah received God's stamp of approval. What a clever, captivating way for The Story to be both extended and exploited!

It would be hard to argue with someone who was "there" when the Messiah received God's stamp of approval.

Speaking of Paul, he makes an appearance of sorts in 2 Peter—toward the end, as the letter appeals one more time to its audience. Early Christians believed that the risen Christ, who ascended to heaven, would return in the near future, after intense changes wrought by God (see, for instance, Matt 10:23; Luke 12:40; 1 Cor 4:5). The author of 2 Peter wants listeners to live honorable lives, so that they will be prepared for "new heavens and a new earth" (2 Pet 3:13). In order to be ready, they are urged throughout the letter to follow sound understanding (i.e., avoid "false teachers")—and 2 Peter recognizes the apostle Paul's standing as one reliable source:

> So also our beloved brother Paul wrote to you according to the wisdom given him, speaking as he does in all his letters. (2 Pet 3:15b–16a)

Even more, this letter grants Paul's writings a status like "the other scriptures." (2 Pet 3:16c)

How remarkable! Within a generation of Paul's ministry, another New Testament document acknowledges legitimacy and fidelity in the prolific missionary's own written words. Second Peter links Paul, whom Simon Peter himself met, with the ancient tradition of the People and Their Story.

In these and other ways, the flow of The One Great Story continues, within the witness of the New Testament, drawing upon a range of episodes and images from the testimony of the Hebrew scriptures. In this chapter, we have seen how That Story was handled by an apostle who spoke primarily to Gentiles, and then by an apostolic tradition that appears to address a more broadly based audience. In the following chapter, we will consider two more New Testament sources—one well-versed in Jewish religious practices, the other a stark and sometimes macabre look at the future. Whether interpreting the meaning of Jesus the Savior through ancient traditions or through foreboding prognostication, these two witnesses both seek to accentuate how Jesus plays a central role in the long trajectory of The One Great Story. Let us see how the Epistle to the Hebrews and the strange book of the Revelation bear witness to this realization, this completion, this turning point.

FOR THE READER

1. Paul the apostle claims among his credentials having been born into the tribe of Benjamin, having achieved membership in the Pharisees, and possessing Roman citizenship. Given these qualifications, which audience do you think had more doubts about his apostolic standing—Jews, of whom he was one (in spades), or Gentiles, who would have been impressed with his imperial status? What reasons would you cite for your answer to this question?

2. What is the distinction that Paul makes in Romans between Abraham the Jewish progenitor and Abraham the follower of God? Why is this distinction so important to Paul?

3. What do you think of Paul overlaying the Christian sacraments of baptism and the Lord's Supper onto the account of the ancient Israelites wandering in the wilderness?

4. Based on discussion in this chapter, which one of the "Peter" letters sounds more uplifting for its audience? About what was the author most concerned in 1 Peter? in 2 Peter?

SUGGESTED ACTIVITIES

*   Read through Paul's letter to the Galatians (just six chapters) and take some notes on evidence that you detect of Paul's use there of The One Great Story. What similarities and differences do you see in Galatians, compared with this chapter's discussion of Romans and 1 Corinthians? How is Paul connecting, in Galatians, his understanding of the gospel to The Story?

*   Sit with a friend, as the two of you look again (as at the end of chapter 9) at a biblical map showing Paul's missionary journeys. As you trace each journey, imagine that you are Paul, traveling by foot and by boat to many locations in the Roman Empire. What do you think it was like for Paul to do all this? Share thoughts with each other about what you think might have kept Paul going.

*   Read Num 22:7–35. What mood from this story do you think its earliest listeners sensed? Next, read 2 Pet 2:12–16. How does 2 Peter use the story from Num 22? In what way might that incident sound different in its retelling?

Chapter 11

Backwards and Forwards

The Story's "Stranger" Worlds

"Therefore, since we are surrounded by so great a cloud of witnesses, . . ."

—Heb 12:1a

"Then I saw a new heaven and a new earth, . . .

See, I am making all things new."

—Rev 21:1a, 6b

Only the most determined of readers can plow through every book of the Bible without blinking! The rest of us—that is, those of us who try to muster up the fortitude—might not want to admit that we pick and choose, selecting books that appeal to our interests, for one reason or another. Sometimes we might not even know why we become fascinated with the many unconventional adventures in Genesis, or the levels of intrigue in 1 Samuel, or Jeremiah's brutal personal honesty, or Mark's fast pace.

My own, second, intentional foray into Bible reading (as I mentioned at the beginning of chapter 1, my first effort was in fourth grade, and I crashed and burned after a few days of befuddled exertion) took me primarily into Paul's letters. At the time, I was not interested in biblical history and story line, or in what the prophets had to say, or even (shockingly) to some degree about what Jesus was up to. But I was pretty resolute then about knowing how to live as a serious follower of Jesus. Consequently, I skipped everything that didn't seem to speak to this singular goal—or, to be fair, I gave those texts a quick once-through and left it at that.

Two of those biblical documents that received my fleeting attention are near the end of the New Testament—ancient tradition bestowed upon these two the names "the Epistle to the Hebrews" and "the Revelation to John." You don't have to spend much time in either of these documents to gain some appreciation for why I chose to limit my time with them. Without some orientation, Hebrews and Revelation—each one in its own way—are hard to understand. You can find "advice for faithful living," as it were, here and there in both documents, but exhortation does not dominate either one.

> *In making their respective claims, Hebrews looks*
> *backward and Revelation looks forward.*

Instead, we find in Hebrews and Revelation long, elaborate presentations of a very different kind. In Hebrews, the presentation revolves around arguing why Jesus as God's Son is better than certain key features of Jewish traditions. The writer of Hebrews looks *backward*, at inherited religious beliefs and practices. Revelation does the opposite: it depicts a vision of the future, of a hopeful world yet to come; it looks *forward*. In spite of this difference in approach, both of these New Testament documents have something in common. They both draw heavily and artfully upon their shared scriptures, the Hebrew Bible. As they do so, they use images and elements of The One Great Story to support their assertions. From this perspective, then, Hebrews and Revelation become much more noteworthy: they do not hang alone, "in the air," but stand as two more of the earliest witnesses to how the Jesus Episode informs the flow of The One Great Story. They might take more unpacking than other New Testament documents, but once done, their contribution to the gospel witness can be appreciated.

We will look first at Hebrews and then—since it is the last book in the Bible—Revelation.

A MORE EXCELLENT WAY

As a child, I remember the occasional argument among kids my age about whose favorite something-or-other was "better than" someone else's. These arguments could get rather heated, as voices got louder, falling into a rhythm something like, "Is that so?" "Yeah!" "Sez who?" "Sez me!" "Oh yeah!" "Yeah—who wants to know?" and so on. Hebrews makes its argument more politely than playground exchanges, but its ancient author is no less earnest. Clearly, the epistle's audience is a community of believers who are familiar enough with contemporary Jewish religious practices that the author can make a case for Jesus that depends on those practices. In a couple of words, Hebrews says that Jesus as the Messiah is "better than" all of them.

> *Hebrews claims that Jesus the Messiah goes one*
> *better than all Jewish religious practices.*

About 100 references to Old Testament texts and stories in Hebrews become woven into this overall rationale. Two dozen of these references appear in the form of quotations, many from the Psalms, others from the Pentateuch (the first five books), and still others from the prophets. Included among all these references are several that are not as directly related to The Grand Narrative. In the first chapter (Heb 1:5–14), for instance, the author quotes six Hebrew Bible passages that refer to angels and one more that the author sees in reference to an as-yet-unknown son of God. Hebrews also spends quite a bit of time talking about the office of "high priest" (Heb 5; 7), not surprisingly arguing that Jesus is better in that office than any of the others (Heb 4:14–15). Continuing with the high priest motif, Hebrews additionally claims that the role of animal sacrifice—unmistakably evident even in the earliest texts of the Hebrew Bible— has been replaced by Jesus' death on a cross (Heb 8–10). These sections of the discussion in Hebrews address issues of great importance to Jews of the day (and thus to the earliest Christians), while elements of the story line itself remain in the background.

FROM THE BULRUSHES

Characters and episodes from The Story are plentiful in Hebrews, however. We already have seen, for instance, how central a role that *Moses* plays in the defining series of events involved in the Israelites' escape from Egypt and years of wandering in the wilderness (see chapter 3 in this book). The man who was pulled from bulrushes as a baby by the Pharaoh's daughter became such an eminent character within The Story that later tradition associated authorship of the first five books of the Bible to Moses himself. We should expect, therefore, that Moses would be featured by Hebrews in support of its thesis—and he frequently does.

Moses is named in Hebrews a number of times, in chapters 3, 7, 8, 9, 10, 11, and 12. He is mentioned in the context of a comment about "the rebellion," that is, the Israelites who did not trust Moses' leadership from God as they traveled through the wilderness (Heb 3:15–19). His time-honored status as author of the Pentateuch receives a passing notice in 7:14. His indisputable role as bringer of God's Ten Words to the People receives recognition, in a reference to the consequences of refusing to live by those Words (Heb 10:26–28). His intercession on behalf of The People, sometimes under startling circumstances, is alluded to (Heb 12:21). His prominent place in a recitation of faithful Hebrew Bible characters cannot be overlooked (Heb 11:23–28). (We will say more about this recitation below; it is a "must-see" on our Hebrews tour!)

> *This epistle distinguishes between Moses, as a*
> *servant, and Jesus, as a son, of God.*

In the face of all the esteem that these references in Hebrews acknowledge for Moses, a major Old Testament figure, the author of this New Testament epistle rocks Moses' boat a little. The long-suffering, reluctant fellow, who had been chosen by the LORD to lead the people from slavery to freedom, whose name overwhelmingly dominates the Hebrew Bible until David appears, comes down a notch—so to speak—in Hebrews. Or, perhaps it would be more accurate to say that a notch was added, above Moses, much later. That notch is filled by no one other than Jesus as the Christ. Hebrews does not deny Moses' place in The Story, remarking that "Moses was faithful in all God's house . . . " (Heb 3:5a). Yet, for Hebrews, it is of great consequence to distinguish between *Moses'* place in The Story ". . . as a *servant*, to testify to the things that would be spoken later" (Heb 3:5b) and the *Messiah's* role in it, as one who "was faithful over God's house as a *son*" (Heb 3:6a). In antiquity, the status distinction between that of a servant and that of a son hardly could be overstated: it is like playing trump in a card game. God's purpose and action through Messiah Jesus becomes a zenith point for The One Great Story.

WHERE THE JOURNEY BEGAN

Less dramatically perhaps, Hebrews appeals more than once to The Story's greatest ancestor of them all, *Abraham*. One of those appeals hearkens back to a moment when the LORD affirmed a promise made to Abraham, that the LORD would "surely bless you and multiply you" (Heb 6:14, see Gen 22:16–18). Hebrews remembers that, even in his and wife Sarah's old age, Abraham trusted God through many years. Isaac was born to Sarah and carried the promise forward; his parents' patience bore out God's faithfulness (Heb 6:13–17).

Another one of the appeals to Abraham is woven into Hebrews' discussion of how Jesus is superior to the Bible's priestly tradition (Heb 6:20–7:22). This discussion gets a little hard to follow, since we today do not readily understand ancient Near Eastern practices of things like tribute or priestly succession. Even more, one of the key characters mentioned by Hebrews here appears outside of Hebrews only twice in the Hebrew Bible! His name is *Melchizedek*, and he briefly appears in Gen 14 (vss 18–20) as "King of Salem," who met Abra(ha)m after the latter helped some other kings recover citizens and flocks that were captured in a battle (Gen 14:10–17). The enigmatic Melchizedek, who also was a priest "of God Most High" (Gen 14:18b), blessed Abra(ha)m in God's name, for his military victory. Then Abra(ha)m presented Melchizedek with one-tenth of their victory's spoils.

What is significant in this episode, to the author of Hebrews, involves the right and status argument that elevates Melchizedek, as a priest, above the Bible's long-standing Levitical priestly tradition. Hebrews alleges that Abraham is involved with that tradition, because one of his descendants would be Levi—whose name subsequently becomes bestowed upon the Israelites' priestly office and inheritance.

Following this point, Hebrews then aims Melchizedek's unique status toward a figure upon whom Hebrews grants an even "higher" status as a high priest—namely, Jesus the Savior. Jesus is viewed in Hebrews as "another priest [who] arises resembling Melchizedek, one who has become a priest . . . through the power of an indestructible life" (Heb 7:15–16). This culmination of the priestly office in Jesus leads to "a better covenant," with Jesus as its "guarantee" (Heb 7:22). In other words, as the author says a little later, "if that first covenant had been faultless, there would have been no need to look for a second one" (Heb 8:7). Thus, Hebrews works with the sacred Levitical tradition to spin another variation on the theme that runs throughout this epistle. As in its treatment of Moses, this New Testament epistle asserts that—in spite of the essential and necessary place of Abraham (and all the others) to The One Great Story—Savior Jesus completes and culminates all elements of This Story.

"BY FAITH . . . "

People who read the Epistle to the Hebrews, however, are much less likely to remember what it has to say about Abraham and Moses as they are about its content in chapter 11. Indeed, this chapter serves as something of a climax to this epistles' direction of ideas. For an obvious reason, it is widely known as the "faith" chapter, since the chapter begins with the words, "Faith is . . ." This word, *pistis*, appears a whopping twenty-five times in this chapter alone, eighteen times as "By faith . . . ," a rhythmic cadence that surely would have stirred and inspired its early audiences. Coincidentally, eighteen names from the Hebrew Bible's installments in The One Great Story are mentioned, as the epistle dramatically summarizes a number of events and episodes. Here we find several well-known characters along with lesser-known ones, such as the judge, Jephthah (Judg 11), and the prostitute, Rahab, who herself was not an Israelite (see Josh 2, 6).

Chapter 11 of Hebrews reads as a tour de force of the biblical witness to faith.

Most of the space in chapter 11 is given to those early, defining generations of persons and incidents with Abraham, Moses, Sarah, Isaac, and Jacob, through the period of settling the Promised Land. Along with unnamed heroes and harrowing, often violent, experiences recounted, this chapter reads as a tour de force of the biblical witness to faith. Noah trusted the LORD in building an ark to save his family from the impending flood; Abraham followed the LORD's call, even without a road map, directions—or an immediate heir; Moses' entire life demonstrates ongoing trust in the LORD, despite a long series of ominous circumstances; and so on, and so on.

Pause to Reflect
Have you ever held an idea or belief about something but then changed it when you found something that you decided was better? What was it like to go through that experience? How were you different because of it?

All of these heroes and experiences display trust in God and what good things happen as a consequence, in spite of crushing circumstances. And yet—while Hebrews applauds them all, it asserts that these faithful persons were living *toward* the Promise, not *in* it. The actions that they took in response to trusting God, Hebrews argues, contributed to the long-awaited Promise gradually—but eventually—coming to fulfillment, completion, fruition. What is that Promise? Hebrews has been developing a rationale for it all along—Jesus the Messiah, who surpasses all previous acts of God. Here, at the end of its lengthy appeal, Hebrews returns to the theme with which it opens: from now on, the divine Son is how we know God and God's purposes in their fullness, their abundance.

Hebrews ends with two chapters devoted to encouraging its audience in its pursuit of faithful living. A few more references to The Story show up in these earnest, moving appeals—to Esau, who gave up his birthright and yearned to get it back (Heb 12:16–17); to Moses again (Heb 12:21); to Abel, killed by his brother Cain of jealousy (Heb 12:24; see also 11:4). These stories, as all of those included in this epistle, provide moral and spiritual instruction to Hebrews's audience. This epistle calls its hearers to live wholeheartedly by faith in the Christ, by drawing their gaze backward. What has gone before them serves as guideposts for their own journey of faith. Enriched by the new chapter about Messiah Jesus, The One Great Story continues to be even more relevant, to continue to speak with power and authenticity.

NO SUGAR PLUMS

While Hebrews aims to encourage its audience by looking *back*, the Revelation to John takes something of an opposite approach. It seeks to uplift its audience by looking *ahead*. It does so by participating in a form of ancient literature that paints pictures of impending, spectacular, and often gruesome events and changes in circumstance. This literature is known as "apocalyptic," in which the great powers of the cosmos battle it out, one of those powers eventually wins, and the world as we know it is changed forever. In Jewish and Christian versions, God the Lord is the winner, after which all creation enjoys everlasting peace and well-being. The Old Testament Book of Daniel includes apocalyptic sections, while Revelation is the only full-blown apocalyptic book in the New Testament.[28]

Entering the world portrayed in Revelation leads
us into turbulent, even baffling, waters.

Entering the world portrayed in Revelation leads us into turbulent, even baffling, waters. No other book in the entire Bible forces us to wrestle with the matter of interpretation as vividly as does Revelation. Although its structure appears as an epistle, the document's intense imagery and cosmic contest can overshadow its pastoral intent (see Rev 1:1–11). Dragons, beasts, plagues, sealed scrolls, sky riders, blaring trumpets, and the like fill descriptions of visions that this John of Patmos (an island in the Aegean Sea) shares with seven named churches (Rev 1:11). It is a wild ride, by any

28. A thorough summary of the pattern and features of apocalyptic literature can be found in Rist, "Apocalypticism," 156–61. A summary of apocalyptic thought from ancient Judaism to the modern day is found in D'Angelo and Matter, "Apocalypticism," 40–44.

modern perspective! Whether or not its first readers understood everything that John was prophesying for them, Revelation has kept religious thinkers—for many centuries and of many traditions—up at night. Beyond a general apocalyptic sense of eventual divine victory over evil, followed by a new order, a new holy city, and a reappearance of Jesus the Lord, most of the original meaning of the book probably is lost.[29]

In spite of these complicated challenges, the last book of the Bible carries abundant evidence of a keen appreciation for The One Great Story. Of its 404 total verses, Revelation alludes to material from the Hebrew Bible in about 275 of those verses—totaling about 400 allusions![30] Although none of these references are quotations,[31] its author drank repeatedly from the life-giving waters of The Story. Images and phrases from Isaiah perhaps are the most frequent; numerous others are recognizable from Exodus, the Psalms, Ezekiel, and other books. A sampling of these references gives us a peek into John's mind, as he shares his visions with his audience.

BUGS, TREES, AND DONKEYS

One of the earliest of The Story's images to appear in Revelation comes and goes quickly, yet its use is arresting. At the end of the message to the first church, Ephesus, those who listen to the Spirit and remain faithful are allowed "permission to eat from *the tree of life* that is in the paradise of God" (Rev 2:7b). The image of the tree of life transports us far back into The Story, immediately following the creation accounts. There, the man and the woman were banished from the Garden for eating from the one tree from which the LORD God had forbidden them to eat (Gen 2–3). The message to Ephesus promises that "everyone who conquers [i.e., remains faithful]" will be able to eat from the prohibited tree. That promise seems to reverse one of The Story's most far-reaching moments. As on the Day of Pentecost (Acts 2), when the confusing of languages at the Tower of Babel (Gen 11) was reversed by the giving of the Spirit, so also the promise of removing the banishment from God's life-giving fruits appears in this last book of the Bible.

---

29. Discussions of these complex matters of interpreting the last book of the Bible can be found in Rowland, "The Book of Revelation—Introduction," 503–58; and in Wainwright, "Revelation, Book of," 389–96. A thorough scholarly approach to Revelation is available to the brave of heart in publications such as Ford, *Revelation*.

30. See Ford, *Revelation*, 27.

31. On the absence of textual quotations as a function of "the prophetic spirit" in prophetic literature, see the Krister Stendahl quotation in Ford, *Revelation*, 27.

The prophet from Patmos frequently weaves vivid pictures from episodes in The Story as he shares his visions. For instance, one of the images that John sees during the blowing of seven trumpets (Rev 8-11) is an *attack of locusts* (Rev 9:3-11). This vision recalls the episode during Israel's enslavement in Egypt, when the LORD sent locusts that devoured vegetation and fruit, the eighth plague (Exod 10:1-20). Later, Israel's *escape from Egypt*—that is, the defining Exodus event (Exod 12:37—14:31)—echoes as the last of seven plagues are noted (Rev 15). Most evident from this section is the use of the phrase "the song of Moses, the servant of God" (Rev 15:3a), which appears at the beginning of a song praising "Lord God the Almighty" (Rev 15:3c) for redeeming the faithful.

> **Pause to Reflect**
> Have you ever had a favorite song or piece of music
> than another artist then performed their own way?
> How did you feel about that "remake" of your favorite?
> How much freedom should people be allowed in
> playing beloved music in a different way?

John's creative capacity for utilizing elements of The Story that originally were not directly connected to each other appears early in the book. In the section where seven churches receive seven messages, the Son of Man (see Rev 1:13) warns the Pergamum church of participating in practices that show lack of trust in the true God. This visionary speaker makes his point by mentioning a character whom we met in the previous chapter, in the discussion of 2 Peter. It is *Balaam* again, the guy whose donkey had to talk to him, to get him to pay attention to what the LORD was expecting Balaam to do. Second Peter's concern was that the faithful stay away from the teaching of greedy persons who lead believers away from right belief and practice (see 2 Pet 2:12-20). The warning to the Pergamum church carries a similar concern about false teachers; now, in Revelation's handling of the Balaam cycle (Num 22-24), Balaam seems to come across as the bad guy. There, he is accused of influencing the Moabite king, Balak, "to put a stumbling block before the people of Israel" (Rev 2:14b), leading them astray.

Revelation's use of the Balaam incident demonstrates how
episodes and incidents from The One Great Story can and
do become understood and emphasized in different ways,
at different times, and from different standpoints.

These two variations on construing the Balaam legacy from Num 22 demonstrate how *episodes and incidents from The One Great Story can and do become understood and emphasized in different ways, at different times, and from different standpoints.* The broad theme of the danger of false teaching appears in both of these New Testament treatments of Balaam, even though they imply contrary views of the character.[32] For their respective purposes, both implications come across as fitting—even though, in the original cycle from Numbers, Balaam remains faithful to the LORD (see Num 24). Our initial task as readers is to appreciate each text on its own, to seek to get inside the meaning that it represents.

FOOD AND KINGS

We have digressed, however, although the question of interpretation remains present in any biblical reading. In the Son of Man's message to Pergamum about false teachers, John of Patmos also heard an image from the escaped Israelites' wilderness wanderings. Those believers who "listen to what the Spirit is saying to the churches . . . [and] conquers . . . [will receive from the messenger] some of the hidden manna . . . " (Rev 2:17ab). We remember *manna* as the food that the LORD provided to the Israelites, when they complained that they were going to starve to death (Exod 16). It appeared every morning, and the People were to gather enough to eat for that day; but it would not keep until the next day. According to the account, the Israelites ate this manna all the years of their wilderness trek (Exod 16:35). Its reference at the end of Revelation's warning to Pergamum suggests that staying faithful to God by avoiding false teaching will result in being wondrously sustained by God.

Neither are we surprised to discover images from The Story's royal episodes playing a part in Revelation's message. One of the most obvious of these references is to "the key of *David*," possessed by "the holy one, the true one" (Rev 3:7). In its context here, the holy and true one fairly clearly seems to be an allusion to Jesus as the Son of God. As we know by now, the earliest traditions that arose around Jesus—even those in the Gospel of Mark—associate Jesus with the lineage of the beloved King David. This association also is declared quite unmistakably at the end of the book, where John hears Jesus speak directly:

> "It is I, Jesus, who sent my angel to you with this testimony
> for the churches. I am the root and the descendant of David, . . . "
> (Rev 22:16)

32. For a brief discussion of the Balaam figure, see Rowland, "The Book of Revelation—Introduction," 578–79.

John hears Jesus called "the Root of David" in a second location (Rev 5:5); this metaphor echoes Isa 11, where the roots of Jesse (David's father) will bring forth a "shoot" upon which will rest "the spirit of the LORD" (Isa 11:1–2a). By the time of Jesus, Jews interpreted this passage from Isaiah to speak of a king to come, one who would reign over the renewed nation-state, Israel. Hopes for political independence remained strong in Jesus' generation, too. We should not be surprised, then, that this "Root of David" image would be seen to pertain to the risen Savior—who will reign over the entire world.

WOE! THEN EXULTATION

Optimistic images of the ultimate outcome for creation might not be as readily obvious in Revelation as we might like! There are plenty of visionary scenes in which distressing and destructive images must have shaken the sensibilities of its early hearers. One of those scenes uses the ancient empire of *Babylon* for its metaphoric purposes. This was the nation that conquered Judah in 586 BCE, sending all its royal court into exile there, effectively bringing the kingdom of the beloved David to a devastating end (see chapter 7). The effect of this loss upon the Israelite identity was expressed plaintively in a late psalm:

> By the rivers of Babylon—there we sat down
> and there we wept when we remembered Zion.
> On the willows there we hung up our harps.
> For there our captors asked us for songs,
> and our tormentors asked for mirth, saying,
> 'Sing us one of the songs of Zion!' (Ps 137:1–3)

So formidable was Babylon within the world of its time that the prophet Jeremiah spoke at length about its eventual demise. His poetic language was strong and graphic:

> You ravaged my patrimony [i.e., Judah];
> but though you rejoice and exult,
> though you . . . neigh like a stallion,
> your mother shall be cruelly disgraced,
> she who bore you shall be put to shame. (Jer 50:11–12a)

These words, written down six centuries before the Book of Revelation, barely scratch the surface of Jeremiah's preoccupation with Babylon—a name that appears in his writings a stunning 170 times! It would have been like an American citizen in the 1950s both worrying about and condemning the Soviet Union.

The image of Babylon the empire expresses for John of Patmos an ultimate cosmic struggle between evil and God's goodness and purpose.

Are we surprised, then, to discover how much space John of Patmos gives to Babylon in his book? Using feminine language, John's visionary messengers unapologetically speak of "the great city" (Rev 17:18) which is "*Babylon*, the great mother of whores and of earth's abominations" (Rev 17:5b). John then spends an entire chapter, with three different voices from heaven, bewailing its destruction:

> therefore her plagues will come in a single day—
> pestilence and mourning and famine—
> and she will be burned with fire;
> for mighty is the Lord God who judges her. (Rev 18:8)

John calls for exultation ("Rejoice over her, O heaven, you saints and apostles and prophets!" [Rev 18:20a]) and is joined by

> the loud voice of a great multitude in heaven, saying:
> Hallelujah! Salvation and glory and power to our God,
> [whose] judgments are true and just;
> [God] has judged the great whore
> who corrupted the earth with her fornication,
> and [God] has avenged on her the blood of [God's] servants. (Rev 19:1–2)

In this way, John draws from a major event in The Story to interpret his visions. He correlates the domination and fall of ancient Israel's nemesis, the empire Babylon, with the domination and eventual fall of the power of evil in the world.

Whether Babylon was intended to represent something more specific, however, has intrigued readers for most of Christian history. Scholars have speculated about a possible veiled message in Revelation concerning an anticipated collapse of the empire that dominated in John's day—that of Rome. Certainly, the known historical context of the time makes Rome an attractive conjecture, although the name "Rome" does not appear anywhere in the book.

Our purpose here is not to enter this debate, since evidence is rather ambiguous, if not confusing.[33] What we certainly can recognize, though,

---

33. A concise discussion of the use of the term "Babylon" in the New Testament,

is that John saw in the old, pivotal episode of Judah's conquest by a world power a symbol of what was to come. The authority of The Story to inform and inspire subsequent generations was not lost on this visionary prophet.

TO WORSHIP AND TO RULE

Indeed—as I have hinted already—along with pictures and scenes of cosmic disaster, Revelation does end on a positive note, and it sprinkles encouraging notes here and there along the way. One of the strongest of these optimistic indications appears fairly early and draws upon two central images from Israel's life with God. I also detect echoes that link these two images with what I see as the banner verse of The One Great Story.

> **Pause to Reflect**
> In today's world, are there "abominable empires" like Babylon was to John of Patmos? What would qualify a nation to be considered so evil by other nations? Who decides?

These two central images—as integral components in The Story—are "priest" and "kingdom." We discover them together in Revelation in two places, the first being in the book's opening salutation,

> To him who loves us and freed us from our sins by his blood,
> and made us *to be a kingdom, priests serving* his God and Father,
> to him be glory and dominion forever and ever. (Rev 1:5c–6a)

And the second just before the Lamb (the Son of God) begins to open, one by one, seven seals on a heavenly scroll:

> You are worthy to take the scroll and to open its seals,
> for you were slaughtered and by your blood you ransomed for God
> saints from every tribe and language and people and nation;
> you have made them *to be a kingdom and priests serving* our God,
> and they will reign on earth. (Rev 5:9–10)

The role of *priest* in the life of The People shows up quite early in The Story. Egypt had priests in their religion; Joseph married the daughter of one of these priests (Gen 41:45); Moses' father-in-law, Jethro, was "priest of Midian" (Exod 3:1a). The traditions that are woven into the accounts of Moses receiving The Ten Words at Mount Sinai assume that Israel's religious practice depended upon specific roles for a priesthood (see Exod 19:22, 24).

---

including Revelation, is found in Minear, "Babylon (NT)," 338.

In fact, the functions of the Israelite priests were so carefully designated that the Book of Leviticus alone uses the word "priest" more than 170 times!

Revelation also draws upon Israel's traditions with a priesthood and with its beloved kingdom.

We also know how important the notion of "*kingdom*" was in the life of The People. Although they lived for many generations by God-appointed judges, without a royal form of government, the People asked for one anyway (see 1 Sam 8–10.). Having its own king "to govern us, like other nations" (1 Sam 8:5c) became such an integral part of Israel's identity: it meant status among other countries, not to mention an accepted way to claim and maintain geographic boundaries. This form of identity was resilient in the Israelite, and later Jewish, culture—so much so, that kingdom language was used freely in Jesus' ministry. There, the concept seems to have been modified significantly, since Jesus spoke of "the kingdom of heaven (as in Matthew)" or "the kingdom of God (as in Mark, Luke, John, and Paul)."

And yet—what do Jesus' followers ask him before his ascension? "Lord, is this the time when you will restore the kingdom to Israel?" (Acts 1:6b). They asked him this question—which sounds pretty political to me!—even though the narrator noted, just three verses earlier, that Jesus spent time "speaking about the kingdom of God" (Acts 1:3c). Clearly, the hope that God's eventual purpose for The People would require real estate again had not faded! The notion of kingdom maintained a strong currency for our biblical ancestors, even after many centuries.

So, then, both priest and kingdom were longstanding components of The Story: for many, they had come to represent to The People who and what they saw themselves to be—whether in fact or in aspiration/calling. It does not surprise me, therefore, to discover far back into The Story a key passage that brings both of these words together. In the scene preparing for God's delivery of The Ten Words, the LORD gives Moses a message for The People:

> Then Moses went up to God; the LORD called to him from the mountain, saying, 'Thus you shall say to the house of Jacob, and tell the Israelites: You have seen what I did to the Egyptians,
> and how I bore you on eagles' wings and brought you to myself.
> Now therefore, if you obey my voice and keep my covenant,
> you shall be my treasured possession out of all the peoples.
> Indeed, the whole earth is mine, but
> *you shall be for me a priestly kingdom and a holy nation . . .* '
> (Exod 19:3b–6a)

Here in this statement from the LORD, we observe major themes that we have seen throughout this book to echo in The Story over and over again—recounting God's rescue and protection of a chosen community of kinfolk; reiterating God's expectation that this People are faithful to God's pact with them; emphasizing the People's unique status with God; and re-stating God's intention for the People's role in the world.

ENLARGING THE TENT

As we have come to see The Story develop throughout the biblical witness, none of these major themes and features can be underestimated or over-looked. What is particularly arresting here, however, is how the words "priest" and "kingdom" are used together. The theological picture that "priestly king-dom" paints is remarkable and compelling. It invites listeners to ponder an image of a nation that serves rather than dominates. Its role is to live among "all the peoples" in a world that belongs entirely to the LORD, for a task unlike any other; as one biblical scholar puts it: "Israel is to embody God's own purposes in the world."[34] This theological affirmation appearing in the second book of the Bible is not accidental. While we can recognize the influ-ence here of later editors within these storytelling traditions, looking back into those traditions and elaborating upon their implications, their impulse to elaborate only highlights what The Story has been saying all along: "and in you all the families of the earth shall be blessed" (Gen 12:3c).

No wonder that John of Patmos uses this phrase from the Exodus epi-sode twice in his apocalypse! No wonder that it appears in 1 Peter as well (1 Pet 2:9—see chap 10 of this book). As narrative currency, "priest" and "king-dom" linked together present a powerful reminder and promise to The Peo-ple of The Story. As Moses stood at the base of the mountain and reminded the wandering Israelites of God's singular action and their distinctive calling, so also John of Patmos sent that 2,000-year-old message ricocheting through his vision of God's future. Whatever John's audience thought of the prospects for their world, he was reminding them that their divinely appointed expec-tation was the same as that of their spiritual ancestors.

Pause to Reflect

Who is part of your community? What kind of variety does it represent? What reasons might be given for including—or not including—any "tribe and language and people and nation" who do not currently live or work in your community?

---

34. Fretheim, *Exodus*, 212–13.

Adding to this reminder of the ancient vocation, just as powerful of an image may be drawn out of John's use of the phrase, "*every tribe and language and people and nation.*" Close variations of this phrase appear several times in Revelation (5:9, 7:9, 10:11, 11:9, 13:7, 14:6, and 17:15). It seems to be used to emphasize that all kinds of people everywhere are included in the particular reference. In some, that inclusion seems to be mostly to describe the action of the particular visionary scene—that massive numbers of people on earth will be involved (as in 10:11, 11:9, and 13:7). In others, however, the tone of the scene is upbeat, positive, favorable—as with the quotation above, referring to "saints from every tribe and language and people and nation" (Rev 5:9d). Similarly, John later sees "a great multitude that no one could count," described the same way, who wave palm branches before the Lamb and the throne, crying out praises to God (Rev 7:9–10). Later, an angel flies high through the sky, announcing "an eternal gospel" to earth's inhabitants, described the same way (Rev 14:6).

Whatever John's audience thought of the prospects for their world, he was reminding them that their divinely appointed expectation was the same as that of their spiritual ancestors.

It is striking to me that John employs this phrase so many times. Throughout his visions, representatives of all human communities on earth face judgment (as Rev 10:11 suggests), stare at the bodies of two slain witnesses who prophesied (see Rev 11:4–10), and endure the rule of a beast from the sea (Rev 13:1–8). These incidents within the many visions clearly express tribulation upon earth's inhabitants. Yet, in other places, the phrase "tribe, language, people, and nation" is part of descriptions of the ultimate triumph of God and the Lamb. When things on earth and in heaven finally move beyond torment, terror, and trouble, God's mercy and favor will govern—*and they will include people of all kinds.*[35] To quote the "new song" again from Rev 5:

> . . . for you [the Lamb] were slaughtered and by your blood
> you ransomed for God saints from every tribe
> and language and people and nation;
> you have made them to be a kingdom and priests
> serving our God, and they will reign on earth. (Rev 5:9–10)

In this first vision in which the Lamb appears, John brings together an *inclusive* view of the world with an ancient, *exclusive*-sounding one. The mission that the LORD gives the Israelites at the time of their wilderness

35. See Rowland, "The Book of Revelation—Introduction," 604, 621.

wanderings—to be ". . . my treasured possession out of all the peoples, . . . a priestly kingdom and a holy nation" (Exod 19:5–6) now merges in the Revelation with a net cast widely. For centuries, the promise in Exod 19 could have been interpreted as only for Abraham's physical descendants. As we have seen above in chapters 9 and 10, though, that narrow interpretation was challenged by early followers of Jesus (Acts and Paul's letters). The chorus singing this new song in Rev 5 expresses the same, more expansive, theological view: God will create this "priestly kingdom" out of folks from everywhere—every place, every tongue, every community, every grouping of human beings.

> *When things on earth and in heaven finally move beyond torment, terror, and trouble, God's mercy and favor will govern—and they will include people of all kinds.*

I can't help but think that this passage in Revelation 5, along with other texts that we have quickly considered here, strikes at the heart of Revelation's main message. To me, it seems to capture the overall movement of The One Great Story, as this Grand Narrative scoops up Jesus in its current and then makes sense out of where it all is going. John's apocalypse looks forward for sure, but it does so by apprehending salient pieces of The Story and rendering them significant for a new age. Indeed, the zenith of John's image-handling comes almost at the end of his explosion of visionary scenes. Once the powers of evil have been uncovered, once the plagues have come and gone, and once Babylon has been thrown down, one more series of visions appears in the Bible's final book. This last series revolves around yet another remarkable, arresting image from The Story.

AS THOUGH STARTING OVER

Six centuries before John of Patmos received his visions of the future, the kingdom of Judah sat in defeat, exile, and despair. We glimpsed in chapter 7 of this book how the prophet Jeremiah perceived that horrifying theological eventuality, drawing as he did quite poetically and with agony, from The Story. Perhaps Jeremiah's most poignant contribution to The Story is the "new covenant" promise (Jer 31:31–34), as the weeping prophet reflected on the covenant of old, broken by The People. John's prophetic mentor seems more to be the Book of Isaiah, and nowhere does this reliance become more apparent than in John's appropriation of the image, *"new heavens and a new earth."* It appears in Isaiah twice, in its final two chapters:

> For I am about to create new heavens and a new earth;
> the former things shall not be remembered or come to mind. (Isa 65:17)
> For as the new heavens and the new earth, which I will make,
> shall remain before me, says the LORD,
> so shall our descendants and your name remain. . . .
> all flesh shall come to worship before me, says the LORD. (Isa 66:22–23)

Pause to Reflect
What are some of the "new things" that you have experienced in your life? What made them new? What relationship, if any, did they have with what had been part of your life previously? How did you respond to the new things? fear? resistance? welcome? What influenced your responses?

As we can appreciate now, this picture of the entire universe being created over again would have appealed to a People whose promising Story seemed to have fallen completely apart. Beyond the many perplexing metaphors that crowd John's visions remains a hope for a future in which God's purposes will not be thwarted but rather achieve a kind of culmination. All demonic, faithless, and dreadful powers will come to an end; God will give all creation an extreme makeover.

Beyond the many perplexing metaphors that crowd John's visions remains a hope for a future in which God's purposes will not be thwarted but rather achieve a kind of culmination.

In a sense, then, Revelation brings full circle The One Great Story and its unlikely, unpredictable, tenacious charisma. The biblical witness to a God who (in the words of one of my pastors years ago) will not let us down, will not let us go, or will not let us off, maintains a remarkable consistency. We have followed that witness from the promise to Abram and Sarai—"in you all the families of the earth shall be blessed" (Gen 12:3)—all the way through Jacob's twelve sons; captivity and escape from Egypt; wilderness, covenant, conquest, judges, kings and kingdoms; prophetic warnings and promises; defeat, exile, return, waiting and hoping; Jesus' ministry, crucifixion, and resurrection; followers of the Way; Gentile inclusion; reinterpretation; and eventual cosmic triumph. It is an immense saga, one that pivots over and over again on God's call, the people's response, and the consequences of faith or the lack thereof.

From this sweeping perspective, then, the final book in the Bible serves The Story well. Revelation offers both a conclusion and a beginning, an endpoint and a starting point, a sunset and a dawn, a book's last page that ends with "To be continued." The Bible has no "the end" in it, anywhere. The One Great Story has a way of continually moving along, moving ahead, inviting its listeners to see their own world through the lenses that The Story brings to life.

In our final chapter, we will take time to reflect, to ponder themes and issues that present themselves anytime that we take seriously being part of The Story's audience. You probably have thought about some of these themes and issues already. Because I believe that The One Great Story sustains its own integrity, we can ask hard and puzzling questions about it. We might not always discover easy or satisfying answers, but we can approach the quest with confidence that The Story needs neither defending or assaulting.

FOR THE READER

1. How does the distinction between Moses as a "servant" and Jesus as a "son" serve the theological argument made in Hebrews? Do you think that the epistle diminishes Moses' standing in The Story? Why or why not?

2. Why is it so important to the author of Hebrews to recite such a long list of faithful characters (Heb 11) from The One Great Story? How does Heb 12:1–3 help you understand the purpose of the long list?

3. How might the Revelation's earliest audiences have reacted to hearing the name "David?" "Babylon?" How do these two names represent the main themes in the book?

4. What do the "kingdom/priests" passages and the "new heavens and new earth" passages share, in terms of what Revelation seeks to impart to its readers?

SUGGESTED ACTIVITIES

- Read Heb 11; which characters and stories mentioned there speak to you the most? Which ones less so? What makes the difference for you, between what is "most" and what is "least?"

- Select from one of these chapters in Revelation—1, 7, 14, or 21—and read it, noting verses and phrases that speak of bad things and those that speak of good things. Where in the world today do you see the "bad" ones at work? The "good" ones? How do you explain your selections?

- If you were to write a final book for the Bible, what would you want it to say? Which aspects of The One Great Story would you want to emphasize? Write down some thoughts for yourself. Invite a friend who has shared some of these previous exercises with you to do the same. Then talk together about your notes and ideas. What insights does your conversation bring out about how The Story appeals to people today?

Chapter 12

The Story Continues—

Even Now

"Now therefore revere the LORD, and serve [God]
in sincerity and faithfulness . . ."

—JOSH 24:14A

It might not be easy to review a story line of such length and detail, but let's give it a try:

A SUMMARY OF "THE STORY"

The God who created the earth and all that is in it—"the heavens and the earth" (Gen 1:1)—brought into existence, over many generations, a community, a People, to bear witness to God's purposes of blessing for all peoples and all creation.

This People often ungratefully strayed in their loyalty to God, who had made them who they were, against all odds. Even when the People—over several centuries—escaped famine, slavery, wilderness threats, many battles with other nations, and became an established state with its own royal

213

house, they continued to seek their own ways, rather than to follow God wholeheartedly.

Internal intrigues and threats from large empires eventually weakened this People, in spite of calls from "true" prophets who reminded them of their special agreement with God, who chastised them for their apostasy and injustices, who warned of impending national disaster, and who finally declared the implausible hope that God once again would act on behalf of the ancient Promise made to this People.

That Promise took flame again through the appearance of Jesus of Nazareth, whose life, ministry of preaching, healing, and teaching ignited fresh hope among the People's common population and resistance among its elite religious officials. In order to undercut a potentially dangerous situation with their own religious authority and with rulers of the current empire, members of the People's elite circles accused Jesus of blasphemy and disruption, entangling him in deliberations leading to his crucifixion by the empire.

> **Pause to Reflect**
> Which episode, chapter, or phase in The One Great Story do you find most intriguing? What is it that makes it that way for you? How does it help you appreciate The Story's overall arc? In what way does this episode, chapter, or phase affect the way that you think about the world today? About your own life?

When Jesus appeared, risen from his execution, his followers were stunned and elated. After he left their presence, they waited in their ancient, beloved capital city, Jerusalem, for what Jesus promised them. God's Spirit then emboldened and empowered them to proclaim that Jesus was the Messiah from God, whose work of healing and restoration was intended, not only for descendants of the ancient People, but for all peoples everywhere. That special agreement was transformed into hope and blessing to any who would receive it.

Through followers like Saul of Tarsus, this message of reconciliation spread throughout many parts of the empire. Saul (Paul) and many others drew from elements of their inherited Story to explain to both descendants and other peoples how Jesus as Messiah ushered in a culmination of the old, old Promise associated far back, to a couple named Abraham and Sarah. That Promise has not reached its ultimate conclusion, however: it remains in the midst of all peoples everywhere, as those who follow Jesus in their own times and places continue to bear witness to what God hopes and seeks for this wondrous, yet still troubled, Creation.

WHEN IS AN ENDING NOT THE END?

This doesn't seem like the end.

There is a sense in which each one of the longest documents in the New Testament conclude without finishing. Matthew's last verses tell of Jesus meeting the eleven and giving them some final instructions and encouragement. Mark has two or three endings, depending on what you think author(s) and editor(s) had in mind, and each one has its own way of leaving things up in the air. Luke ends with Jesus disappearing "into heaven" after telling his followers to stay in Jerusalem and wait for what was to come. John's final chapter (21) feels like a second ending, too, and concludes with a musing about how many books it would take to write down all the things that Jesus did. The Acts of the Apostles leaves Paul under house arrest but free to preach and teach the gospel. As we just saw in chapter 11 of this book, the Revelation to John ends with the promise of new heavens and new earth, with the expectant words, "See/Surely I am coming soon" appearing three times (Rev 22:7a; see also 12a, 20b).

Oh, sure, it's not that any of these witnesses to Jesus as Savior end in a mid-sentence, as though the person responsible for its final form nodded off to sleep at the writing desk, or the last leaf of the original document fell in the fire and never got replaced, or—sillier yet—that the writer couldn't think of how to finish. Rather, in one way or another, each one of these New Testament books suggests a trajectory shooting out of its last words—that, although their recording of testimony is concluded, there is more to come. The Story itself is not contained, limited, stifled, devalued, or discarded just because the particular words in those particular documents stopped where they did.

The One Great Story is the original "never-ending story." *Characters* emerge, play out their scenes with opportunity, intrigue, challenge, and occasional achievement, and then move aside in death as others take center stage. *Locations* shift many times until the era of conquest and kingdom, and then eventually shift again. *Conditions* change dramatically over the centuries, from nomadic life to slavery to wilderness wandering to conquest to settlements to kingdom to international reputation to division to double defeat to exile to rule by empires.

Yet, in spite of all the changes of circumstance and time, the characters, locations, and conditions hang together. They share a thread of purpose, articulated often enough that it is hard to miss. This thread of purpose, this pervasive message, keeps calling its biblical listeners ahead. The way that the People are expected to live out their call and blessing serves as a model and an invitation. By the time that we hear it from Paul and Peter and Hebrews and Revelation, we can't escape it reaching out to us—and even beyond us.

> *The Story's characters, locations, and conditions share a thread*
> *of purpose, articulated often enough that it is hard to miss.*

If we accept The Story's declaration that hope in God's forgiveness and blessing indeed extends to people everywhere, then how do people today relate to it? For those who take on the mantle of being "followers of the Way," how does one find a place in such a Story? These are the central questions that guide this final chapter. First, we will reflect on several general ruminations that help position us to engage The Story authentically. Then we will identify what I consider to be several themes that emerge along the way as key elements of The Story's trajectory. Finally, we will think a little more deeply about the matter of interpretation—how we legitimately go about understanding The Story as it is and then associating ourselves in valid ways with it. I am hoping that these three sets of reflections will answer some of the questions that you have formulated throughout the reading of this book. This way, I trust that you will feel more confident to continue reading—reading The Story directly, better prepared than I was in fourth grade, or even in seminary!

RUMINATIONS ON HEARING "THE STORY" TODAY

The Bible tells a strange story—that an unlikely band of folks living mostly on the fringes of the world stage could carry a divine promise of blessing for all peoples.

There is a sense in which, as we review The Story, we are struck by the thought that no one could make this up. Over and over again, this ancient story line conveys a quality, an ambience, that is dramatic yet still realistic. Even scenes early in The Story, in which the LORD is presented with human characteristics such as getting angry, being impatient, or changing plans, sustain a tone that allows hearers to relate to it. We are not listening to fantasy or mythology as much as people and events that feel compelling, while also stirring us with their appealing improbability. Traditions and narratives from other ancient sources have heroes and tragedies, too, but nothing like this. The Story, through all of its twists and turns, is like no other.

Biblical storytelling is often startlingly honest, especially when its main characters turn out to be as faltering as the rest of us.

When I was a child in Sunday school, I gained the impression that biblical characters were quiet, even-tempered people who somehow had a way of effortlessly following God. How little I knew then! It would be years before that impression radically changed—when I realized that Noah got drunk after the ark came back to dry land, that Sarai denied laughing when she overheard the LORD's messengers promising Abraham and Sarah a son (earlier, Abraham lied to Pharaoh about Sarah being his wife), that Jacob cheated his twin brother Esau out of the birthright, that Moses complained over and over again to the LORD during the People's wilderness wandering, that the People in the wilderness built a golden calf to worship, that the great prophet Samuel's sons were worthless scoundrels, that beloved King David impregnated Bathsheba and then had her soldier husband killed in battle, that Peter denied knowing Jesus, that—well, the list could go on and on!

One of my uncles once commented, after her death, that my grandmother had had a way of ignoring her children's "indiscretions." The Story will have none of that! It sugarcoats nothing; it recounts the People's memories, warts and all.

What appears as good news to one biblical character or group not infrequently is bad news to someone else.

This rumination will help us think more about interpretation later in the chapter. It is not merely a matter of The Story's events and episodes being filled with "good guys" and "bad guys"; there is plenty of struggle throughout much of The Story with nations who want the People out of their way. More subtly, especially within the life of the People themselves, actions would lead to certain kinds of consequences, depending on whether or not the People expressed trust in the God who called them. The Israelites knew better, but as a whole they tended to stray from that special agreement with the LORD and do what they wanted. That stubbornness on their part resulted in bad news, of one kind or another. Yet, in spite of this persistent lack of memory and gratitude among the People, there typically remained one or two folks whose faithfulness kept the Promise alive. Good news sometimes only flickered, often on the edges of the bad news that the People as a whole needed to face.

The Story starts coming alive when we begin to take it seriously
without getting stuck in literalistic quagmires.

> **Pause to Reflect**
> When was a time in your life in which you admitted that you
> had failed at something really important? What was it like to
> face that failure? What did you do next? In what ways might
> that difficult admission have helped you in the long run?

Many earnest readers of the Bible today have had trouble with this insight
about the nature of the ancient documents comprising the Hebrew Bible
and the New Testament. Arguments about the meaning of divine inspiration come into play, which we will not seek to summarize or evaluate here.
It is enough for our purposes to emphasize this: acknowledging that biblical
texts by nature function differently than our modern assumptions about
literal precision and historical neutrality does not have to take away from its
capacity to speak genuinely and convincingly.

Good news sometimes only flickered on the edges of the
bad news that the People as a whole needed to face.

In my particular tradition, for instance, one of the ordination questions for both pastors and ruling elders (church members elected by the
congregation) says:

> Do you accept the Scriptures of the Old and New Testaments to
> be, by the Holy Spirit, the unique and authoritative witness to
> Jesus Christ in the Church universal, and God's Word to you?[36]

A question like this affirms what Christians throughout the centuries
have recognized for the Bible—its unparalleled, distinctive place in the life
of those who follow Jesus. Yet we insult the Bible when we insist that it must
adhere to assumptions about reality (a universe with galaxies, a round earth
that spins, etc.) and truth (scientific and exact) that emerged in the Western
world only in recent centuries. When we do so, we put ourselves at a disad-
vantage, seeking to fit the Bible into our worldview, rather than engaging the
Bible on its own terms. Otherwise, the Bible turns into a laborious collection

---

36. The Constitution of the Presbyterian Church (U.S.A.), Part II, *Book of Order*,
2015–2017.

of ancient manuscripts, in which perplexing phrases, circumstances, and actions become ignored or awkwardly explained away.

I hinted at this insight somewhat in chapter 1, and I realize that some contemporary Christian traditions find this view troubling or offensive. However, we discover that the Bible—and the Grand Narrative that weaves it together—comes alive when we stop trying to squeeze it into our own comfortable mold. To paraphrase from a story about theologian Paul Tillich, we don't have to "grasp the Bible;" instead, we need to let "the Bible grasp us."

It is dangerous to read one part of The One Great Story in isolation from another.

Abraham/Sarah, Isaac/Rebekah, Jacob/Rachel, Joseph, Moses, Miriam, Joshua, Ruth, Hannah, Samuel, David/Bathsheba, Solomon, Jeremiah, Hosea, Ezekiel, Malachi, Mary, John the Baptist, Jesus, Peter, Paul: these characters, and many others, make The Story what it is. That is, they not only *contribute* to it, they also in an important sense *inherit* those episodes, chapters, and events that precede them. Each one thus makes sense as part of the trajectory, the flow. We seek to understand across their many generations, as we listen both backward and forward.

This insight suggests three others:

- We don't read the Old Testament as though Jesus is "in there"—but we do read about Jesus as though the Old Testament is there.

    This point might sound completely off-base at first, but its purpose is to keep things in appropriate perspective. The many full-bodied, pre-Jesus elements of The Story maintain an integrity of their own: they grew out of rich experiences and memories that were valued and preserved in their own right. As the generations came and went, and The People's circumstances changed, various elements of The Story were evoked to explain present conditions and to articulate reasons for hope. Jesus' active presence stimulated probably the most intense recollection and reframing of Their Story ever undertaken.

Jesus as Savior brings to The Story a realization of its foundational plot.

    As we have seen, Jesus as Savior brings to The Story a realization of its foundational plot. This realization explicitly links Jesus with the long-awaited Promise. No wonder, then, that we discover such a feast of direct and indirect references to the Hebrew Bible in the New Testament documents!

- Christians can't ignore the Old Testament and expect to fathom the authentic power of the New Testament.

    Hopefully, you can appreciate this statement, now that you have read this far in this book. The message of the New Testament—the "gospel," the good news—flows out of a story line populated by people, events, and places going all the way back into Genesis. Trying to disconnect the story of Jesus and its significance from the Hebrew Scriptures is like telling an orphan that it doesn't matter where she or he came from, or like pulling a plant out of the soil and expecting it to live. The Story does not begin with Jesus; it reaches a pinnacle of sorts with him, but it starts a long time earlier. Those who seek to follow Jesus find themselves called back into those early episodes and chapters of That Story.

- The Bible and its Story look more like a tapestry than a treasure chest. Given the sheer size of the library that makes up the Bible, I suppose that it is not surprising to find some versions of Christian teaching and preaching that treat the Bible like a treasure chest. One opens the lid and searches for some shiny, precious stone that appeals to them at the time. This metaphor carries a certain appeal, I realize, since followers of the Way typically seek to be informed, supported, and encouraged by studying "what the Bible has to say." At the same time, though, the Bible as treasure chest implies that one's faith is strengthened by collecting assorted gems of knowledge and wisdom as though their relationship to one another could be arbitrary or—even more troubling—insignificant.

    In this book, I have attempted to make the case that the Scriptures are woven together by a narrative, a story line that is remembered, passed on, enlarged, and interpreted generation after generation. The One Great Story reads as we would study a medieval tapestry, with its various distinct scenes, moving as on a path, from one episode to another. You can appreciate each scene for what it specifically represents, yet it is all the scenes together that make the tapestry what it is. Such is the case with the Bible: we understand it best and most authentically when we treat each part as it contributes to the whole.

The Story is much more about "us" than it is about "me."

Pause to Reflect
Think about a time when you were surprised to find
out that your impression of a particular person was not
accurate. What happened to trigger this new awareness?
What was it like to realize that you were "off"?

When we pay attention to human presence in various parts of The Story, we eventually must come to terms with a perspective on human nature that differs from what we today take for granted. In the Bible, as in virtually all of human history, "being a person" meant being part of a community. One's identity was defined first by the village or tribe into which one was born; one's actions in life reflected upon that village or tribe, bringing either honor or shame upon it. When, for example, Joshua says, "As for me and my household, we will serve the LORD" (Josh 24:15d), he is reflecting this community understanding. Decisions are made for the benefit of the community, rather than by individual persons for their own personal interest and gain. By contrast, persons who are cut off from their community are considered suspicious: what have they done to become alienated from "their people?"

Self-in-community, as a concept taken for granted in the Bible, carries some significant implications for thinking about what it means to follow Jesus today. We will touch on these implications below, in the upcoming section.

Many churchy and popular images of Jesus fall short; they don't capture the Jesus of the four Gospels.

One of the strongest dangers in listening to The Story is not realizing where and how we might be imposing our own views on what we hear. Our unconscious assumptions can filter what we think we are seeing in any part of The Story—especially when Jesus is involved. For instance, if we carry a "gentle Jesus, meek and mild" picture in our minds, we might not fully recognize the import of passages in the Gospels in which Jesus confronts religious authorities (see, for example, Luke 5:17–26 and Mark 3:22–27) or says things to people that we might be surprised to hear him say (such as, "You faithless and perverse generation, how much longer must I be with you? How much longer must I put up with you?" [Matt 17:17]).

It is tempting to try to fit Jesus into our image of what we want him to be. We would rather that he not confuse or challenge us. Yet, Jesus lives fully within the flow of The Story when he—in the words of twentieth-century theologian Reinhold Niebuhr—"comforts the afflicted and afflicts the comfortable." In doing so, Jesus echoes the longstanding condition of the Promise—that the People are called to remain faithful to the LORD, in order to carry the blessing. Hence, Jesus stands in the tradition of the biblical prophets, who were not known for winning popularity contests!

> *It is tempting to try to fit Jesus into our image*
> *of what we want him to be.*

THEMES THAT ENDURE THROUGHOUT "THE STORY"

As we have journeyed from Genesis to Revelation, tracing The Story throughout many witnesses and many generations, we begin to notice certain broad themes. These themes grow out of our attention to topics and ideas that appear over and over again, as The Story develops along its various twists and turns. Let us, then, consider the following list as an effort to provide illuminating expression to these themes.

The People's Journey as Founded on Marginality and Vulnerability

Throughout the many generations from Abraham and Sarah to King David, the People spend most of their time on edges. For a long time, they live as nomads, escaping starvation by settling in Egypt, only to become slaves of Pharaoh. After escaping, they wander for many years before conquering what would become their land. Even after all the tribes receive their territorial allotments, the People are threatened for many years by their neighbors. Establishing a kingdom provides them with some level of political stability but, in the long run, the kingdom is conquered. The People live in exile, their identity threatened with assimilation to the empire, later with insecurity under occupation. It is a Story saturated with threat, deception, conspiracy, deals kept and broken, holding on frequently by a thread of someone's faith in the Promise. The journey toward blessing is not a comfortable and triumphal one; it rarely commands esteem from halls of status and power.

Creating and Sustaining a Community that Witnesses to God's Purposes for the World

On the surface, The One Great Story appears driven by characters, events, and localities that can overwhelm the listener with detail. Remember that my fourth-grade mind could not sort it all out! The "forest" that is given shape by all those "trees" revolves around a community emerging for a unique mission. That community—whom I have called here "the People"—remains central to The Story's trajectory, even as we see it culminating in Acts and the Pauline letters. The People of the Promise were called to "enlarge the tent" (Isa 54:2), in order that Christ "might create in himself one new humanity in place of the two" (Eph 2:15b), that is, make from The People and all the rest of the nations, one community. Because of Jesus' witness to The Story, no groups of human beings are excluded from God's gift of blessing.

The implications of this theme for life today are deeper and more challenging than much of what American Christianity has emphasized. In a century in which technology continues to make the world smaller, the population larger, and all kinds of diversity more evident, creating and sustaining community is not easy. It flies in the face of a "me-first, get-as-much-as-I-can" culture. Still, if we listen carefully to The Story, we cannot avoid how it is couched in collective terms: the call is for a People of God, not Individuals for God.

The Persistent and Threatening Appeal of "No-gods"

Reflecting back on my earlier experiences with reading the Bible, I have become aware of a number of "filtering" patterns that were unconsciously at work in me. One of them was reading quickly, without much thought, sections and references to religious characters and practices from the other nations. I did not pay much attention to Molech, Astarte, the Baals, or the people who were their followers. They typically represented these "gods" with carved wooden or stone figures—hence, the frequent translation of several biblical terms all rendered as "idol." One of those terms, "*aelil*," means "a nonentity (that is, something that actually does not exist)" and sounds similar to a general term, "el," referring to Israel's God.[37] This wordplay could suggest that the storytellers were reminding their listeners that they must be careful not to confuse other things for the One Who called them.

37. See Gray, "Idol," 673–75.

How can followers of the Way live faithfully when idols
of wealth, status, and power meet us daily?

This ancient reminder seems relevant even now. Today's world contains plenty of things that vie for our allegiance—perhaps most evidently,
the drive to get more and more stuff. Jesus knew that the tiny wealthy class
of his time were tempted to seek greater wealth (see Luke 12:13–21; Matt
19:21–24; and even Matt 6:25–33). Who could have imagined in those days
that entire societies many centuries later would be tempted to suppose that
having more things would guarantee a good life? Wealth, status, and power
might look different today than they did in Jesus' time, but they certainly
rank high in popular culture. How can followers of the Way live faithfully,
when these idols meet us daily?

God's Community Being "Counter Cultural" and Accepting Some Appropriate Stance of Marginality

I don't think it is a stretch to say that the People got into the most trouble
when they tried to be like everyone else around them. Following God the
Creator, trusting in God's purposes and guidance, meant that the People did
not "fit in" (remember "You must be holy, for I am holy?" [Lev 11:45; see
also Lev 20:26]). There is something about divine expectations for the People that sets them apart from seeking power, advantage, wealth, and status.

A word that helps me to think about this theme from The Story is
"marginality." The apostle Paul's admonition speaks to this point: "Do not
be conformed to this world, but be transformed by the renewing of your
minds" (Rom 12:2). Followers of the Way claim different values and standards, which put them at odds with popular ideals and practices, which give
followers a different perspective on lots of things.

As I read The Story, I see believing communities called to give witness
in the world to a God whose purpose of blessing involves mercy, justice,
humility, and well-being for all peoples everywhere. News headlines on
any given day give witness to the wider world's drive for achievements that
exclude—and harm—others. Remaining committed to the Way takes courage: the community learns to live creatively with the edges toward which its
faith beckons it. Slipping into a stance of comfortable convention slowly but
surely drains the community of its Spirit-offered strength for God's work.

*Recognizing that Jesus as the Savior Brings to The One Great Story More **Con**-tinuity Than **Dis**-continuity.*

It oversimplifies The Story to say that Jesus brings love and grace to an old narrative that is dominated by law and retribution. Those who passed on and interpreted the Jesus episodes of The Story did so with careful attention to what those episodes contribute to—not how they disrupt—that Story. Matthew emphasizes this point when Jesus says, "Do not think that I have come to abolish the law or the prophets; I have come not to abolish but to fulfill" (Matt 5:17). Our society often thinks in terms of "either-or," as if something "this" way is totally the opposite of "that" way.

Not so in The Story! Its witness to God's purposes is more complex and subtle—characters that are neither fully saints or sinners; bumps along the road toward Promise, as the People waffle in their trust of the LORD; unexpected links along the way (remember the five women in Matthew's genealogy of Jesus?); the central character, Creator God, whose persistence over the centuries just boggles the mind. What makes the Jesus episodes "new" is less a break with the past and more a bringing-to-completion of the ancient Promise. Understood in this way, studying the Old Testament becomes a lively, even if sometimes outlandish, testimony to God's hope and purpose.

Preparing for the Unexpected as Part of the "New Thing"

At the same time, the Story gradually wraps the Promise of blessing with a motif of surprise. Perhaps it was because the People got stuck in a rut, supposing that a monarchy was the "be-all and end-all" of the Promise—or, after the kingdoms both were conquered, supposing that restoration of their nation-state was the only thing that God had in mind. As we have seen, Jesus himself startled many of his contemporaries with his own vision of the kingdom—a vision that led to his crucifixion.

The God who promises blessing also energizes
followers of the Way, with God's very Spirit.

Pause to Reflect
What is something in your life that caught you off-guard but turned out to be something beneficial? What was it like to

> realize eventually that your hesitation was not well-founded?
> How has that awareness influenced your life since then?

By the time we get into the thick of The Story in the Acts of the Apostles, it becomes quite clear that the ancient Promise involves two astonishing features. One, that Promise is to encompass Gentiles, that is, nations and groups who were not part of the original twelve tribes of Israel. Two, the God who promises blessing also energizes followers of the Way, with God's very Spirit. A net thrown as wide as it could be; divinely granted strength to live as witnesses of the Promise: what could be more unforeseen? What could be more gracious and hopeful?

Being Open to and Led by the Holy Spirit

It behooves us here to reflect a little more about the Holy Spirit. As the later documents in the New Testament offer their testimony, readers become aware that the Spirit played a significant role in the life of the early Jesus movement. Indeed, the word "Spirit"—referring to God—appears fifty-seven times in the Acts, at least eighty-eight times in Paul's letters, and fifteen times in the Revelation.

In the history of the church, though, the Holy Spirit has been treated in pretty passive and tame ways, if it was acknowledged at all. It has been much easier for church thinkers over the centuries to elaborate upon ideas about God and Jesus—both of which receive extensive attention in the biblical testimonies—than to ponder the Spirit. Perhaps this task has seemed too ambiguous or elusive. Yet we cannot avoid acknowledging that, by the time the four Gospels began to circulate, the presence and activity of Divine Spirit had become integrated into the experience and testimony of early Christians.[38]

The One Great Story calls people today to allow the Holy Spirit to help them live out fresh episodes of that Story.

Their testimony, however, has not sustained clear or widespread acceptance of the role of God's breath and wind in the midst of today's world. In a few historically recent Christian movements and traditions, the Holy Spirit is afforded a role that gives rise to dramatic expressions of praise,

38. For a short and readable twentieth-century discussion of the Holy Spirit in historical and theological context, see Van Dusen, *Spirit, Son, and Father.*

worship, and faith. These movements have been criticized by some Christians for excessive emphasis on specific demonstrations of what it means to follow Jesus fully.[39] Still, we cannot overlook the presence of Spirit in the Bible generally and in the New Testament specifically.

I believe that The One Great Story calls people today to allow the Holy Spirit to help them live out fresh episodes of that Story. Following the Jesus of the New Testament does not mean legalistic, literal imitation of Jesus, Peter, Paul, or any of the other characters named there. The "new thing" of Isaiah, the "new covenant" of Jeremiah, the "new heavens and new earth" of Revelation become possible in our day through the wonder-filled life that is available through the Holy Spirit. This means an adventurous attitude, shared in community, admitting uncertainty on the journey—but also acknowledging (as our ancestors in The Story occasionally did!) that, when blessing comes, it was not by human power alone.

"Conditional" Clause a Big Part of The Story: "If Faithful, Then Blessing; but if Unfaithful, then Disaster."

Finally, I suggest that those who listen to The One Great Story today embrace an inherent tension in its message. God's promise of blessing for all peoples has a paradoxical quality: it requires a response, an acceptance of what God expects from us, in order that this blessing can flourish. Many, many times, The Story testifies to the People turning away from God and ending up in a lot of hot water as a result. Despite some of the gruesome elements in some of those episodes, I don't believe that God is vengeful or cruel in character. Rather, what I think The Story seeks to show is that there are consequences in life for the People in abandoning their special agreement with the One who gave them the Promise. Blessing comes with responsibility; grace is given freely, but it can be frittered away—or, worse yet, rejected. Followers of the Way, in all times and places, choose every day—every moment—whether to stay true to the Giver of all life and blessing.

THE ONGOING TASK OF INTERPRETATION

As we conclude these several reflections on The One Great Story and how we engage it, we cannot avoid the reality of interpretation. Every time someone hears or reads something from this Story, some kind of process of

---

39. I speak here of the Pentecostal movement, which began around 1900, and the charismatic movement, which emerged among established Christian bodies in the 1960s and 1970s. To learn more, see Quebedeaux, *The New Charismatics*.

"making sense" out of it is taking place—and we most often don't even know it. Let's reflect also, therefore, on what a "making sense out of" process and experience might entail—and what it might need.

We begin by recognizing that *interpretation occurs in the Bible itself.* The most obvious examples of this kind of interpretation are things like:

- When Matthew (and other Gospel writers) quote a passage from the Hebrew Bible (for example, Matt 3:3, 11:10, and 12:17–21), in order to explain why something is happening in one of their episodes about Jesus.

- When the Gospels report Jesus referring to something from The Story (for example, Mark 2:23–27, 7:5–13; and Luke 11:30–32) as part of his teaching ministry.

- When Paul discusses Abraham's faith in God's promise (Rom 4), Isaac's place in the promise (Rom 9:6–16), and the People being sustained during the wilderness wanderings (1 Cor 10:1–7).

This type of interpretation seems more readily justified, because the burden is on the New Testament documents to make persuasive connections between Jesus and the Hebrew Bible phases of The Story. What Christian readers might not realize at first, however, is that interpretation of episodes and elements of The Story also occurs within the Hebrew Bible itself. For instance, on a broad scale, the history of the People—from Adam through the time of the Persian Empire—that is recounted in 1 and 2 Chronicles draws heavily from other Hebrew Bible documents (mostly 1 Sam 31 through the end of 2 Kings). The Chronicles corpus leaves out many details from those stories, lacks the sense of closeness to events, and expresses a different narrative tone than the documents on which it depends.

Interpretations of characters and events within The One Great Story occur throughout much of the Old and New Testaments.

Pause to Reflect

Think of a person, event, or situation with which you became familiar in years gone by. How do you understand that person, event, or situation at this point in your life? To what would you attribute the comparison—and, if no change, why not?

Hebrew prophets also incorporate images, characters, and episodes from The Story into their reflections and pronouncements (for example, the Exodus from Egypt in Isa 43:15–19; the wilderness covenant in Jer 7:21–26; and priestly responsibilities for the ancient covenant, in Mal 2:4–12.). Even earlier documents in the Hebrew Scriptures show signs of interpretive attention, perhaps most dramatically when Joshua calls for a covenant at Shechem by reciting a version of the People's Story from Abraham to settlement of the land (Josh 24:2–13). At the level of the texts as we have received them, therefore, it becomes clear that interpretation is part of the ball game. What continues to make The Story alive involves re-telling, re-handling, explaining, emphasizing, reframing, and connecting—tasks that seek to underscore the relevance of The Story for other times and places.

What, then, does interpretation of the Bible and Its Story involve? If someone prays hard, opens up the Bible, flips through some pages, sticks their finger down on a random text, and begins reading, what guarantee do they have that they will understand what that text means? Does "whatever comes to mind in that moment of reading" count as valid? What might later treatments in the Bible of earlier elements of The Story suggest about how to interpret The Story authentically, reliably, and faithfully?

The Bible's own evidence of interpretation implies—if nothing else—that listeners to The Story should learn to *pay attention to three distinct, but related, worlds. First* and foremost is the world out of which any particular part of The Story emerges. That world is primarily defined by ancient Near Eastern geography, history, cultures, and the like—then later by the Roman Empire. We have sought in this book to bring some of those features into focus; learning to account for these features takes some effort, but it helps to make The Story come alive.

As we get more accustomed to that biblical world, we become aware that a *second* world in play is our own. Whoever we are, we have been deeply influenced by many factors that involve history, location, family, ethnic origins, social and economic standing, and so forth. The factors of "our world" serve as filters, lenses through which light from The Story becomes shaded and refracted in our minds. Hence, "our world" often encounters the Bible with a degree of strangeness: we don't readily understand actions and statements reflecting ancient cultural practices. Learning to pay attention to *that* world helps to make us more aware of the things that make *our* world what it is. Learning, then, to move back and forth between these two worlds creates a kind of dialogue, in which we can discover more about ourselves as we listen more deeply to The Story.

Interpretation does not stop there, however. It might seem that these two worlds—that within The Story and that within us—cover the waterfront for making sense out of the Bible. Yet I urge us to think about a third world, or rather, a third set of worlds. This set of worlds has to do with communities and locations that are different from our own. In large cities, for instance, it is easy to observe communities living fairly close together and representing a wide variety of races, classes, gender and gender identities, countries of origin, and other distinctions. What might people in these communities see and hear in a particular biblical episode? For instance, which listener is closer to understanding the original parable in Luke (15:3–7): the American pastor who refers to it as "the lost sheep," or the Russian Orthodox priest who refers to it as "the incomplete flock?"[40] None of us should be surprised to discover that communities different than our own could understand a story differently, depending on how they discern their own world relating to the story. After all, for whom was the Exodus from Egypt good news? Certainly not for the Pharaoh!

Let's follow this line of thought a little further. I think that *a principal task for interpretation is to give high regard to the persons in a story line who are most like us, and with what elements of that story relate most closely to us.* In simple terms, I am referring to "who" and "what," or "players" and "possibilities." To illustrate, I cannot imagine the Egyptians putting themselves in the Exodus episode as the enslaved, harassed characters needing rescue, or officers in Pilate's military guard identifying with the plight of Jewish peasants. In the same way, the challenge for all hearers of The Story is to seek honest equivalents between the "who" and "what" of The Story, of their own context, and of the context of other hearers. Not every episode of The Story speaks the same message about everyone within that episode; neither does it speak the same message in other worlds of hearing.

The meaning of an incident or episode from The One Great Story does not change, but its significance to various audiences in various times and places can and will change.

We are speaking here of a critical distinction between the "meaning" of a text and its possible points of "significance." Simply stated, a text's "*meaning*" has to do with what an oral tradition, an author or editor(s), intended to convey to readers or listeners; by contrast, "*significance*" has to do with how someone associates a particular meaning with something else (e.g., a person, a community, a set of circumstances, an idea, etc.). The meaning of an incident or episode from The One Great Story does not change, but its

40. This distinction in naming this well-known parable was told to me by my former colleague, Rev. Jim Watkins.

significance to various audiences in various times and places can and will change. These two concepts—meaning and significance—clearly are related to each other, but the starting point always needs to be with meaning: as far as we can determine, what were those responsible for the text as we have it seeking to communicate?[41]

> **Pause to Reflect**
> What was your favorite song when you were thirteen years old? What memories and feelings were associated with it at that time in your life? When you hear that song now, what is different for you—thoughts, feelings, memories? What has not changed? How does this reflection help you to think about our experiences with interpretation?

Once we are clear about distinguishing between meaning and significance, it is easier for us to appreciate why we want to take note of "who" and "what," of a text's players and possibilities. One of my seminary professors liked to call a version of this process of interpretation "dynamic analogy," in which readers today "should look for the persons and figures in [a text] who might represent different folk today dynamically." If, for example, we always focus on Jesus in stories that include him, we have a hard time understanding the reactions that other characters in those stories had to what Jesus was doing.[42] Putting ourselves in the place of various characters in a story ("who/players") allows us to see the "possibilities" that those characters directly or indirectly might be entertaining. As I have suggested already, this kind of process is at work within The Story Itself, especially within its later episodes: the prophets, for instance, reflect on the Promise and the covenant as they speak (often of doom in consequence) to the People's actions. Even earlier (as has been mentioned previously), Joshua is remembered to have recited a synopsis of the People's earliest episodes as a prelude to renewing their covenant with the LORD (Josh 24). For biblical tellers, the meaning of The Story continued to address, generation after generation, its descendants, those inheritors of that central Promise: it spoke with significance—time and again—to their time, place, and new circumstances.

However, not every imaginable dynamic analogy might be faithful to the text. For instance, we should be careful not to identify with biblical

41. My source for distinguishing between "meaning" and "significance" is Hirsch, *Validity in Interpretation*. The discussion there is academic and therefore technical, but Hirsch provides in a few places concise summaries of the two terms; see 8, 62–3, 140, 141, 143, 211, 255.

42. Sanders, *God Has a Story Too*, 20.

characters in *economic* crisis if we ourselves do not experience economic distress. We should be careful not to see ourselves as a downtrodden biblical *outsider* if we are part of a supportive community that enjoys privilege. We should be careful to acknowledge when the "who" in a biblical episode is about a group, a *community*, and not simply about individuals. These three quick examples begin to point us in the direction of seeking points of significance that are valid and authentic, in which the possibilities that we hear from the text flow out of an honest dynamic analogy of players within its world to players in our own (or someone else's) world.

Another way of making this point is to say this: As "players" listening to a text, we might not always be the "good guys." Because of our own location in our world, we might have to recognize that a valid point of significance places us more with characters with whom we rather would not identify. Over the years, for instance, I have ruminated on Jesus' searing comments to the Jewish religious authorities of his day, scribes and Pharisees (see, for instance, Matt 23:1–36). What would be a valid point of significance today? Who might be "players" in today's world who would create a dynamic analogy between text and today? Being an ordained Protestant minister, I find myself thinking about the role of pastor of a congregation. I can imagine Jesus' woes against scribes and Pharisees acting as warnings to today's clergy—not to set bad examples (as Matt 23:3), not to place weighty religious expectations on church members (as Matt 23:4), not to seek attention and status (as Matt 23:5–7), and so on. As uncomfortable as I might feel in making this connection, it seems to be a justifiable—and valid—one.

At the same time, we want to avoid a simplistic, "either-or" view of dynamic analogy. Earlier in this chapter, we noted that one of the themes that recurs in The Story speaks to how the Promise is available. "If" the People accept their part in living toward the blessing, "then" wonderful things can happen ("a land flowing with milk and honey" and the like). But "if" the People turn away from the LORD, following gods who are not part of the Promise, "then" they can expect that their life will unravel. Life with God is conditional—not because God is capricious or vindictive, but because the Promise travels on a two-way street. Beyond tragedies such as the prophetic fall of the kingdom, The Story proclaims the chance for repentance, return, and renewed hope. The same can be said about locating the significance of troubling elements of The Story for today: even when we realize that we are more like the bad guys in an episode, there still remains a way out for us. We can heed the warnings, we can give up destructive ways, we can open ourselves once again to the God who is far more interested in fresh beginnings than in dreadful endings.

Even when we realize that we are more like the bad guys in an episode of The Story, there still remains a way out for us.

By learning to face our blind spots and struggle to acknowledge our own valid connections to challenging messages, we discover even more profoundly the depths and breadth of the Promise that echoes and calls throughout The One Great Story.

"As it was in the beginning is now and ever shall be; world without end, Amen."

We have traveled a long journey together. The Grand Narrative that makes the Bible what it is reads like a saga, with its many characters extending across countless generations, full of plot kinks and spins, seemingly more low points than high ones, peppered with strange tales and gruesome scenes, littered with the foibles of human ambition and failure—all the while managing to maintain a spark, a flame, a still small voice of expectation. The God who doesn't let us down, doesn't let us go, and doesn't let us off maintains a sometimes baffling persistence. Our complex world in some ways appears to resist the astonishing Promise that The Story refuses to abandon.

It has been my purpose in this book to make This Story more accessible and inviting to you. I am trusting that my rendering of This Story is not only faithful to it, but that—in this rendering—you have begun to catch its vision. I encourage you to explore that vision, to enter The Story Itself, as you read more of it on your own. This book can serve as a guide, but the guide is valuable only as you make use of it. So consider the invitation, pack your bags, and allow yourself to experience the voyage that can last a lifetime.

Welcome to The One Great Story!

FOR THE READER

1. Of the ruminations listed in the first section of this chapter, which one (and why):

    - does not surprise you?
    - gives you the most trouble?
    - surprises you the most?
    - leaves you wanting to do more reading in the Bible?

2. Of the themes noted in the second section of this chapter, which one (and why):

    - appeals to you the most?
    - would never have occurred to you?
    - seems the hardest to accept?
    - would be the easiest for you to mention in a conversation with your friends?

3. How does the distinction between the "meaning" of a text and a possible point of "significance" with that meaning help you to think about reading the Bible? What is it like for you to focus first on what an episode from The Story says? How might you most often find yourself as a "player" in an episode? How do you hear an episode's "possibilities" differently when you consider people outside of your own world?

SUGGESTED ACTIVITIES

- Sit with a friend and share with each other one of the responses that you gave to one of the parts of question one. How does hearing your friend's response help you appreciate her or his thinking on that subject?

- Sit with a friend (hopefully the same one) and follow the same process above, this time for question two. Then ask each other how this experience of sharing (both in speaking and in listening) helps you to think about the value of The One Great Story today.

- Read Luke 10:29–37. Do your best (with or without a published commentary) to determine what Jesus was trying to get across to the man who asked him the question. Whom do you think Jesus considered to be the central character of this parable? With whom do you most identify in the parable? How does pondering these two questions help you to think, first, about the meaning of this parable and, second, about its possible points of significance?

Bibliography

Achtemeier, Elizabeth. "Typology." In *The Interpreter's Dictionary of the Bible, Supplementary Volume*, edited by Keith Crim, 926–27. Nashville: Abingdon, 1976.

Black, Matthew. "Pharisees." In *The Interpreter's Dictionary of the Bible*. 4 vols. Edited by George Arthur Buttrick, 3:774–81. Nashville: Abingdon, 1962.

Brown, Robert McAfee. *Unexpected News: Reading the Bible with Third World Eyes.* Philadelphia: Westminster, 1984.

Brueggemann, Walter. *The Bible Makes Sense*, revised edition. Cincinnati: St. Anthony Messenger Press, 2003.

The Constitution of the Presbyterian Church (U.S.A.). Part II, *Book of Order.* 2015–2017.

Conzelmann, Hans. *1 Corinthians.* Translated by James W. Leitch. Philadelphia: Fortress, 1975.

Culpepper, Alan. "Luke." In *The New Interpreter's Bible*. 12 vols. Edited by Leander E. Keck, IX:1–490. Nashville: Abingdon, 1995.

D'Angelo, M. R. and E. A. Matter. "Apocalypticism." In *Dictionary of Biblical Interpretation*. 2 vols. Edited by John H. Hayes, A–J:40–44. Nashville: Abingdon, 1999.

Ford, J. Massyngberde. *Revelation.* Anchor Bible 38. Garden City: Doubleday, 1975.

Fretheim, Terence E. *Exodus.* Interpretation: A Bible Commentary for Teaching and Preaching. Louisville: John Knox, 1991.

Gealy, F. D. "Centurion." In *The Interpreter's Dictionary of the Bible*. 4 vols. Edited by George Arthur Buttrick, 1:547–48. Nashville: Abingdon, 1962.

Grant, F. C. "Roman religion." In *The Interpreter's Dictionary of the Bible*. 4 vols. Edited by George Arthur Buttrick, 4:109–12. Nashville: Abingdon, 1962.

Gray, J. "Idol." In *The Interpreter's Dictionary of the Bible*. 4 vols. Edited by George Arthur Buttrick, 2:673–675. Nashville: Abingdon, 1962.

Hamilton, Michael P., ed. *The Charismatic Movement.* Grand Rapids: William B. Eerdmans, 1975.

Hirsch, E. D. Jr. *Validity in Interpretation.* New Haven: Yale University Press, 1967.

Horsley, Richard A. *Jesus in Context: Power, People, and Performance.* Minneapolis: Fortress, 2008.

Kelber, Werner H. *The Oral and the Written Gospel: The Hermeneutics of Speaking and Writing in the Synoptic Tradition, Mark, Paul, and Q.* Philadelphia: Fortress, 1983.

Mays, James Luther. *Psalms.* Interpretation: A Bible Commentary for Teaching and Preaching. Louisville: John Knox, 1994.

McDonald, Lee Martin. *Formation of the Bible: The Story of the Church's Canon.* Peabody, MA: Hendrickson Publishers, 2012.

McKenzie, John L. "The Hebrew Community and the Old Testament: Part II, 'Oral Tradition.'" In *The Interpreter's One-Volume Commentary.* Edited by Charles M. Laymon, 1073–74. Nashville: Abingdon, 1971.

Minear, Paul S. "Babylon (NT)." In *The Interpreter's Dictionary of the Bible,* 4 vols. Edited by George Arthur Buttrick, 1:338. Nashville: Abingdon, 1962.

Mudge, Lewis. "Paul Ricoeur on Biblical Interpretation." In Paul Ricoeur. *Essays on Biblical Interpretation,* edited with an introduction by Lewis S. Mudge, 1–40. Minneapolis: Fortress, 1980.

Napier, B. D. "Prophet, Prophetism." In *The Interpreter's Dictionary of the Bible,* 4 vols. Edited by George Arthur Buttrick, 3:896. Nashville: Abingdon, 1962.

Olson, Dennis T. "The Book of Judges." In *The New Interpreter's Bible.* 12 vols. Edited by Leander E. Keck, 2:721–888. Nashville: Abingdon, 1998.

Quebedeaux, Richard. *The New Charismatics: The Origins, Development, and Significance of Neo-Pentecostalism.* New York: Doubleday, 1976.

Ricoeur, Paul. *Interpretation Theory: Discourse and the Surplus of Meaning.* Fort Worth: The Texas Christian University Press, 1976.

Rist, Martin. "Apocalypticism." In *The Interpreter's Dictionary of the Bible.* 4 vols. Edited by George Arthur Buttrick, 1:156–61. Nashville: Abingdon 1962.

Rohrbaugh, Richard. *The Biblical Interpreter: An Agrarian Bible in an Industrial Age.* Philadelphia: Fortress, 1978.

Rowland, Christopher C. "The Book of Revelation—Introduction." In *The New Interpreter's Bible.* 12 vols. Edited by Leander E. Keck, 12:501–58. Nashville: Abingdon, 1998.

Sanders, J. A. "Dispersion." In *The Interpreter's Dictionary of the Bible,* 4 vols. Edited by George Arthur Buttrick, 1:854–56. Nashville: Abingdon, 1962.

———. *God Has a Story Too: Sermons in Context.* Philadelphia: Fortress, 1979.

———. *Torah and Canon.* Philadelphia: Fortress, 1972.

Sample, Tex. *Ministry in an Oral Culture: Living with Will Rogers, Uncle Remus, and Minnie Pearl.* Louisville: Westminster/John Knox, 1993.

Sampley, J. Paul. "The Second Letter to the Corinthians—Introduction." In *The New Interpreter's Bible.* 12 vols. Edited by Leander E. Keck, 11:3–35. Nashville: Abingdon, 2000.

Seitz, O. J. F. "Letter." In *The Interpreter's Dictionary of the Bible,* 4 vols. Edited by George Arthur Buttrick, 3:113–15. Nashville: Abingdon, 1962.

Sparks, H. F. D. *The Johannine Synopsis of the Gospels.* New York: Harper & Row, 1974.

Thompson, George B. Jr. "The Beckoning of Scripture: Meaning and Significance in Biblical Interpretation." STD diss., San Francisco Theological Seminary, 1989.

Van Dusen, Henry P. *Spirit, Son, and Father: Christian Faith in Light of the Holy Spirit.* New York: Charles Scribner's Sons, 1958.

Wainwright, A. W. "Revelation, Book of." In *Dictionary of Biblical Interpretation.* Edited by John H. Hayes, K–Z:389–96. Nashville: Abingdon, 1999.

Wall, Robert W. "Introduction to Epistolary Literature." In *The New Interpreter's Bible.* 12 vols. Edited by Leander E. Keck, 10:369–91. Nashville: Abingdon, 2002.

Watson, Duane F. "The Second Letter of Peter." In *The New Interpreter's Bible.* 12 vols. Edited by Leander E. Keck, 12:321–61. Nashville: Abingdon, 1998.

Wright, N. T. "The Letter to the Romans—Introduction." In *The New Interpreter's Bible.* 12 vols. Edited by Leander E. Keck, 10:393–412. Nashville: Abingdon, 1998.

CPSIA information can be obtained
at www.ICGtesting.com
Printed in the USA
FSHW020059220920
73985FS